W9-DFW-262

## ATLA Monograph Series
## edited by Dr. Kenneth E. Rowe

1. Ronald L. Grimes. *The Divine Imagination: William Blake's Major Prophetic Visions.* 1972.
2. George D. Kelsey. *Social Ethics Among Southern Baptists, 1917-1969.* 1973.
3. Hilda Adam Kring. *The Harmonists: A Folk-Cultural Approach.* 1973.
4. J. Steven O'Malley. *Pilgrimage of Faith: The Legacy of the Otterbeins.* 1973.
5. Charles Edwin Jones. *Perfectionist Persuasion: The Holiness Movement and American Methodism, 1867-1936.* 1974.
6. Donald E. Byrne, Jr. *No Foot of Land: Folklore of American Methodist Itinerants.* 1975.
7. Milton C. Sernett. *Black Religion and American Evangelicalism: White Protestants, Plantation Missions, and the Flowering of Negro Christianity, 1787-1865.* 1975.
8. Eva Fleischner. *Judaism in German Christian Theology Since 1945: Christianity and Israel Considered in Terms of Mission.* 1975.
9. Walter James Lowe. *Mystery & The Unconscious: A Study in the Thought of Paul Ricoeur.* 1977.
10. Norris Magnuson. *Salvation in the Slums: Evangelical Social Work, 1865-1920.* 1977.
11. William Sherman Minor. *Creativity in Henry Nelson Wieman.* 1977.
12. Thomas Virgil Peterson. *Ham and Japheth: The Mythic World of Whites in the Antebellum South.* 1978.
13. Randall K. Burkett. *Garveyism as a Religious Movement: The Institutionalization of a Black Civil Religion.* 1978.
14. Roger G. Betsworth. *The Radical Movement of the 1960's.* 1980.
15. Alice Cowan Cochran. *Miners, Merchants, and Missionaries: The Roles of Missionaries and Pioneer Churches in the Colorado Gold Rush and Its Aftermath, 1858-1870.* 1980.
16. Irene Lawrence. *Linguistics and Theology: The Significance of Noam Chomsky for Theological Construction.* 1980.
17. Richard E. Williams. *Called and Chosen: The Story of Mother Rebecca Jackson and the Philadelphia Shakers.* 1981.
18. Arthur C. Repp, Sr. *Luther's Catechism Comes to America: Theological Effects on the Issues of the Small Catechism Prepared In or For America Prior to 1850.* 1982.
19. Lewis V. Baldwin. *"Invisible" Strands in African Methodism.* 1983.
20. David W. Gill. *The Word of God in the Ethics of Jacques Ellul.* 1984.

# The Word of God in the Ethics of JACQUES ELLUL

by

David W. Gill

*ATLA Monograph Series, No. 20*

The American Theological Library Association and
The Scarecrow Press, Inc.
Metuchen, N.J., & London
1984

The author gratefully acknowledges permission given to reprint the following:

Excerpts from The Ethics of Freedom (1976), The Politics of God and the Politics of Man (1972), and The Judgment of Jonah (1971), all by Jacques Ellul and translated by G. W. Bromiley. Copyright © by William B. Eerdmans Publishing Co. Used by permission.

Excerpts from Autopsy of Revolution (1971; translated by Patricia Wolf), The Political Illusion (1967; translated by Konrad Kellen), and The Technological Society (1964; translated by John Wilkinson), all by Jacques Ellul. Copyright © by Alfred A. Knopf. Inc. Used by permission.

Excerpts from Jacques Ellul's To Will and to Do: An Ethical Research for Christians. Translated by C. Edward Hopkin. Copyright © 1969 by United Church Press. Used by permission.

Excerpts from Apocalypse: The Book of Revelation (1977; translated by George W. Schreiner), False Presence of the Kingdom (1972; translated by C. Edward Hopkin), Hope in Time of Abandonment (1973; translated by C. Edward Hopkin), The New Demons (1975; translated by C. Edward Hopkin), The Presence of the Kingdom (1967; translated by Olive Wyon), and Violence: Reflections from a Christian Perspective (1969; translated by Cecelia Gaul Kings), all by Jacques Ellul. Copyright © by Seabury Press. Used by permission.

---

Library of Congress Cataloging in Publication Data

Gill, David W., 1946-
The word of God in the ethics of Jacques Ellul.

(ATLA monograph series; no. 20)
Bibliography: p.
Includes index.
1. Word of God (Theology)--History of doctrines--20th century. 2. Bible--Criticism, interpretation, etc.--History--20th century. 3. Christian ethics--History--20th century. 4. Ellul, Jacques. I. Ellul, Jacques. II. Title. III. Series.
BT210,G54 1984 241'.2 83-20165
ISBN 0-8108-1667-9

---

FOR LUCIA

ma femme, mon amour, mon amie

CONTENTS ☐

## EDITOR'S NOTE ☐

Since 1972 the American Theological Library Association has undertaken responsibility for a modest dissertation series in the field of religious studies. Our aim in this series is to publish two dissertations of quality each year at a reasonable cost. Titles are selected from studies in a wide variety of religious and theological disciplines nominated by graduate school deans. We are pleased to publish David W. Gill's study of the word of God in the ethics of Jacques Ellul as number 20 in our series.

Following undergraduate studies in the University of California, Berkeley, Gill received a master's degree at San Francisco State University in 1971 and took the doctorate in social ethics at the University of Southern California in 1979. He spent the summer of 1982 studying with Jacques Ellul in Bordeaux. Articles and reviews of Ellul's work by Mr. Gill have appeared in *Fides et Historia*, *Themelios* (London), *Christianity Today*, *Reformed Journal*, *Radix*, *Catholic Agitator*, and the *Journal of the Evangelical Theological Society*. He currently serves as Dean and Associate Professor of Christian Ethics in the New College for Advanced Christian Studies in Berkeley.

Kenneth E. Rowe
Series Editor

Drew University Library
Madison, New Jersey

## FOREWORD

This volume comes from the pen of one of the most active American interpreters of the thought of Jacques Ellul. Indeed, David W. Gill was once himself in the position of writing an introduction to a book about Jacques Ellul. In his Introduction to the American edition of a series of interviews with Ellul, published under the title In Season, Out of Season (Harper & Row, 1982), Professor Gill traces the manner by which Ellul's thought found its way into the American scene. Ellul's work was recognized first as a provocative form of social analysis and, after that, as a contribution to theological and ethical thinking. Gill's introduction to that book was an example of the skillful interpretation and analysis that is found in the pages that follow. Gill has produced many other articles about Ellul's thought and reviews of Ellul's books, and his name is already well known in the circles of contemporary scholars of Ellul.

The interpretative literature about Jacques Ellul available to the American reader is relatively modest. The 1982-83 subject guide to Books in Print has no listings under Ellul as a subject. Two volumes of essays about various aspects of Ellul's thought are useful. One, entitled Introducing Jacques Ellul, was edited in 1970 by James Y. Holloway and contains a series of articles that first appeared in Katallagete, the journal of the Committee of Southern Churchmen. The second, edited by Clifford G. Christian and Jay M. Van Hook, was published in 1981 and treats both the social/analytical and the theological/ethical dimensions of Ellul's thinking. It is not without significance that this second volume, entitled Jacques Ellul: Interpretative Essays (University of Illinois Press), concludes with a bibliography that was assembled by David Gill. At that time Gill listed nine unpublished dissertations about Ellul written in the 1970's, of which his own was one. This is the first of that list to be published and made conveniently available. It should be emphasized that the original dissertation format has been revised to make this book more useful for the general reader without losing the careful analytical posture of disciplined scholarship.

The thought of Jacques Ellul tantalizes those who explore it. It does not lend itself to easy appropriation as a basis for sycophantic discipleship. People from a variety of positions in the intellectual landscape are attracted to it, but it has never been the object of massive attention. For instance, Ellul's sociological writings have attracted the attention of many Americans who are not normally identified as theologians, but rather as social critics, as diagnosticians of culture, or as futurists. In an interesting juxtapositioning, his theological and ethical thought has generally proven most appealing to a kind of antiestablishment evangelical rather than to what might be called (in slippery phraseology) mainline Protestant scholars. Consider, for instance, the great interest shown over the years by graduate students and others in the thought of Barth, Brunner, Bonhoeffer, the Niebuhrs, and Tillich in comparison with the limited attention shown Ellul.

It is difficult to categorize Ellul neatly. James Holloway suggests how Ellul demands that as Christians we stand utterly without a "strategy" or "plan of action" as we face the world. This is hardly a recipe with which to produce a cadre of followers. Robert Nisbet believes that many people are turned away from Ellul because they wrongly perceive him as attacking technology. For Nisbet, Ellul is a modern social critic who sees more clearly than most others how the acids of modernity are attacking our spiritual vitality. Martin Marty characterizes Ellul as the "quintessential Protestant" who wars against the artifacts of both political and religious structures--not least, Marty adds, because as a lay theologian and professor of law Ellul does not draw a paycheck from the church. Vernard Eller compares Ellul to Kierkegaard and suggests how massive is the dialectic in each--a dialectic that makes it impossible ever to synthesize reality into a coherent pattern. Gill's own suggestion, apparent in the introduction to In Season, Out of Season, is that Ellul is a prophet who disturbs the status quo, puts to question everything that is taken for granted, and sheds new light upon old issues by simultaneously uprooting and planting, destroying and building, overthrowing and affirming.

Nobody has a "last word" on Ellul. All that any of us has is a new and different way of attempting to describe the elusive quality of a perennial subtlety that defies coherent consistency. Yet, a careful study can be produced about this kind of thought, and David Gill has done just that. We are indebted to him for careful scholarship, a judiciously cautious loyalty, a clarity of exposition, and an ongoing attention to this prophetic law professor from Bordeaux whose challenge is always as unpredictable as it is insistent.

Edward LeRoy Long, Jr.
Professor of Christian
Ethics and Theology
of Culture

Drew Forest
Whitsun Week 1983

# PREFACE

In the fall of 1971 I discovered and then reviewed The Meaning of the City by Jacques Ellul for a special issue of Radix Magazine (Berkeley) on Christianity and urban problems. This first encounter with the thought of Jacques Ellul was provocative and stimulating but not entirely satisfying. However, in the spring and summer of 1972, this time in search of critical perspectives on Christianity and politics as I prepared to cover the Democratic National Convention in Miami Beach, I read (or, more accurately, devoured) four more of Ellul's books: The Political Illusion, The Politics of God and the Politics of Man, Presence of the Kingdom, and False Presence of the Kingdom. This time I was hooked! Both Ellul's sociology and his theology were stunningly accurate and illuminating in relation to both political events and the content of Scripture.

During the dozen years since my discovery of Ellul I have seldom been very far from some project related to his thought. I have read and reread most of his forty books along with many of his essays. Since 1972 I have been in correspondence with him periodically. After several unsuccessful attempts to get him to America (by arranging a speaking tour), I was finally able to interview him in person when I traveled to Bordeaux in the summer of 1982. Both in correspondence and personal encounter, Jacques Ellul has always been patient, willing to respond to my questions, open and friendly in debate about my objections, and encouraging of my work. Even more than his brilliance and productivity, his humanity, integrity, and piety are what have impressed me. He insists, I should add, that none of the "prophetic fury" contained in his writings is intended as a personal attack on anyone; he wishes to debunk certain ideas, not decapitate (verbally) the authors of those ideas.

The Word of God in the Ethics of Jacques Ellul is a revised version of my Ph.D. dissertation, completed at the

University of Southern California in June 1979. I have edited down my review of Hiers, Gustafson, Kelsey, Birch, and Rasmussen in Chapter One, and I have taken the liberty of updating a few matters, chiefly bibliographical. Despite the growing attention Ellul is receiving in various publications, the subject of my work here has not been pursued in detail anywhere else. And yet, the relationship of Jesus Christ and Scripture to Christian ethics continues to be central both to Ellul's agenda and to that of many other Christian ethicists.

Despite Ellul's growing influence, it cannot be taken for granted that very many readers will have consumed all (or most) of Ellul's books germane to this subject. But as Ellul said recently in an interview (Le Monde, September 13, 1981): "The fact is, it is correct to say I haven't written books, but 'one' book of which each is a part. It's a bit crazy to believe there will be readers patient enough to see how my 36 works fit into one another." Not wishing to presume on the patience of some, but at the risk of repetition for the "crazy," my first task in this study is to review, summarize, and correlate the various "chapters" Ellul has penned on my subject. My second objective, then, is to briefly outline the discussion of Jesus Christ, Scripture, and Christian ethics as it is proceeding in the contemporary ethical guild. And third, I intend to give my own analysis and evaluation of Ellul's work. As suggested by the title of my concluding chapter, while I believe (with Ellul!) that Christian ethics must go "beyond" him, most certainly it will be greatly impoverished if it does not take time to work "through" Ellul.

* * *

Next only to Jacques Ellul himself, I am most indebted for the present work to my USC mentor, John P. Crossley, Jr., Professor of Theological Ethics and now Director of the School of Religion. For those fortunate enough to have studied with him, Crossley's lack of a national reputation as an author of great books on ethics is more than compensated by his brilliance as a lecturer and seminar leader and his unending care for his students. In particular, I appreciate his masterful guidance through many volumes of Søren Kierkegaard and Karl Barth--two of Ellul's most important sources. Neither Professor Crossley nor any of the other persons mentioned below should, however, be held responsible for what emerges here as the final product!

Professors John B. Orr, Donald E. Miller, Henry B.

Clark, and Ronald F. Hock, all of the University of Southern California, also contributed a great deal to my understanding of Christian ethics in general and Jacques Ellul in particular. It was also at USC that I was privileged to study with then visiting Professor of Social Ethics, John Coleman Bennett. Then, and in many conversations since, Bennett has engaged me in lively, productive debate about Ellul's positions (and my own). During my four years in southern California, University of LaVerne Professor Vernard Eller provided me with a nearby friend and superb partner in many discussions revolving around our mutual interest in Ellul. Four other friends and colleagues who have helped me in one way or another with my work on Ellul are John Howard Yoder (Notre Dame), Joyce Hanks (University of Costa Rica), Katherine Temple (New York City Catholic Worker), and Lewis Smedes (Fuller Theological Seminary).

Before as well as after completing the original version of this study, my understanding of Ellul's thought was greatly assisted by encounters with colleagues and students when I delivered lectures and papers at meetings of the American Academy of Religion, American Historical Association (Conference on Faith and History), Pacific Coast Theological Society, American Scientific Affiliation, Evangelical Theological Society, Westmont College, Fuller Theological Seminary, Mennonite Brethren Biblical Seminary, Trinity Episcopal School for Ministry, and the Los Angeles Catholic Worker.

Bill and Barbara Moore and the late Esther Ware provided me with places to which I could retreat for the writing and revision of this book. It is quite safe to say that I never could have finished without this help. Ward and Laurel Gasque, David and Thelma Cole, Charles and Lucerne Beal, Fred and Betty Vann, Jay and Susan Boone, and many others provided support and encouragement for my research.

As my dissertation was being written, New College for Advanced Christian Studies was being born. In many respects and for many of its founders, New College Berkeley was inspired by Jacques Ellul's ringing call for Christian reflection on the meaning of life and work for the Christian laity today. Ellul's own attempt to launch various "Associations of Protestant Professionals" was similar in spirit and intent to New College. I owe a great deal to my students at New College, especially those who have sat through my lectures and seminars on Ellul. I have also been immeasurably assisted by the contributions of my New College faculty colleagues Douglas Anderson, Joan Terpstra Anderson, Bernard Adeney, and Tony Petrotta. My administrative assistants Debra Sands Miller and Christine Carlisle held the fort for me while I was writing and revising this work. I am especially grateful to Chris for typing the final version of the manuscript.

Jacques Ellul has often stressed the importance of life and experience in the discernment of reality and truth. I have been accompanied during these years of my study of Ellul by my wife, Lucia, and our children, Jodie and Jonathan (whose births in 1971 and 1972 coincided with my discovery of Ellul; they learned how to say "Jacques Ellul" before "Big Bird" or "Donald Duck"). The little man with the twinkle in his eye, a dog named Pearl, a wife named Yvette, and all those books are a part of their experience as well as mine.

Friendship and companionship would be more than enough in themselves, but I have had the additional good fortune (since I studied only German in high school and as an undergraduate) to be married to someone fluent in French! In my reading and translation as well as in personal conversation with Jacques Ellul--and in life as a whole--Lucia has been my invaluable associate and has saved me from a multitude of errors. "Elle est le sel de notre monde et la lumière de notre vie."

D. W. G.

New College Berkeley
Berkeley, California
February 1983

CHAPTER ONE

# THE WORD OF GOD IN RECENT CHRISTIAN ETHICS

Historically, the primary source of the "ought" in Christian ethics has been understood to be God, specifically the "Word of God" which expresses the "Will of God." Christians have often understood this Word of God to be mediated by the Church and its leadership as well as through individual experience of revelation or "God's leading." However, especially for Protestantism, the term "Word of God" has come to have two primary referents: Jesus Christ and Scripture. It is through them that God speaks most clearly and frequently in the experience of the Protestant churches.

Jesus Christ is described as the definitive Word of God in New Testament passages such as these:[1]

> In the beginning was the Word, and the Word was with God, and the Word was God....
> The Word became flesh and lived for a while among us.

> In the past God spoke to our forefathers through the prophets at many times and in various ways, but in these last days he has spoken to us by his Son.... The Son is the radiance of God's glory and the exact representation of his being.

The designation of the broader biblical corpus as Word of God is less explicit but nevertheless strongly implied by biblical authors in the frequent and authoritative "Thus says the Lord," "It is written," and other formulae. Many Christians find additional support for this assumption that Scripture is the Word of God in passages such as these:[2]

> Above all, you must understand that no prophecy of Scripture came about by the prophet's own interpretation. For prophecy never had its origin in the

> will of man, but men spoke from God as they were carried along by the Holy Spirit.
>
> All Scripture is God-breathed and is useful for teaching, rebuking, correcting and training in righteousness, so that the man of God may be thoroughly equipped for every good work.

It is, of course, an interesting and important question to ask why Jesus Christ and/or Scripture should be regarded as the Word of God (and whether such a view is adequately grounded in biblical passages such as those I have cited). My interest here is not in *why* Jesus Christ and Scripture are so viewed, but rather *that* they have this status. For, whatever textual or theological arguments can be mustered with respect to these questions, it remains given that in Christian tradition Jesus Christ and the Bible are regarded as the Word of God.

While the expression "Word of God" carries with it connotations of transcendence and authority (hence its centrality for normative, prescriptive ethics) it is, in the cases of Jesus Christ and Scripture, applied to phenomena thoroughly rooted in human history. Neither Jesus Christ nor Scripture has the character of an abstract, timeless universal; they are both ancient historical phenomena immediately related not to us but to past historical-cultural milieux. However, despite periodic arguments to the effect that Jesus Christ and Scripture are substantially irrelevant to contemporary Christian ethics because of this historical-cultural chasm, the Christian Church at large continues to insist on the central importance of Jesus Christ and Scripture as primary sources for its morality. The issue will not go away. As we shall see below, a growing number of biblical scholars, theologians, and ethicists, in appreciation of the brute fact of this situation in the Church and in service of that Church, are attempting to go beyond the negative stances of some of our predecessors to a more positive, creative, and affirmative stage in the discussion.

We are faced with two major questions (or sets of questions) as we approach this subject. The first concerns the character of biblical theology and ethics and has three parts: What is (or was) the ethical teaching of Jesus of Nazareth? What ethical teaching is given in the broader canon of Scripture? How does this broader biblical teaching cohere internally (if at all), and how does this biblical canon-as-Word-of-God relate to Jesus Christ-as-Word-of-God in biblical ethics? This first set of questions is primarily historical in nature and any conclusions should be controlled by the actual content of the biblical texts. Nevertheless, it must be remembered that all historical research is bound up to a certain extent with presuppositions and influences from the present. Additionally, some degree of creativity and speculation is always required in historical reconstruction.

If the first set of questions concerns our understanding of the ancient Scriptures and of the Jesus Christ known in those documents (i.e., biblical ethics), the second concerns the application of that material to our situation in the late twentieth century. In short, how may the ancient religious text and its central figure function authoritatively for contemporary Christian ethics? The goal of this study is to contribute to the ongoing search for answers to this and the preceding question through a critical analysis of the work of the French author Jacques Ellul.

My intention in this first chapter is ambitious, but the task is essential. Two general objectives will be pursued. First, the broader subject of the relationship between the Word of God (in Jesus Christ and Scripture) and ethics has arisen with increasing frequency and urgency during the past generation, especially among American and British Protestants. It is essential to attempt a sketch of the shape of this discussion in recent literature. To develop this "map" we will examine first two contemporary works, one by John Howard Yoder and the other by Jack T. Sanders, to establish the poles (or "borders" if we stick to the map image) of the discussion. Then we will turn to four recent works by Richard Hiers, James M. Gustafson, Bruce C. Birch and Larry L. Rasmussen, and David H. Kelsey as we identify the main contours of the debate.

Second, and growing out of this first investigation, an adequate methodological framework for the remainder of this study must be established. "Adequacy" here has reference to its potential for illumination, analysis, and criticism of Jacques Ellul's ethics as well as to the importance of relating Ellul's work to that of others approaching the same issues. Owing to the paucity of secondary literature on Jacques Ellul, some introduction to the man and his work will be provided in a kind of preliminary justification of his contemporary importance for our subject. This will have only "preliminary" significance, of course, in that a decision on his relevance to contemporary ethics will be rendered best at the conclusion of this study--not prematurely on the sole basis of the prodigious quantity and rhetorical flash of his writings.

Nevertheless, the position to be argued here is that this French social critic, lay theologian, and ethicist is among the most significant contributors to the current discussion and that his contributions take us a fair distance toward a viable solution of the problems stated earlier. Following this first chapter, the second and third will consist of a clarification and analysis of Ellul's "theoretical" positions on the nature and role of ethics, Jesus Christ, and Scripture. The fourth and fifth chapters will consist of detailed analyses of two test cases for Ellul's ethics: urban-technological civilization and politics and the nation-state, respectively. The sixth and final chapter will be devoted to a critical summation of Ellul's contribution and to my own proposals for going beyond (and in some cases against) Ellul's positions.

## JESUS CHRIST AND SCRIPTURE IN RECENT ETHICAL THOUGHT

At one extreme in the contemporary debate about the relationship of Jesus Christ and Scripture to Christian ethics, we may place Jack T. Sanders, a New Testament scholar who teaches at the University of Oregon. Sanders' Ethics in the New Testament (1975) addresses the relation of Jesus Christ and the New Testament to ethics and asks "whether and to what degree an Occidental of the modern day may look to the New Testament for any guidance or clues for behavior."[3] Sanders' conclusion, offered on page one (sic) and at every other point of his investigation, is a vigorous "No." Jesus and Scripture (New Testament, specifically) are of virtually no importance for contemporary ethics.

On what basis does Sanders argue this position? It will be helpful to list his major objections since these have to be faced by advocates of a more positive position. (1) Following Henry Cadbury, Sanders argues that Jesus' teaching was purely individualistic in nature and is thus an impossible base for a social ethics.[4] (2) Following Albert Schweitzer, Sanders argues that Jesus' teaching was an "interim ethic" valid only in light of an immediate Parousia. Since Jesus and the Synoptic authors as well were mistaken in their eschatology, their ethics are irrelevant.[5] (3) Siding with what he understands to be modern psychological knowledge, Sanders rejects other aspects of Jesus' teaching as simply outdated, unenlightened, or wrong (e.g., Jesus' condemnation of lust).[6]

(4) Paul comes in for criticism on the same grounds as Jesus and the Synoptic writers. His only "saving grace" is that he is inconsistent and in places appears to be moving toward a qualitative rather than temporal understanding of transcendence.[7] (5) The Deutero-Pauline writings and I Peter manifest an "unreflected ethics that is indistinguishable from good citizenship" and are therefore at best unnecessary.[8] (6) John's Gospel and Letters are "intriguing" but evidence "weakness and moral bankruptcy" in their narrowing of love to "one another" as well as in their overriding concern about whether one "believes."[9] The remainder of the New Testament continues this retreat from ethics to an emphasis on "keeping faithful to the received teaching." Sanders sees this retreat as the "basic evil of the Apocalypse."[10] (7) The only hint of any "valid" ethical guidance for today is in the Letter of James and its "visceral humanitarianism." But even James' injunctions are "unrelated to one another," "all too briefly glimpsed," and require other external criteria before we can pass on their validity or acceptability today.[11]

"A few may wonder whether a study having such overwhelmingly negative conclusions should have been carried through to completion." Aside from a few crumbs of promise in James and Paul, Sanders concludes: "Throw out the New Testament as an aid to ethics once and for all."[12]

> The ethical positions of the New Testament are the children of their own times and places, alien and foreign to this day and age. Amidst the ethical dilemmas which confront us, we are now at least relieved of the need or temptation to begin with Jesus, or the early church, or the New Testament, if we wish to develop coherent ethical positions. We are freed from bondage to that tradition, and we are able to propose, with the author of the Epistle of James, that tradition and precedent must not be allowed to stand in the way of what is humane and right.[13]

And how are we to establish what is "humane and right"?

> Ethical criteria are perhaps best derived from

> the context, from one's active involvement in the life, in the society about one, from one's realization, not derived from the New Testament at all, that some things are not right, that some things must be changed.[14]

Sanders thus epitomizes the extremely pessimistic pole of the continuum. The very fact that the book was written and published testifies to the continuing urgency of the subject. And the book testifies as well to the continued existence of the critical "No" to the question, Are Jesus Christ and Scripture relevant or helpful for contemporary ethics?

Before leaving Sanders it is important to analyze briefly some of the dynamics of the argument given in his book. First, we must note the "damned if you do, damned if you don't" approach to the distinctiveness (or lack of it) of the New Testament ethical approach(es). Jesus and the others are frequently and vehemently rejected precisely on the grounds that their teaching is archaic and incommensurate with our enlightened age (Sanders' "progressive" view of history could, of course, be challenged in its own right). And yet, when he does find strands of ethical teaching in the New Testament that fit with his perception of acceptable contemporary ethics, he concludes that we know all of this anyway on other, independent grounds. Where Jesus Christ and New Testament are distinctive and challenge our contemporary ethics, they are dismissed as naive, mistaken, or irrelevant. Where Jesus Christ and the New Testament agree with contemporary ethics they are dismissed as unnecessary and redundant.

After Sanders' 130 pages of debunking Jesus Christ and the New Testament, one is tempted to respond, "So what?" No one denies (or needs to deny) the diversity within the canon or the time-conditioned character of its teaching. In fact, a primary characteristic of biblical faith is its historical character. That is, it partakes of specific milieux; it is expressed by different writers in different styles; it addresses different situations; it manifests change and development. That very dynamism may be seen as a virtue rather than a failing.

The corollary of the above is that Sanders totally ignores any possible continuity or coherent, intentional development within the canon. Continuity and complementarity are overlooked completely in the search for discontinuity and contradiction. What is true for the biblical canon is also true for history: the differences between cultures granted, there remain substantial similarities between the first-century Mediterranean world and our own. Why should the latter be absolutized anyway?

The most obvious problem with Sanders' approach is that he does not speak from or to the standpoint of Christian faith (or the Church). From the standpoint of Christian faith, if that is the best term, Jesus Christ and Scripture are in fact affirmed not only as relevant but as normative in some profound sense. The brute fact is that multitudes of Christians do confess this authority, internally consistent or not, twentieth-century scientific, philosophical, and historical perspectives notwithstanding. Their question, far from being ruled out of order, deserves critical and constructive response from Christian ethicists: how best may we understand and apply that Word of God in Jesus Christ and Scripture to our own moral life?

Sanders' book represents a critical "No" to our question.[15] This negative position is, in turn, based on four pivotal decisions: (1) Ethics must be valid for the world and not just for the Church. The "community of faith" is ignored. (2) The discontinuity and contradiction in Jesus Christ and Scripture are more significant than any continuity. (3) The ancient world of the Bible was radically different and, indeed, inferior to our own in its psychology, cosmology, understanding of history, and so forth. (4) There is no a priori reason for granting Jesus Christ or Scripture any special authority in ethics: the "standpoint of faith" taken by masses of Christians is ignored rather than recognized.

* * *

At the opposite pole in the contemporary debate about the relationship of Jesus Christ and Scripture to Christian ethics, we may locate John Howard Yoder, a church historian and ethicist who teaches at the University of Notre Dame and at the Associated Mennonite Seminaries (Goshen, Indiana). Like Sanders, Yoder, in his widely circulated Politics of Jesus (1972), begins with the question of how Jesus Christ and Scripture may or may not be related to contemporary ethics, lays before us a sampling and interpretation of Jesus Christ and Scripture (mainly New Testament), and interacts with a variety of critical scholarship.[16] Yoder's approach, presuppositions, and conclusions are diametrically opposite to those of Sanders. Yoder represents a critical "Yes" to our question. For him virtually everything he sees in Jesus Christ and Scripture is the Word of God relevant to our contemporary ethics.

In marked contrast to Sanders, Yoder debunks several modern assumptions about the irrelevance of Jesus Christ and Scripture. Among these are the argument that Jesus Christ and Scripture offer us an irrelevant "interim ethic" based on a wholly future but temporally imminent eschatology; the assumption that the environment of the first-century community was simple, rural, apolitical and thus radically discontinuous with our own situation; and the allegedly ahistorical, individualistic or purely dogmatic/forensic interest of the kerygma.[17] Unless these assumptions or judgments are seriously called into question (and Yoder believes that recent scholarship provides ample reason to do so), they threaten to feed back negatively into New Testament studies obscuring the possibility of seeing new or unexpected ways of relating Jesus Christ and Scripture to contemporary Christian ethics.

Yoder's argument proceeds as follows: (1) Biblical scholarship is not unanimously committed to the irrelevance of Jesus Christ and Scripture for contemporary ethics. In particular, Yoder refers to the work of the "biblical realists" such as Otto Piper, Markus Barth, Paul Minear, Hendrik Kraemer, and Claude Tresmontant. "It has become thinkable that there might be about the biblical vision of reality certain dimensions which ... stand in creative tension with ... our age."[18]

(2) Jesus of Nazareth is "according to the biblical witness, a model of radical political action."[19] "There is a bulk of specific and concrete content in Jesus' vision of the divine order, which can speak to our age ... if it can be unleashed from the bonds of inappropriate a prioris."[20] Yoder "reads" the Jesus story for us, primarily through Luke's Gospel, pointing out the sociopolitical significance of the "temptation of Christ," the proclamation of the Kingdom, and other words and deeds from the Annunciation through the Trial and Crucifixion. He concludes, "It is quite possible to refuse to accept Jesus as normative; but it is not possible on the basis of the record to declare him irrelevant."[21]

(3) The Old Testament provides the stuff of which Jesus' proclamation is made (e.g., the Jubilee legislation, the promise that "God will fight for us"). Jesus' "platform"

in Luke 4, for example, recalls and defines Old Testament themes. (4) The New Testament does not violate but rather elaborates and fills out the central thrust of Jesus' teaching and ethics. To illustrate this contention, Yoder examines several themes and passages in the New Testament letters. He argues that the complementary themes of discipleship and participation in Jesus Christ illustrate a strong sense of continuity of vision between Jesus (as known in the Gospels) and the early Church. The cosmology and its derivative understanding of the "powers" (exousia) are common to Jesus and the Apostolic authors, such as Paul. The emphasis on servanthood and subordination, for example, in the Haustafeln of Colossians, Ephesians, and I Peter is continuous with Jesus' teaching even in the Sermon on the Mount. In fact, even the Pauline emphasis on "justification by faith through grace" has a social as well as personal meaning in Yoder's view. In sum, Yoder concludes, "What we have been describing are several significant strands of corroborative evidence for the survival of the social stance of Jesus into the church of the Apostolic Age."[22]

> A social style characterized by the creation of a new community and the rejection of violence of any kind is the theme of the New Testament from beginning to end, from right to left. The cross of Christ is the model of Christian social efficacy, the power of God for those who believe.[23]

Certainly no less than Sanders, Yoder brings an "interest" to his research. It is not surprising that this leading Mennonite scholar concludes his study by arguing that alternative community and pacifism (arguably the two central distinctives of the Anabaptist/Mennonite heritage) are the common unifying core of Jesus Christ and Scripture and that these positions (and, incidentally, the Mennonite movement itself) are relevant today.

A much more serious question about Yoder's work concerns the (inevitable) selectivity of themes and passages. Where, for example, are we to place the biblical emphasis on Creation, with its more inclusive, universal, and positive implications for social and political ethics? It is also fair to question the alleged "neutrality" of choosing Luke's Gospel as the primary source. Matthew, for example, would have tilted the study in a slightly different direction.[24] Nevertheless, Yoder neither hides from the critical research of the present, even when he contradicts majority opinion, nor fails to deal with biblical material traditionally difficult to reconcile with pacifist-communitarian ethics.

What kinds of presuppositions and judgments are involved in Yoder's vigorous "Yes" to our question about the relevance of Jesus Christ and Scripture for contemporary ethics? We can identify four general points: (1) The world may be wrong. The majority opinion of scholars, theologians, politicians, or psychologists may not be as valid or desirable as some alternative perspective. Similarly, the ancient world is not necessarily less wise or understanding than our own age. (2) Ethics "must, if it is to be our business as Christians to think about them, be rooted in revelation, not alone in speculation, nor in a self-interpreting 'situation.' "[25] That is, Christian ethics must presuppose the existence of a "Word of God." The community of faith and the perspective of faith are essential factors from the outset.

(3) "This will of God is affirmatively, concretely knowable in the person and ministry of Jesus."[26] The central figure of Christianity is granted central importance and authority in the quest for guidance in Christian ethics. This Jesus was socially and politically relevant to the circumstances of his own time and place, though in a fashion quite different from what the world, then and now, might expect. (4) While differences of emphasis and perhaps even contradictions may exist in Scripture, the unity and complementarity of the combined voices in the canon are much more impressive and significant. This unity is to be understood most fruitfully in the ways that Jesus' message is echoed, interpreted, and applied in the New Testament and anticipated in the Old Testament.

The contrast between the approaches of Sanders and Yoder could hardly be more striking. Each man has approached the same body of literature with a distinct set of presuppositions and a distinct interest. Sanders stands as witness to the possibility of continuing the argument that Jesus Christ and Scripture have little to offer in the search for a contemporary ethics. Yoder, on the other hand, provides us with a powerful counter-example. Yoder's _Politics of Jesus_ is an ingenious, well-argued case for a Jesus-centered biblical ethics that takes the contemporary world (including its biblical scholarship and political character) with great seriousness. Sanders finds virtually nothing of help in Jesus Christ and Scripture; Yoder finds, it would seem, that everything fits together and is somehow helpful.

These, then, are the poles of the continuum, the borders of the map.[27]

* * *

Jack T. Sanders and John Howard Yoder, two contemporary ethicists, supply us with the borders on the map, the poles of a continuum along which others work in relating Jesus Christ and Scripture to ethics. A step removed from the kind of primary work Sanders and Yoder have undertaken are several recent studies surveying various ways Jesus Christ and Scripture are being used in Christian ethics. The following brief reviews of four of these important secondary, methodological studies will hardly do them justice but it will be helpful in indicating the broader context within which Jacques Ellul's contribution must be assessed.

Richard Hiers' Jesus and Ethics: Four Interpretations (1968) focuses attention on four major thinkers: Adolf von Harnack, Albert Schweitzer, Rudolf Bultmann, and C. H. Dodd.[28] Hiers' (and his subjects') interest is, for the most part, restricted to the historical Jesus of the Synoptic tradition. Harnack, the classical spokesman for nineteenth-century Liberalism, believed that Jesus was of enduring importance for Christian ethics and that the "essence of Christianity" "contains something which, under different historical forms, is of permanent validity."[29] Harnack's proposal was to discard the outdated historical "shell" of the New Testament era, especially Jewish nationalistic, apocalyptic eschatology, and retain three themes as permanently valid guidance: (1) the idea of the kingdom of God and its coming (interpreted as the rule of God over the individual), (2) the fatherhood of God and the infinite value of the human soul, and (3) the "higher righteousness" and the "love command."

Albert Schweitzer, in contrast to Harnack, insisted that whatever little we can know about the historical Jesus emphatically rules out the tame nineteenth-century liberal Jesus-without-eschatology. The primary thrust of Schweitzer's work was to suggest that Jesus' ethics were not eternally valid truths but rather specialized short-term instructions, an "interim ethic" valid only in light of the brevity of time before the eschaton (which, Schweitzer argued, did not occur). Yet, after all, Jesus does have something to offer Christian ethics, according to some of Schweitzer's writings. Hiers suggests that Schweitzer found four themes relating the "personality," "spirit," or "will" of Jesus to the modern situation: (1) devotion to the kingdom of God (demythologized by Schweitzer after all, in contradiction to his earlier position), (2) self-devotion to others, (3) reverence for life, and (4) the ethic or religion of love.[30]

For Rudolf Bultmann, Jesus' eschatology continued to be a major problem. Bultmann solved the problem by demythologizing, i.e., by a radical reinterpretation of Jesus' message out of first-century categories and into modern existentialist terms.[31] For Bultmann, the contemporary meaning of Jesus' proclamation is "radical obedience" expressed in a self-authenticating decision. "Love of neighbor" remains a central theme but the content of this stance is not spelled out for it is known only in the existential moment of decision.

C. H. Dodd, Hiers' fourth case study, proposes still another resolution of the problem of Jesus' eschatology.[32] According to Dodd, Jesus taught a "realized eschatology" (rather than a temporally imminent future kingdom) in which the kingdom of God is the transcendent, absolute, and infinite reality which stands (Platonically) over against (but breaking into) our world. Jesus is then relevant but chiefly by way of analogy and example. Jesus provides a direction and quality to our actions rather than a systematic ethical code. Guided by his example we are to incarnate the absolute in our situation.

Hiers' study is valuable for showing the centrality of the problem of eschatology in dealing with Jesus' ethical relevance and for describing four distinctive, classical approaches to this problem. The two weaknesses of Hiers' study are (1) the failure to deal with mediating interpretations of the "realized/future" eschatology of Jesus (e.g., T. W. Manson, A. N. Wilder, O. Cullmann, D. Bonhoeffer, K. Barth) and (2) his erroneous assumption (with Harnack, Schweitzer, and Bultmann) that contemporary, educated Christians cannot relate to an imminent, apocalyptic eschatology. Whether that is true for most theologians and ethicists, it is certainly not so for masses of Christians today. Rightly or wrongly, millions of Christians live in apocalyptic expectation of the Parousia. That this expectation characterized Jesus and the early Church would not, necessarily, render the ethics of Jesus and the New Testament irrelevant, at least for a large segment of the Church. The question remains, Given this faith of the Church in the centrality of Jesus Christ (often including belief in an imminent eschaton), what ethical implications may be derived for our age?

A more positive impression of the relationship of Jesus Christ to Christian ethics is gained from James M. Gustafson's Christ and the Moral Life (1968).[33] Gustafson's focus is broader than Hiers' in that he does not restrict his view to the historical Jesus of the Synoptic tradition, nor is his sample of theologians and ethicists as narrow. Gustafson's organizing question is this: "What claims for the significance of Christ for the moral life do theologians explicitly make or apparently assume?"[34] Gustafson follows "Jesus Christ" wherever he goes in ethical discussion, whether he is viewed as the Synoptic proclaimer of a new order, as "Christ the Creator," or as something else.

The first of Gustafson's categories (or types) includes those whose ethics emphasize the nature and locus of "the good," i.e., the (nonmoral) value situated above or beyond questions of specific action or character. In such an approach, he argues, Jesus Christ is viewed primarily as "the Lord who is Creator and Redeemer." Here the question is not, first of all, What ought I to do? but rather, What has already been done for you in Jesus Christ? The answer to the ethical question is not found in ethical systems per se but in turning to the locus of value, Jesus Christ. The ethical life is seen in terms of conformity to Reality, not obedience to specific rules. Karl Barth, Dietrich Bonhoeffer, F. D. Maurice, and Jacques Ellul are Gustafson's examples of this first general approach.[35]

A second general style of relating Jesus Christ to the moral life is that of making claims for a change in the moral self as a result of Jesus Christ's work as Sanctifier and Justifier.[36] The emphasis is on "being" and "character" rather than on "doing" and "obligation." The focus is on moral value, on questions of virtue and good and evil. Again, the emphasis is less on following laws and rules and more on the formation of moral character. John Wesley, F. D. E. Schleiermacher, and Barnard Häring represent examples of the reliance on Jesus Christ as Sanctifier (the One who makes holy) in ethics. Martin Luther, Rudolf Bultmann, and Reinhold Niebuhr are Gustafson's examples of using Jesus Christ the Justifier (the One who sets free) in ethics.

The third general place where Jesus Christ is brought to bear on ethics is, in contrast to the preceding, on "doing" and "obligation."[37] The quest is for specific criteria, models, and principles to help identify right and wrong decisions and courses of action. Newman Smith, Charles Sheldon,

Thomas à Kempis, William Law, and others exemplify the use of Jesus Christ the Pattern, the ethical model to imitate. T. W. Manson, Walter Rauschenbusch, and others exemplify a reliance on Jesus Christ the Teacher, the provider of authoritative ethical norms and principles.

Gustafson points out that few if any ethicists fit neatly or totally into the typology he has constructed.[38] In many cases it is rather a matter of priority and emphasis. The teachings of Jesus, for example, play an important role for many thinkers, even if they are subordinated to a greater emphasis on character formation or on the ultimate Good. For Gustafson himself, Jesus Christ has particular importance for the moral life by affecting and shaping the moral agent's "perspective and posture," "disposition," and "intentions," as well as by remaining a "norm" and the source of norms.

> Jesus Christ is normative for the Christian's moral purposes whether it is convenient for him to be so or not. He is a standard by which my purposes are judged, he is an authority that ought to direct and inform my activity, if I acknowledge him to be my Lord.[39]

Jesus Christ is not the only factor or norm in ethical reflection, according to Gustafson, but he does condition and illuminate each situation and decision as the essential, primary, and most important norm.

The issue of how to relate Jesus Christ to Christian ethics leads rather directly into a study of the biblical text since there are no other primary sources (of any substance, at least) on Jesus Christ. But, although he is the fullest and clearest revelation of God, Jesus Christ has rarely been regarded as the exclusive Word of God. Christians commonly believe that the whole canon of Scripture is, contains, or mediates the Word of God. How does or can the Bible, in this more inclusive sense, relate to Christian ethics?

James Gustafson is often quoted in discussions of this subject:

> In spite of the great interest in ethics in the past thirty years, and in spite of the extensive growth of Biblical studies, there is a paucity of materials that relate the two areas in a scholarly way.

> Writers in ethics necessarily make their forays into the Bible without the technical exegetical and historical acumen and skills to be secure in the way they use Biblical materials, but few Biblical scholars have provided studies upon which writers in ethics can draw.[40]

Yale Old Testament scholar Brevard Childs makes the same point from the opposite side of the divide:

> In spite of the great interest in ethics, to our knowledge, there is no outstanding modern work written in English that even attempts to deal adequately with the Biblical material as it relates to ethics.[41]

The urgency of this matter is due to a growing ferment concerning the character, function, and authority of Scripture for theology and the Church. This ferment cuts across the spectrum from conservative to liberal.[42] Specific ethical issues in business, government, law, sexuality, medicine, scientific research, and so on, press in on the Church with all of their relentless complexity and ambiguity. The Church turns to its book--but how should this book function in this ethical questioning?

Bruce C. Birch and Larry L. Rasmussen have contributed to the discussion of the relationship of Scripture to ethics with their recent book, Bible and Ethics in the Christian Life (1976).[43] After reviewing (and applauding) the recent efforts of John Howard Yoder, James Muilenburg, Victor Paul Furnish, James M. Gustafson, Edward LeRoy Long, Jr., Brevard Childs, C. Freeman Sleeper, H. Edward Everding Jr., and Dana W. Wilbanks, Birch and Rasmussen develop their own proposals for relating Scripture to ethics.[44] The task of Christian ethics, in their view, revolves around two closely related concerns. First and most important is character formation ("being"). Second is decision and action ("doing"). In both tasks, the ethicist must carry out both a critical task (description and assessment) and a constructive task (normative ethical prescription).

"The starting point for moral identity is with the Bible in the life of the church as the gathered community."[45] In this process of character formation, Birch and Rasmussen argue, it is important not to engage in "genre-reductionism." Not only the overtly ethical-didactic sections but all the various stories and images in the canon provide helpful ways of seeing, intending, and acting. These stories and images mold character, an ethical task that has too often been underplayed and undervalued. In fact, the "most effective and crucial impact of the Bible in Christian ethics is that of shaping the moral identity of the Christian and the church."[46]

Second in importance to character formation, but essential nonetheless, is the role of Scripture in decision making. The Bible relates to decision-making situations in at least two ways. First, it assists in analysis of a given situation. With careful exegesis analogous situations in Scripture can be discerned which illuminate current moral dilemmas. Second, the Bible may provide, directly or indirectly, norms and standards for a situation. These may function negatively by indicating boundaries or overruling certain norms in the world around us. Or they may function positively by authorizing, taking up, and transforming other norms. Again, Birch and Rasmussen warn against "norm-reductionism," that is, the assumption that only a single biblical norm is relevant or applicable in each situation.[47]

Christian ethics is at root a relational or response ethics. The Bible is diverse and the community context is essential for moral discernment. As the Bible is used in the decision-making process, this dynamic character must not be obscured. Christian ethics is worked out in the tension between standards and obligations on the one hand and the gift of freedom on the other. The role of imagination can also be significant, for in making a decision the context and our question are our starting points (rather than Scripture, as is the case in character formation). The very choice of biblical passages, as well as the order in which they are consulted, involves the imagination to some extent. Since imagination expresses character, Birch and Rasmussen remind us that we are brought full circle back to the primary importance of the formation of that character by the Bible in the gathered community.

Like John Howard Yoder and James M. Gustafson, discussed earlier, and unlike Jack Sanders and Richard Hiers, Birch and Rasmussen assume the ongoing importance and authority of Scripture in the confessional community, the Church. Scripture, they argue, does not have exclusive authority, but it does have primacy over science, philosophy, and other authorities which must be taken into account. This primacy and authority of Scripture is a confessional stance and not an empirically verifiable truth. Birch and Rasmussen explore the relationship of biblical authority to character formation (the ethics of virtue) and decision and action (the ethics of obligation). Although it is, perhaps, implicit in their study, they neglect the third possible emphasis (see Gustafson above) on the nonmoral good. In brief, the missing component or type would argue that the Bible functions not so much to form character or provide norms as to put us in touch with the Good, i.e., with God. The point of Scripture, then, would be to redirect our attention beyond the immediate ethical dilemma to God. It would put us in a position or relationship to God in which we then would see the situation differently and hear the will of God more clearly.

A fourth and final example of recent attempts to map out and analyze the relationship of Jesus Christ and/or Scripture to ethics is David H. Kelsey's The Uses of Scripture in Recent Theology (1975).[48] Though Kelsey does not specifically address the problem of ethics, Christian ethics is a species of theological reflection and argument and thus his analysis is highly relevant. Kelsey first examines several recent theologians and their varied uses of Scripture. Then he maps out the range of possible uses of Scripture by means of a typology. Finally, he draws out some implications of his study for the theologian (or ethicist) bent on using Scripture to authorize his or her proposals.

Kelsey's case studies fall into three general categories. First, the authoritative aspect of Scripture can be considered the doctrine or concepts it teaches, an intrinsic (rather than functional) property of the text (B. B. Warfield, Hans-Werner Bartsch).[49] Second, the biblical narrative or recital of the being and action of God, the functional "rendering present" of the living God, can be considered the authoritative aspect (G. E. Wright, K. Barth).[50] Third, by means of its literary images, pictures, religious symbols, and kerygmatic myths, Scripture can trigger a subjective faith response and, for this reason, be authoritative (L. S. Thornton, P. Tillich, R. Bultmann).[51] The questions raised by these case studies revolve around decisions on how to construe the text: What patterns are appealed to? What function in the Church's common life shall they serve? What logical force is ascribed to the text?

Kelsey then turns to a more detailed discussion of how the biblical text may be used. Employing Stephen Toulmin's The Uses of Argument, he analyzes the constituent parts of theological argument and shows where biblical material might enter the argument.[52] In roughest form, any argument is composed of data and conclusion. The move from data to conclusion is authorized by warrants (reasons given for drawing the conclusion from the data), which are themselves supported by some kind of backing (reasons given for accepting the warrant as valid). The conclusion itself is usually qualified with conditions of rebuttal (indication of factors that would prevent or exclude the otherwise valid conclusion).

Kelsey's analysis suggests that the biblical material (in any of the three general styles listed earlier) may be brought to bear on theological arguments at any point from data through conclusion. There is no one prevailing way of bringing Scripture to bear in an argument. The use of Scripture may be direct or indirect and it may occur at any point in the argument. Finally, Kelsey notes, Scripture may bear on life in less direct a fasion than that of a component in an argument. It may "non-informatively express" in order to transform lives, and not merely serve in doctrinal or ethical statements and arguments.

Finally, Kelsey argues that what is decisive in the whole process of relating Scripture to theology is basic decision about the very point of doing theology. A "single, synoptic, imaginative judgment" is made in an attempt to "catch up what Christianity is basically all about."[53] Theological criticism is guided by such a discrimen, defined as "a configuration of criteria that are in some way organically related to one another as reciprocal coefficients."[54] At one level this discrimen is simply the conjunction of certain uses of Scripture with "the presence of God." Stated differently, the discrimen is an imaginative judgment about the mode in which God is present. As evidenced in his case studies, Kelsey argues that this can be an ideational mode (doctrine or concepts), the mode of concrete actuality (e.g., rendering an agent present), or the mode of ideal possibility (e.g., the possibility of "authentic existence" or "new being").

## JACQUES ELLUL: BACKGROUND AND INTRODUCTION

It is in the context of the preceding discussions that Jacques Ellul's work will be examined. Ellul holds a triple fascination for this subject. First, he has articulated theoretical positions on the nature and interrelationship of ethics, Jesus Christ, and Scripture. Second, he has applied this perspective to actual problems of Christian ethics (the state and politics, the city and technology, violence, money, etc.). Third, he has been personally engaged in the kinds of situations he deals with in his ethics; he is not merely an "armchair ethicist."

Ellul's biographical background is, perhaps, more important to an accurate understanding of his thought than is the usual case.[55] He was born January 6, 1912, to a poor, "not especially Christian" family in Bordeaux, a port city on the Garonne River near the southwest coast of France. He began earning his own living at age sixteen and continued to do so throughout his university studies in law, history, and sociology. His work at the University of Bordeaux culminated in the Doctor of Laws degree in 1936. He has also received honorary doctorates from the University of Amsterdam and the University of Aberdeen.

While a student in 1931, Ellul "chanced" to read Marx's _Das Kapital_ and became an enthusiastic Marxist. He studied Marx's writings a great deal but never joined the Communist Party because it then seemed to be so far from Marx. At about the same time, Ellul also began reading the Bible and by 1934 was converted, he says, "with a certain brutality." He participated in the personalist movement and its journal _Esprit_ (with Emmanuel Mounier, the Catholic father of "personalism" who so powerfully influenced Peter Maurin, Dorothy Day, and the Catholic Worker movement).[56] Ellul's great concern in those years was to know if he could be both Marxist and Christian. By 1938 he "chose decisively for Christianity" and broke with the _Esprit_ group on three grounds: (1) they seemed to be headed toward "ordinary socialism"--Christianity was being swallowed up by Marxism in the attempted synthesis; (2) Mounier was too "uncompromisingly Catholic"--from 1935 or 1936 Karl Barth became Ellul's favorite theological writer (along with Kierkegaard and the biblical authors); and (3) their sociology and theology seemed "superficial" to Ellul--this charge has continued to be Ellul's opinion of all forms of "social Christianity" from that day to this.

In 1935 Ellul also wrote his first article on _la technique_. "Since 1935 I have been convinced that on the sociological plane, technique was by far the most important phenomenon, and that it was necessary to start from there to understand everything else."[57] Ellul has said that his sociology follows in the tradition and method of Marx, but that in the present day that leads to a perception of technique as the critical factor. Ellul argues that if Marx were alive today he would agree that technique, rather than the distribution of wealth and class struggle, is the key to sociological understanding.[58]

After his graduation in 1936, Ellul taught at the University of Strasbourg until the German occupation began and he was dismissed from his post by the Vichy government in 1940. Ellul's own father was arrested and detained during the Nazi occupation. Ellul spent the next four years working in the French Resistance, studying theology, and eking out an existence on a small farm.

At the end of the war, Ellul was appointed an assistant to the Mayor of Bordeaux but decided not to continue in political office two years later, partly out of frustration at the incapacity of the government and partly out of a desire for an academic career. From 1944 to his retirement in 1980 he was Professor of the History and Sociology of Institutions in the Faculty of Law and Economic Sciences at the University of Bordeaux. From 1947, he also held a chair at the Institute of Political Studies at Bordeaux.

Between 1936 and 1946 Ellul published a half-dozen articles and two historical studies (on French military recruitment and on the Reformed Church of France). Since 1946 his literary output has been monumental: some forty books (twenty-three in English translation) and over 250 articles and reviews. There are two relatively distinct sides to Ellul's work over the years. On the one hand, he is formally trained in and a professor of the history and sociology of institutions (especially law). This is what he teaches at Bordeaux and is the subject of about half of his books and articles. On the other hand, he is a widely respected lay theologian and churchman. He has served on the national synod of the Reformed Church of France and on various committees of the World Council of Churches. Since 1969 he has been editor of _Foi et Vie_, a highly respected quarterly theological journal.

Thus, Ellul sees his work as having two more or less distinct sides to it: the sociological examination of the modern world, and theological-biblical studies of the Word of God and Christian life.

> I have sought to confront theological and biblical knowledge and sociological analysis without trying to come to any artificial or philosophical synthesis; instead I try to place the two face to face, in order to shed some light on what is real socially and real spiritually. That is why I can say that the reply to each of my sociological analyses is found implicitly in a corresponding theological book, and inversely, my theology is fed on socio-political experience. But I refuse to construct a _system_ of thought, or to offer up some Christian or prefabricated socio-political solutions. I want only to provide Christians with the means of thinking out _for themselves_ the meaning of their involvement in the modern world.
>
> Such is the essential goal of my work. It ends, necessarily, in a Christian ethics--but _only_ therefore an ethics that is indicative.[59]

The question of how interdependent or independent the two sides of Ellul's work really are is somewhat tangential to the purpose of this book. He argues that his sociological and theological methods are specified by their respective subjects, but there is an obvious similarity of method and substantive conclusion in the two phases of his work.

For the sake of perspective, it should be mentioned that Ellul's professorial _magnum opus_ is the five-volume _Histoire des Institutions_ (1951-1956), from Ancient Greece to the West of World War I.[60] His sociological reputation in America, however, rests primarily on his three major studies, _The Technological Society_ (translated and published at the urging of Aldous Huxley and the Center for the Study of Democratic Institutions in 1964; original French edition, 1954), _Propaganda: The Formation of Men's Attitudes_ (1962; ET,* 1965), and _The Political Illusion_ (1965; ET, 1967), each of which debunked the conventional wisdom of the time. _The Technological Society_, in particular, established Ellul as a leading critic of modernity, especially of the triumphant spirit of Western rationality, artificiality, science, bureaucracy, and efficiency. Over the past thirty years Ellul has also published important studies of revolution, art, class structure, public relations, the history of propaganda, juvenile delinquency, and the sociology of religion. _The Betrayal of the West_ (1976; ET, 1978) gives a remarkable and pas-

*ET refers to English translation throughout.

sionate analysis of the rise and fall of Western civilization. A closer look at aspects of his sociology will follow when his understanding of urban-technological society, the nation-state, and politics is considered below.

Ellul's first theological book was The Theological Foundation of Law (1946; ET, 1960). This was followed by The Presence of the Kingdom (1948; ET, 1951), still one of the best brief and synoptic introductions to Ellul's overall vision and concern. Among his other theological books is a sequel to The Presence of the Kingdom called False Presence of the Kingdom (1964; ET, 1972). He has published four biblical studies: The Judgment of Jonah (1952; ET, 1971), The Politics of God and the Politics of Man (II Kings) (1966; ET, 1972), Apocalypse: The Book of Revelation (1975; ET, 1977), and The Meaning of the City (1975; ET, 1970), a biblical study of the city from Genesis to Revelation. A study of Ecclesiastes is forthcoming. L'homme et l'argent (1953), a biblical study of money, is not available in English translation but has recently been reprinted in France (1980). Among Ellul's other topical theological studies are these: Violence: Reflections from a Christian Perspective (1972; ET, 1969), Prayer and Modern Man (1971; ET, 1970), Hope in Time of Abandonment (1973; ET, 1973), L'Idealogie Marxiste-chretienne (1979), La Foi au prix du doute (1980), and Le Parole humiliée (1981). To Will and to Do: An Ethical Research for Christians (1964; ET, 1969) and The Ethics of Freedom (1973/74; ET, 1976) are the first major installments of Ellul's ethics. Most of these volumes will come into the discussion later on, so a more complete introduction can be left to a more appropriate context.

Ellul's scholarly output is prodigious in its size and scope. A major reason for his importance to the subject of this book is precisely this willingness to elaborate his approach in a variety of ways. His work provides ample opportunity for the examination of the strengths and weaknesses of his positions. We rarely, if ever, have to speculate on "what Ellul might say about...." A final reason for Ellul's (at least preliminary) importance for this study is the breadth of his impact across various boundaries. His work has been condemned and praised by both Catholics and Protestants, by biblical exegetes and ethicists, by American Evangelicals and Ecumenical Liberals, by Reformed Calvinists and Radical Anabaptists. Somehow his message cuts across most of the boundaries and provides many of us with a subject of (un)common interest in our pursuit of a better formulation of the relationship of the Word of God in Jesus Christ and Scripture to our contemporary Christian ethics.

Jack T. Sanders and John Howard Yoder have provided us with working examples of two poles in contemporary Christian ethics insofar as the relevance of Jesus Christ and Scripture are concerned. For Sanders, virtually nothing can be salvaged; certainly nothing is treated as though it mediated a "Word of God." If an ethical norm is deemed valid, it is so on grounds other than those associated with Jesus Christ or Scripture. For Yoder, on the other hand, virtually everything is presented as powerfully relevant to contemporary Christian ethics. While Yoder's style is not classically preachy, he is clearly advocating a normative ethics deeply dependent on Jesus Christ and Scripture and mediating the Word of God.

It became clear in reviewing Sanders and Yoder that certain assumptions and attitudes have conditioned their different styles and their radically different conclusions. These assumptions include their evaluations of biblical scholarship, comparative history, psychology, and so forth. Psychological factors, although difficult to define, also appear to be at work in their respective compulsions toward contradiction and harmony.

For a variety of reasons the question has been raised with new vigor in the contemporary Church and in the theological-ethical guild: Can we find a normative Word of God for ethics today by "returning" to Jesus Christ and Scripture? If so, how best can this be accomplished? Richard H. Hiers, James M. Gustafson, Bruce C. Birch and Larry L. Rasmussen, and David H. Kelsey have provided us with some description and analysis of many of the ways this quest for the ethical relevance of Jesus Christ and Scripture is being carried out.

The studies we have examined raise the major questions in terms of which the rest of this study will proceed. The first task will be to describe and analyze Jacques Ellul's understanding of (1) Christian ethics and (2) the Word of God, as he interprets it in relation to both Jesus Christ and Scripture. Primary reference will be made to Ellul's explicit (theoretical) statements on these subjects.

We will ask how Ellul conceives of the task and role of Christian ethics. What are its potentialities and limits?

What are its constituent concerns and which of these receive emphasis (the nonmoral "good"? virtue and character formation? obligation and action?)? On what grounds is his understanding of Christian ethics commended?

We will then ask how Ellul conceives the Word of God and how, in turn, this relates to Christian ethics. What is meant by the Word of God? How does the Word of God relate to Jesus Christ? How does it relate to the parts of Scripture and to the canon as a whole? How do Jesus Christ, Scripture, and Word of God interrelate?

Drawing on Hiers and Gustafson, we will ask how Ellul views Jesus Christ. What does Ellul do with the historical issues so critical for Hiers and Sanders? What about the problem of Jesus' eschatology? What aspects of Jesus Christ receive emphasis--teaching? example? redemption? sanctification? justification?--and on what grounds? In short, how does Ellul construe Jesus Christ?

The same kinds of questions must then be directed at Ellul's view of Scripture. Drawing on Birch and Rasmussen and Kelsey we will ask where, if at all, concepts like revelation, inspiration, and authority fit into his view of Scripture. What aspects of Scripture are authoritative and why? Is there a _sensus plenior_ in the canon as a whole? How are we to deal with the historical conditioning of the biblical materials? With what _discrimen_ does Ellul approach Scripture and the ethical task?

As these questions are raised, we will attempt not only to identify the ways Ellul resolves various issues, but also to clarify his presuppositions, prior "faith commitments," and the problems or issues he has sidestepped, mishandled, or even newly raised. What are the conditions of rebuttal and qualifiers acknowledged or implicit in Ellul's perspective?

The second major task of this work will be to describe Ellul's use of the Word of God in Jesus Christ and Scripture in the actual formulation of his urban ethics (Chapter Four) and his political ethics (Chapter Five). In each case study we will examine his description of the character of the situation and its ethical dilemmas. What aspects of urban-technological society receive his attention? How then does he proceed to develop a Christian ethical argument? How and where do Jesus Christ and Scripture get introduced into the argument? What is illuminated by these approaches--and what has been discounted or overlooked by Ellul?

Finally (Chapter Six), the question will be raised whether the weaknesses or omissions in Ellul's Christian ethics are a logical necessity, given his general framework, or whether there are ways of improving his approach. The promise of Ellul, as a corrective and a challenge, to Liberal and Conservative theological and social ethicists will be summarized. The problems raised by his ethical method, his biblical hermeneutics, his Christology, and his all-encompassing dialectical perspective will be summarized as we search for a way beyond his ethics.

The method and procedure of this study are thus eclectic and intended to respect the work that has already been done at various points on the "map." At the same time that they are eclectic, the method and procedure are relatively simple and straightforward, and they should permit an analysis and conclusion which will, in fact, advance the current discussion of the possible relevance of Jesus Christ and Scripture as Word of God for contemporary Christian ethics.

## NOTES

1. John 1:1, 14: Hebrews 1:1-3. This and all biblical quotations are from the New International Verson (Grand Rapids, Mich.: Zondervan, 1978).
2. II Peter 1:20-21; II Timothy 3:16-17.
3. Jack T. Sanders, Ethics in the New Testament: Change and Development (Philadelphia: Fortress, 1975), p. xi.
4. Sanders, p. 1; see also Henry J. Cadbury, The Peril of Modernizing Jesus (New York, 1937).
5. Sanders, pp. 2-3; see also Albert Schweitzer, The Quest of the Historical Jesus (English translation, London, 1954).
6. Sanders, p. 45.
7. Ibid., p. 66.
8. Ibid., p. 88.
9. Ibid., p. 100.
10. Ibid., p. 114.
11. Ibid., p. 128.
12. Ibid., p. 129.
13. Ibid., p. 130.
14. Ibid., p. 90.
15. Almost as negative on similar grounds is J. L. Houlden's popular introduction, Ethics and the New Testament (Baltimore: Penguin, 1973).

16. John Howard Yoder, The Politics of Jesus (Grand Rapids, Mich.: Eerdmans, 1972).
17. Ibid., pp. 15ff.
18. Ibid., p. 5.
19. Ibid., p. 12.
20. Ibid., p. 6.
21. Ibid., p. 99.
22. Ibid., p. 215.
23. Ibid., p. 250.
24. Ibid., pp. 23-24.
25. Ibid., p. 239.
26. Ibid.
27. Rudolf Schnackenburg's The Moral Teaching of the New Testament (New York: Seabury, 1973) is another example of a more positive approach to the unity and relevance of biblical ethics.
28. Richard Hiers, Jesus and Ethics: Four Interpretations (Philadelphia: Westminster, 1968).
29. Hiers, p. 14. Hiers is citing Adolf Von Harnack, What Is Christianity? (New York: Harper and Brothers, 1957 ed.), p. 14.
30. Ibid., pp. 47-61.
31. Ibid., pp. 79ff.
32. Ibid., pp. 115ff.
33. James M. Gustafson, Christ and the Moral Life (New York: Harper and Row, 1968).
34. Ibid., p. ix.
35. Ibid., pp. 28-29; In general, this is an accurate judgment about Ellul. The question is how precisely this theme is developed by Ellul and how the other areas (moral self, specific norms) are seen.
36. Ibid., see pp. 81-115 on "Jesus Christ the Sanctifier" and pp. 116-149 on "Jesus Christ the Justifier."
37. Ibid., pp. 150-237, on "Jesus Christ the Pattern" and "Jesus Christ the Teacher." It is often stated rather too quickly that American Fundamentalists and Evangelicals propose Jesus' teaching as a "new law" (or restatement of the old law) to be literally, woodenly applied. One has only to observe the affluent lifestyles of these groups and their leaders to realize that they neither "Give to everyone who asks of you," nor practice the Jubilee legislation of Moses and redistribute their wealth! As James Barr has pointed out recently, Fundamentalists use the rhetoric of "literalism" when it suits them, freely allegorize and "spiritualize" at other times, and are unswerving only in their espousal of "inerrancy." Fundamentalism (Philadelphia: Westminster, 1978), pp. 40ff.

In some ways the recent "radical Evangelicals" connected with Sojourners magazine (Washington, D. C.) and The Other Side (Philadelphia) are the true "wooden literalists" in their unqualified refusal of violence, capitalism, etc. They are, however, considerably more politically and hermeneutically sophisticated than the stereotype would have it. Also on the fringe of American Evangelicalism, Greg Bahnsen (Theonomy in Christian Ethics, Nutley, N. J.: Craig, 1977) and his father-in-law, Rousas J. Rushdoony (The Institutes of Biblical Law, Nutley, N. J.: Presbyterian and Reformed, 1973) are in the front lines of the conservative Calvinist argument for total, literal adherence to biblical (including Mosaic) law.

38. This threefold categorization of ethical approaches is common in philosophical ethics; see William Frankena, Ethics (Englewood Cliffs, N. J.: Prentice-Hall, 1973).

39. Gustafson, p. 265.

40. James M. Gustafson, "Christian Ethics in America," in his Christian Ethics and the Community (Philadelphia: Pilgrim, 1971), pp. 67-68; this essay was also published in Paul Ramsey, ed., Religion (Englewood Cliffs, N. J.: Prentice-Hall, 1965). Gustafson also has written on this subject elsewhere, notably in his Theology and Christian Ethics (Philadelphia: Pilgrim, 1974), pp. 122-159.

41. Brevard S. Childs, Biblical Theology in Crisis (Philadelphia: Westminster, 1970), p. 124; it is of more than passing interest that in Childs' recent Old Testament Books for Pastor and Teacher (Philadelphia: Westminster, 1977), Jacques Ellul is commended for his books on Jonah and II Kings.

42. For example, on the "liberal" side of the spectrum: James Barr, The Bible in the Modern World (New York: Harper and Row, 1973), and James D. Smart, The Strange Silence of the Bible in the Church (Philadelphia: Westminster, 1970); on the (very) "conservative" side, Harold Lindsell, The Battle for the Bible (Grand Rapids, Mich.: Zondervan, 1976), and James Montgomery Boice, ed., Foundation of Biblical Authority (Grand Rapids, Mich.: Zondervan, 1978); in the "middle" I would place Brevard Childs, Jack Rogers, ed., Biblical Authority (Waco: Word, 1977), and Stephen T. Davis, The Debate About the Bible (Philadelphia: Westminster, 1977). These are some of the more important publications, but they are only a small part of a deluge of recent publications on the subject.

43. Bruce C. Birch and Larry L. Rasmussen, Bible and Ethics in the Christian Life (Minneapolis: Augsburg, 1976).
44. On biblical ethics, see the volumes mentioned earlier by Sanders, Yoder, and Schnackenburg, and also these: James Muilenburg, The Way of Israel: Biblical Faith and Ethics (New York: Harper and Row, 1961); Victor Paul Furnish, Theology and Ethics in Paul (Nashville, Tenn.: Abingdon, 1968); The Love Command in the New Testament (Nashville, Tenn.: Abingdon, 1972); Amos Niven Wilder, Eschatology and Ethics in the Teaching of Jesus (New York: Harper and Brothers, rev. ed., 1950); L. H. Marshall, The Challenge of New Testament Ethics (New York: Macmillan, 1947); E. Clinton Gardiner, Biblical Faith and Social Ethics (New York: Harper and Brothers, 1960); T. B. Maston, Biblical Ethics: A Survey (Waco, Tx.: Word, 1969); John Knox, The Ethic of Jesus in the Teaching of the Church (New York: Abingdon, 1961); and William Lillie, Studies in New Testament Ethics (Philadelphia: Westminster, 1963).

    On relating Scripture to ethics, see James M. Gustafson, Theology and Christian Ethics, (Philadelphia: Pilgrim, 1974), pp. 121-159; Edward LeRoy Long, Jr., "The Use of the Bible in Christian Ethics: A Look at the Basic Options," Interpretation, 19 (April 1965): 149-162; Brevard Childs, Biblical Theology in Crisis (Philadelphia: Westminster, 1970); C. Freeman Sleeper, "Ethics as a Context for Biblical Interpretation," Interpretation, 22 (October 1968): 443-460; H. Edward Everding, Jr., and Dana W. Wilbanks, Decision Making and the Bible (Valley Forge, Pa.: Judson, 1975); also Hendrik Kraemer, The Bible and Social Ethics (Philadelphia: Fortress, 1965).
45. Birch and Rasmussen, p. 111.
46. Ibid., p. 104.
47. Ibid., p. 115.
48. David H. Kelsey, The Uses of Scripture in Recent Theology (Philadelphia: Fortress, 1975).
49. Kelsey, pp. 14ff.
50. Ibid., pp. 32ff.
51. Ibid., pp. 56ff.
52. Ibid., pp. 125ff. See Stephen Toulmin, The Uses of Argument (Cambridge, 1969).
53. Kelsey, p. 159.
54. Ibid., p. 160.
55. In addition to the random comments Ellul makes about

himself throughout his books and articles, and the various introductions to his books provided by translators and editors, Ellul's article "Mirror of These Ten Years," Christian Century, 87 (February 18, 1970): 200-204, is particularly insightful for its autobiographical materials. The best two sources of biographical detail are Jacques Ellul, In Season, Out of Season (San Francisco: Harper & Row, 1982), and Jacques Ellul, Perspectives on Our Age (New York: Seabury Press, 1981).

56. Despite his often harsh rejection of this Catholic "social Christianity" it is remarkable to observe the common orientation on many issues between Ellul, Mounier, Dorothy Day, and the Catholic Worker movement in America. See also Emmanuel Mounier, Be Not Afraid: Studies in Personalist Sociology (London: Rockliff, 1951); Eileen Cantin, Mounier: A Personalist View of History (New York: Paulist, 1973); and William D. Miller, A Harsh and Dreadful Love (Garden City, N. Y.: Doubleday, 1974).

57. "From Jacques Ellul," in James Y. Holloway, ed., Introducing Jacques Ellul (Grand Rapids, Mich.: Eerdmans, 1970), p. 6; this volume is a reprint of articles about Ellul which appeared originally in Katallagete: Be Reconciled (Winter/Spring 1970), the journal of the Committee of Southern Churchmen.

58. Ellul is quoted to this effect by David Menninger in the latter's "Jacques Ellul: A Tempered Profile," Review of Politics, 37 (April 1975): 235-246.

59. "From Jacques Ellul," op. cit., p. 6; see also "Mirror of These Ten Years," op. cit.

60. Complete bibliographical and publication data on Ellul's published books is contained in the bibliography at the end of this volume. For the sake of chronological awareness, the dates of the original publication and the original English publication (ET) are both given. In a few cases, the English translation of Ellul's manuscript was rushed into print before the French.

## CHAPTER TWO ☐

# THE SHAPE AND TASK OF ETHICS IN ELLUL'S THOUGHT

Although Ellul has played the role of Christian ethicist at many points in his writings, explicit and sustained attention to ethics is provided only in To Will and to Do: An Ethical Research for Christians (1964) and The Ethics of Freedom (1973/74).[1] These two books are only part of a much longer series on ethics which Ellul has planned. To Will and to Do is the "first half of the first volume" that will be the Introduction to Ellul's ethics. To Will and to Do deals with the origin and character of various "moralities of the world" and shows their relation to biblical Christian ethics. The unpublished second half of the Introduction will "sketch the conditions which a Christian ethics should fulfill and ... outline the problem of social ethics."[2]

The three main volumes of Ellul's ethics are planned around the Pauline theological virtues of faith, hope, and love. The Ethics of Freedom corresponds to hope and has been published first because Ellul believes that hope and its partner are the "site" of the decisive conflict of our era. Eventually, Ellul plans to complete the series by publishing an ethics of holiness (corresponding to faith) and an ethics of relationship (corresponding to love).

In this chapter we will examine first Ellul's critique of ethics (the "impossibility" of a Christian ethic) as given primarily in To Will and to Do. This is an essential setting of the stage for the next task, which is to examine his own proposed Christian ethic (the "necessary" Christian ethic). These tasks accomplished, we will look in the following chapter more specifically at Ellul's understanding of the Word of God in Jesus Christ and Scripture, especially as related to Christian ethics.

As this discussion proceeds, Ellul's work will be

located in relation to the discussions and categories of the previous chapter. Few analyses of Ellul's ethics have been published, but reference will be made when appropriate to what is available. Two other figures who will enter the discussion periodically are Ellul's two primary theological mentors: Karl Barth and Søren Kierkegaard. With respect to Barth, Ellul frequently confesses a debt to his thought, though he is not an "unconditional Barthian."[3] In a recent article, "Karl Barth and Us," Ellul says:[4]

> When I rethink my progress over these last twenty years, it seems that I received from him two great principles and a "mission." The two principles: freedom and universal salvation--not the themes classically thought of when speaking of Barth.

The "mission" Ellul received from Barth was to work out a better ethics:

> I had the impression that the ethical consequences of Barth's theology had never been elicited. I was not satisfied with his volumes of ethics and politics, which seemed to be based on an insufficient knowledge of the world and of politics. However, there was everything there necessary to formulate an ethic without losing any of the rediscovered truth, being totally faithful to the Scriptures, but without legalism or literalism. But this work seemed possible to me only if one conserved the groundwork laid by Barth and did not start over.

Ellul's explicit references to Kierkegaard are much fewer in number than those to Karl Barth but they are without exception positive and approving. Anyone reading both Kierkegaard and Ellul will soon be struck by the close similarity of their thought and often their language. The relationship to Kierkegaard is made explicit in one of Ellul's most important American articles, "Between Chaos and Paralysis":

> What then do I mean when I say that our hope lies in starting from the individual--from total subjectivity?
>
> . . .
>
> This radical subjectivity will inform ... the three human passions which seem to be the essential ones--the passion to create, to love, to play. But

> these mighty drives of the human heart must find a particular expression in each person. It is in the building of a new daily life.
>
> . . .
>
> I am convinced that Christians are absolutely the only ones who can attempt it--but here too on condition that they start from zero. Kierkegaard, it seems to me, alone can show us how to start.[5]

More will be said about both Barth and Kierkegaard as this study proceeds, but it is essential to recognize their critical influence on Ellul from the beginning.

## PROLEGOMENON: A CRITIQUE OF ETHICS

A traditional concern of ethics has been with "the good." Ellul begins his critique of ethics by arguing that, from a biblical Christian perspective, the good is not an independent reality which can be known naturally, generally, abstractly, or a priori.[6] Rather, the good is the will and command of God, known in a certain relationship with God in Jesus Christ, and it is concrete and specific. The people of God can only reflect the goodness of God; they cannot put forth any natural goodness before God. Without putting it in these terms, Ellul is arguing that the term "good" should be conceived in terms of the nonmoral value situated over and above any normative ethical discussion. The second important aspect of Ellul's argument here is that the locus of nonmoral value ("the good") is God--transcendent, personal, speaking, acting, willing. What we have in Ellul's opening move is, of course, precisely what James M. Gustafson identified as a characteristic of the "Jesus Christ the Lord who is Creator and Redeemer" ethical style.[7]

In Ellul's biblical theology, the origin of morality itself is bound up with the fall. With the fall humanity became aware of the good--not in possession of it but aware of something lost. Since the fallen creature cannot fully know the good (in the biblical sense of knowledge as participation of the whole being), humanity creates and defines its own good and evil. In the Eden story (which reveals the fundamental spiritual reality of morality) the fall brings with it the need to express shame, fear, and accusation, and a corresponding need for self-justification, leading to a rabid interest in morality. Thus Ellul stigmatizes morality, per se, as a product of sin or disobedience. Morality is of the "order of the fall."[8]

But, morality is also of the "order of necessity":

> It is neither nothingness, nor the absurd, nor incoherence. It is an order, an organization, a stability, embracing whatever is necessary to maintain life (relatively) and creation (also relatively).[9]

Before the fall there was freedom; the fall brought chaos and confusion. Order ceased to be the free gift of God and became a matter of external restraint. In fact, the world and humanity cannot survive without this total network of physical, legal, social, and other restraints. Without the system of duties and obligations we term morality, the group cannot survive. "The moral structures, the defining of the good, are ideological expressions of the social and biological determinants with which the individual lives."[10] This critique exhibits Ellul's roots in a Marxist sociology, in seeing morality (in its ideological expression) as a kind of "superstructure" and as "the truth of a false condition." There is, of course, a radical difference in perception of the good which judges empirical morality for Marx (the telos of the "classless society") and Ellul (the Wholly Other God).

Thus, the radical incapacity of humanity to know and do the Good is not the end of the discussion.[11] There is also a relative, human good characterized by degrees (while God's Good is always either/or). There is a necessary human morality (which may or may not coincide with the divine Good at various points) which varies in form and content according to the setting and is adaptable to changing cultures. Human moralities are a defense against anguish and chaos. They are social in origin and individual in application. Moral values are thus conditioned, unstable, limited, and relative.

It is essential to recognize these two incommensurable moralities: (1) Christian "morality," which is the relationship to God whereby his command, the revelation of his will, is his own choice and decision, and (2) morality of the world, as described above. Christian "morality" (the command of God) unmasks, devalues, and relativizes human morality and moral pretensions. Nevertheless, human morality is essential, serious, and necessary for human existence in the world.

To the extent that the command of God does not intervene in opposition, Christians should do what is right, good, and honorable in the sight of all people.[12]

Before proceeding with Ellul's analysis of human morality we should note the similarities between his approach and that of Søren Kierkegaard. Kierkegaard's three "stages on life's way"--the aesthetic, the ethical, and the religious--do not (as Walter Lowrie and other Kierkegaard scholars have pointed out) exist as completely discrete spheres. As the ascent is made upward from the aesthetic to the ethical and finally to the religious, the lower stages are dethroned, relativized, and given their true value and meaning in relation to the higher. The highest stage, which Kierkegaard calls the "religious" (Ellul, following Barth, would prefer to make "religion" refer to a relative, human phenomenon and call this highest stage of essential Christianity "revelational," discipleship, or something to that effect--but the substance is the same by whatever term we use) is the dynamic existential relationship to God.

Two quotations from Kierkegaard's <u>Concluding Unscientific Postscript</u> make plain the parentage of Ellul's view:

> The comparative, the conventional, the external, the legal conception of the ethical may be useful enough in common intercourse, but in case it is forgotten that the substantial value of the ethical must be in the inwardness of the individual, if it is to be anywhere at all ... that generation is nevertheless impoverished ethically in an essential sense, and is essentially bankrupt.
>
> ...
>
> In connection with the human crowd ... it is all right to apply a comparative standard, but in case this use of the comparative standard gets so much the upper hand that the individual in his inward man applies it to himself, then the ethical is done for.[13]

The crucial point for disciples of Christ is that the "substantial value of the ethical" in the subjective, spirit-to-spirit relationship with the Wholly Other must always have the "upper hand."

The "morality of the world" is thus exclusively on

the human level, not transcendent, and the object of this moral life is the fulfillment of what is in a given time and place called the good. Ellul then makes a distinction between objective and subjective morality.[14] Objective morality is defined as "a system of values or imperatives, whether formulated or not, which are set forth as possessed of an objectivity indispensable to all members of the group."[15] Objective moralities are always based on pragmatic arguments that have three constituent elements: (1) "theoretical morality"--where the imperatives are drawn up by a religious authority or philosopher, (2) "sociological morality"--where the imperatives spring from collective necessity, and (3) "moral custom"--where the imperatives are derived from past authority, custom, and antiquity.

Subjective morality is comprised of two elements: (1) the imperative of conscience--the origin of which is unknown (Ellul, with Barth, rejects arguments based on Romans 2 that God has implanted his law in everyone's heart in the form of conscience) and (2) choice or decision--the ethical situation is the situation requiring choice or decision (to obey or not to obey, etc.). Theoretical justification may be formulated later on, of course. The phenomenon of human morality, in Ellul's view, always displays these objective and subjective features.

Ellul also makes a distinction between theoretical and lived morality. Theoretical moralities (for example, those of Confucius, Kant, or Bentham) are innumerable. They are characterized by idealization, absolutization, rationalization, and systematization. They can be prescriptive or descriptive in style. Their great weakness is their lack of applicability. They remain in philosophers' studies and libraries. Still, theoretical moralities give us one picture, one indication, of a society at a particular point. They can have a marginal influence on lived morality if they are carefully formulated in relation to a living context.

The lived moralities are located not primarily in philosophers' studies and university lecture halls but at the social level. Morality and society are closely connected in at least two ways. First, no society can survive in the absence of a morality with both individual/psychic and social/political power. As noted earlier, morality is of the order of necessity. Second, human morality owes its very origins to the social group and its evolution. It is never arbitrary but has a principal motif related to the complex of interrelationships within the group.

Values are related to this central motif and to what is "the sacred" in a given society.[16] Ellul uses the term "value" in three ways: (1) beliefs--convictions which provide controlling reasons for acting and judging; (2) "certain existing facts and powers" (e.g., equality, work, history) to which are attributed the status of value; and (3) "certain definitely existing realities" desirable to the people, possessed of a grandeur, in function of which people act and judge but--in contrast to (2)--which are independent of all synthesis and intrinsic meaning. Values, in any of these three senses, can be revolutionary or stabilizing and institutional. Usually "value instigates both an order and a will to transgress that order."[17]

There has always been a certain distance between the person as moral agent and the morality itself. Persons take a certain stance in relation to morality. At the extremes are moralism and immoralism. Moralism is the practice of using morality as a means of justification and a "good conscience," as an organization for convenience (establishing predictable behavior, classifying and judging people, etc.), or as a means for self-determination and revolution. Moralism uses morality as a tool to be exploited for one's own ends, and it results in depersonalization on the one hand and usurpation of God's judgment on the other.

Immoralism can take the form of following one's own passions and propensities, which reduces to slavery to the self. It can take the form of repudiating a declining morality in the name of a contemporary morality, which is then slavery and conformity to the average, the normal, and the status quo. Or, thirdly, it can take the form of a theoretical or scientific criticism of all morality per se, which is finally illusory, for destruction of a given morality inexorably leads to the establishment of a replacement; morality is inescapable.

Finally, Ellul turns to the current form of lived morality, which he not surprisingly calls "technological morality." Technological morality aims to bring behavior into harmony with technique. As Christian morality (actually, "Christendom's morality") declines, new virtues and values in subordination to technique (the new "sacred") appear. Technological morality has two primary characteristics: It is a morality of behavior and conduct, not of intentions, and moral questioning is excluded and the "one best way" is sought every time.

This contemporary morality has three values on its scale: (1) technique, the decisive criterion, the source of meaning, promise, justification, and motivation; (2) the normal, which replaces the "moral"--adjustment and behaving "normally" (rather than "well") are what is important; and (3) success, which, with failure, replaces "good and evil"--and the means to success are technological, of course. Technological morality demands commitment and the practice of its virtues, such as work, loyalty, self-discipline, responsibility, and increased production. Other moral values, such as the family or humor, are progressively subordinated or eliminated. Humanity is thus being adapted to technique by morality. Objective, external behavior is the standard of conduct.

At best, then, morality of the world is a pale imitation and pursuit of what has been lost since the fall of the human race. It is of the order of necessity in the double sense of being needful for life to continue and being characterized by a significant degree of external constraint. At its worst (read: today), it is the means and expression of terrible bondage to a civilization crushing its individual citizens under the yoke of unbridled technique.

The whole saga of human morality from the fall to the technological society stands over against the Word of God and leads Ellul to argue the "impossibility of a Christian ethics." "All morality, Christian or not, is destructive of freedom."[18] The "biblical concept of the good as the will of God immediately prohibits us from formulating an ethic."[19] An ethic is always, ultimately, the formulation of a good in itself and is thus an usurpation of God and an assumption that the good is immanently knowable, permanent, and universal.

Christians confess that the good is the will of God, knowable only by revelation of a living God.

> Either the revelation is a present, living Word and it cannot be systematized into a morality, or it is a dead letter which isn't worth using in preference to anything else in the building of an ethic.[20]

The will of God remains free, not frozen into principles. The Bible records history, not philosophy. Thus, the Christian life is a "being," a certain kind of life, a "walking worthy," a bearing of the fruit of the Spirit, an action inspired and guided by that Spirit, not the doing of works nor compliance with a system of ethical rules.

What Ellul proposes (as we shall see in the next section) is not a doctrinaire nihilism nor an ethical casuistry, but a life. Christianity must be lived or it is nothing. And there are many "Christian lives," not just one. The Christian faith tells us that we should live, now how. Christian life is eschatological, and we cannot make a valid, systematic description of the End in the present time. Much of the "how" we live is left to our invention at the point of contact between our concrete situation and the Holy Spirit's requirements. The responsibility of the particular person is to discover how the Spirit's eternal requirement can be embodied in today's world, conflicts, and events. Thus, our decisions will often be prosaic, microscopic, and opposed to the world. They will seldom be grandiose and never codified or hardened.

Historically, of course, Christians have formulated moralities.[21] This was a process that grew over the first several centuries, motivated by three circumstances in particular. First, there was the legitimate desire for the "cure of souls" and for concrete spiritual guidance. Second, the wedding of Church and State in the fourth century imposed the requirement of formulating a morality for politics and citizenship. Third, the desire of the Church to manage society in Christendom led to an ever more aggressive formulation of moralities beginning in the Middle Ages.

In all attempts to formulate a Christian morality, Ellul complains, it has proved impossible to avoid the importation of foreign material such as Stoicism, Neo-Platonism, Aristotelianism, rationalism, or Marxism, thus polluting and betraying the Word of God. The long-range results have been catastrophic as the specific witness of Christianity has been accommodated and lost. The relationship with God has been transformed from personal dialogue into impersonal systematization. This objectification "binds" God and relieves his people of the burden of being called into question. Even the Reformers failed, in Ellul's view, to extend their theological reformation into a rejection of morality of the world.

We have noted earlier the similarity of Ellul's critique of ethics to that of Kierkegaard. It is important also to listen briefly to Karl Barth's language on the nature of the Good and on Ellul's "morality of the world." "Good human action is action set free by the command of God, by His claim and decision and judgment."[22] "Man's action is good insofar as it is sanctified by the Word of God which as such is also the command of God."[23] Statements like these could be multiplied, showing Barth's conception of the Good to be identical to that of Ellul.

Barth rejects what Ellul calls the "morality of the world" but under the rubric of "formal casuistry" (Ellul's "necessary" ethic corresponds to what Barth calls "practical casuistry"). A formal casuistry is unacceptable for three reasons: (1) It sets up the moralist on God's throne as a judge and is thus an usurpation making God's will and command the prisoner of the moralist's law and his or her application of it. (2) It makes "the objectively untenable assumption that the command of God is a universal rule, an empty form, or rather a tissue of such rules and forms." (3) It is also an "encroachment in relation to man's action under the command of God, a destruction of the Christian freedom, in which alone this can be a good action."[24]

There are clear affinities of this approach with some of Bonhoeffer's ethics on the same basic point; a radical distinction between systematic, philosophical, and natural ethics, on the one hand, and Christian ethics, defined as a living, personal relationship to the Good, commanding God, on the other. Ellul's distinctiveness in this critique of ethics is not in its general outlines but in his more extensive analysis of both the biblical story of the origin and character of morality and the contemporary manifestations of human morality. This is explained by the fact that Ellul is a sociologist (of the technological society) and ethicist, in contrast to the anti-Hegelian philosopher (Kierkegaard) and the dogmatic theologian (Barth).

At the end of the next section we will locate Ellul in relation to the categories and questions of the first chapter of this book. For now, the question may be raised as to how successful Ellul's critique is. As a rhetorical "strategy," first of all, Ellul is a profound success. By that we mean that from several angles he has successfully emphasized the distinctiveness of biblical Christian ethics. Anyone who shares Ellul's basic theological commitments might rejoice at this carving out of a unique place and approach for what is regarded as a unique faith in a unique God.

As an exercise in ethical criticism, however, Ellul's success is ultimately very modest. First, to relativize (or even reject) normative ethical systems (or "formal casuistry") in the name of a nonmoral value ("the good") is not the exclusive prerogative of Christian ethicists. Any number of alternative possibilities could be suggested (happiness, erotic love, etc.). Second, the existentially dynamic character of ethics can be preserved in other than Christian ethical approaches (my own will or Sun Myung Moon's will, if established as the good, are partly novel and partly constant, analogously to the will of God). It will not do to stigmatize my examples as "immoralism" and slavery, for obedience to the will of God is also "slavery" in one respect. Thus, what will differentiate Ellul's Christian ethics (or Barth's) from other ethics is only partially this matter of its form. Primarily it will be differentiated by its content, that is, by the will of *this* God.

There is a sense in which Ellul's doctrines of the fall and the incarnation are (despite their apparent radicalism) arrested. That is, "fallen" morality, the "quest for what has been lost," can imitate even the dynamism and the form of a Divine Command ethics. It is not limited to the form of a legal code or philosophical system. And, on the other hand, if God can be faithfully incarnated in an existentialist ethic, why not a step or two further in a code? After all, he found it possible to be limited to the body of a man for thirty years. Why not an ethical code for a few years?

In the end, of course, all of this critiquing by Ellul is not the end: an ethics is necessary and possible after all. The point has been to identify its positive distinctiveness and to differentiate it negatively from its competitors and its various "betrayals."

## THE "NECESSARY" CHRISTIAN ETHIC

Already, in his critique of ethics, Ellul has admitted that there is no escaping the need for a Christian ethic. To avoid the problem is to acquiesce to some morality of the world. Yet Christians are to be a "foreign element" in the world, a contradiction, the "salt" and the "light" of the earth.

The Christian who is involved in the material his-

> tory of this world, is involved in it as representing another order, another Master (than the "prince of this world"), another claim.... The opposition between this world and the Kingdom of God is a total one.[25]

Thus, a Christian ethic is indispensable at the level of individual conduct as guidance for Christian disciples. The triple danger of inward spiritual pietism, indifference, and excessive worldliness must be avoided. Theologians, in particular, must propose an ethics as an instrument of reflection and explanation concerning people and their problems. Ethics serves theologians as well as the laity, by reminding them to be committed in the world as a register of commitment to the Word. Ethics indicates the limits and conditions of that involvement.

The Church, as a society or social group itself, also stands in need of an ethics for its corporate life. Ellul suggests four marks of authenticity for such an ethic: It should be conscious, aware of its relativity, humble and under judgment, and in the service of the faithful, not imposed on them.[26]

Christian ethics must be temporary ethics. "Morality should express our way of being present to the world. Hence it should change as the world changes."[27]

> We are not concerned with formulating principles, but with knowing how to judge an action in given circumstances.... The Scripture teaches us that its ethic varies in form, and in concrete application to situations and places.... We must not imagine that this ethic will give us the permanent solution of all problems.... It needs to be continually revised, re-examined, and re-shaped by the combined effort of the Church as a whole.[28]

Thus, Christian ethics must avoid the extremes of biblicistic immediate application and pure conformity to the changing world. What is required is realism and understanding in relation to both Scripture and the world.

Christian ethics will thus be not a system of general principles but rather a call, a requirement, a spur, deriving from faith and related to the revelation of God. It will be indicative, not imperative, and hortatory, not dogmatic. It will be the application of the requirement and promises of faith in Jesus Christ to particular, concrete situations of Christians. It will be addressed to faith, calling faith to fulfillment. "There are no normative ethics of the good, but there are ethics of grace, which are quite the opposite."[29] Once again, despite Ellul's protest, it is not really that there are no normative ethics; it is rather that the status of such ethics is always relative and subordinate to both God (the nonmoral "good") and to the situation. If there were really no normative ethics, we would simply point to God and be quiet!

Ellul is quick to point out that he is not advocating pure situationism. Ethics does have continuity, especially during periods of the "silence of God" (as he sees our era) when a good deal of "remembering" is called for. While not permanently codifiable, neither is Christian ethics discontinuous, incoherent, or indescribable.

> There are consequences of faith which can be objectively indicated. To say the contrary suggests that we are all angels, that we are already in the Kingdom of God, and that our flesh no longer offers any resistance to the action of the Spirit.... But this elaboration must not be substituted for the fight of faith, which every Christian must wage; that is why it is indicative, not imperative.[30]

Freedom does not mean inconsistency, arbitrariness, or absurdity. God is free and unconditioned but He is also "the same yesterday, and today, and forever." God does not deceive us; He is not a despot, but a loving Father. Thus it is legitimate that we should look into past revelation for ethical guidance. The Holy Spirit will enable us to translate the biblical revelation into Word of God for our current situation.[31] In what is probably his clearest definition, Ellul says:

> Ethics is there precisely to bring down to the level of the tangible problems, the demand of the absolute which the Christian experiences within himself, and to oblige him to take seriously the relativity of human situations.[32]

As a final characteristic of this "necessary" Christian ethic, Ellul insists that it be "apologetic." This is not the same as an intellectual apologetics, but rather that our "works done in virtue of, and in consequence of, the Christian ethic, ought to appear in the light of Jesus Christ as veritable good works."

> We must see to it that our works proceed so directly from the action of Jesus Christ in us, that the world will see them in their true light ..., that these "works" are of such a quality that they lead men to praise God. When they do this, they constitute an apologetic. Our ethic as a whole will have no meaning unless it is directed toward this conflict with the world which should end in giving glory to God.[33]

The Ethics of Freedom is the first systematic statement by Ellul of what this necessary, temporary, apologetic, relative, conscious, and humble ethic in service of the faithful might be for our time and place. Ethics, as he has stated, ought to "flow out of the relationship with Christ."

> Some mediation, however, is needed, and I think I have found it ... in the theological virtues which are presented by Paul. To each of these a sector of the Christian life seems to correspond, and every question needs to be seen from the standpoint of these three virtues. But each expresses a specific type of behavior. Thus it seems to me that hope corresponds to an ethics of freedom, faith to an ethics of holiness, and love to an ethics of relationship. I resolved in 1960 to write the ethics of freedom, even though hope does not come first, because I was becoming increasingly convinced that freedom is the location and condition and arena of all Christian ethics and that holiness and relationship are possible only on the basis and in terms of the functioning of freedom. The other two parts of ethics would then be closely linked to one another. Thus holiness as separation, service, and witness for God, or as the conflict of faith, expresses the distinctiveness of incarnate Christianity, but separation has a place only for the sake of mission. The break has to come first, but it implies a rediscovery of the world, society, and one's neighbor in a new type of relationship.[34]

Ellul promises to defend this choice of faith, hope, and love as the means of developing Christian ethics, in the second half of his "Introduction."

Ellul's decision to write the ethics of freedom once again puts him in the footsteps of Karl Barth (and Kierkegaard, for that matter).[35] It would be a mistake, however, to think that Ellul is merely reproducing Barth's approach. As we have seen, his self-stated position is that of a "conditional Barthian." Thus, while both Barth and Ellul regard the "gift of freedom" as the "foundation of evangelical ethics," there are differences leading up to, as well as from, that common affirmation. In briefest terms, Barth arrived at this affirmation of the centrality of freedom via his theology of God and the Word of God. Ellul, by contrast, arrived at the same point at least as much via sociological studies and personal experience as theological study. From the starting point of freedom, Barth intended to mediate the elaboration of the rest of his ethics through the doctrines of Creation, Redemption, and Reconciliation, raising ethical questions first from one and then another of those perspectives. Ellul, whose Christology is not nearly so thoroughly developed as Barth's (and in this respect reminds one more of Kierkegaard), intends to proceed to faith/holiness, and love/relationship as the perspectives complementing hope/freedom in the threefold raising of the ethical question.

Hope in Time of Abandonment (1973) is one of Ellul's most important books for understanding his ethics.[36] In this work he describes the way his sociological studies led him into a blind alley. Civilization seemed headed for catastrophe and death. Worse yet, his perception of the current condition of the Church and his biblical studies led him to conclude that God has turned away in silence and that we are "abandoned," in a sense. Our era is like the time between the Old and New Testaments when God was silent (despite the flood of apocryphal literature pretending to be the voice of God). It is like the time at the end of the Judges in Israel. It is a sad realization of the worst fears of the Psalmist who begged God not to turn away (Psalm 74). God has not turned away from all individuals, but from the culture and perhaps even from the Church on a general level.

We persist in centering all on faith, Ellul complains. But the modern world is filled with "faiths" (though the sacred is transferred to the cultural and social level in these faiths, according to Ellul). "How witness to Christian faith in the midst of all these beliefs and new myths?" This is an appropriate question for today's evangelism. But the proclamation of hope is more decisive today than either faith or love. In a time of abandonment, hope is central and prior to all other questions. Thus, he says, we must proclaim the radical exclusiveness of hope in Christ.[37]

Theologically, of course, faith, hope, and love are inseparable. But it is proclamation (not theologizing) that is decisive, and hope is what the modern world needs most to hear. Hope is exactly what the Church still has, even while theological definition founders. Hope is dynamic rather than static, and yet it is factual, a "dialectic of the concrete." As opposed to faith, which is more static and intellectual, hope is headed toward the future. This means that a Christian ethics of freedom is inexorably an eschatological ethics.

> Thus the principle of the Christian ethic begins here. We must search the Scriptures for the way in which we ought to live, in order that the end, willed by God, should be present amongst men.[38]

The quotation above from Ellul's 1948 book, Presence of the Kingdom (and there are many other similar comments in that work), indicates that the choice of hope/freedom is not just a function of the particular character of our era. It is also a conclusion about the fundamental outlook of the Bible. The Ethics of Freedom makes this quite clear:

> For Christians all ethics must be eschatological. The starting point must be the end, the last things ..., the final recapitulation, and the ultimate creation.... The movement of the return of Christ is the movement which gives point to our history and which already presses with all its weight on time as it now is.
>
> We have to understand this fact as the constitutive basis of ethics because here alone do we learn how God views our activity, how he judges it, and how he finally assumes it.[39]

So faith and love are not excluded, but hope is the dominant factor.[40]

Hope is also

> man's answer to God's silence ..., the absurd act of confidence placed in those who declared that it was the Word of God which they have received ..., that this Word of God might once again be spoken, be born, be decisive.[41]

Hope is a demand that God turn again, a protest before God, a resolute will to make God change, a kind of violence against God. The attitude of Job, the wrestling of Jacob, the "importunate woman" of Jesus' parable--these are examples of what Ellul means by "hope in time of abandonment."

Hope has "enormous ethical and politico-social consequences."[42] "Freedom is the ethical expression of the person who hopes. Hope is the relation with God of the person liberated by God."[43] This freedom is "the only freedom not based on other slaveries."[44] Ellul's earlier description of the Christian life in The Presence of the Kingdom illuminates this approach: "The heart of this ethic may be expressed thus: it is based on an 'agonistic' way of life; that is to say, the Christian life is always an 'agony,' that is, a final decisive conflict."[45] The fundamental dialectical opposition is that between God, the Wholly Other, the source of life, on the one hand, and the world, closed off from God, closed in on its path to death, on the other. The Christian is inexorably part of both realities; the dialectical opposition is never resolved philosophically; it is resolved in life, the life of struggle and hope.

This struggle of hope expresses itself in "waiting," and "realism," but chiefly in prayer.[46] Prayer is the primary mediation of hope; and as God's gift in response to our hope, freedom is the possibility for living out hope concretely and effectively from day to day. What is required, then, is an ethics of freedom, the articulation of a call, a requirement, a spur to a faithful living out of the freedom granted by God in answer to our hope.

Ellul's "necessary" ethics of freedom proceeds in four stages, to which we now turn. In part I of The Ethics of Freedom, "Alienated Man and Liberation in Christ," he describes the determining and conditioning forces making our contemporary world, a world of "necessity" and "alienation" (alienation from the self, from work, and so forth). "It is alienation in the multiplicity, complexity, crushing rigor, the non-criticizable rationality of social systems." It is the fact that "man is less than the master of his own life."[47]

Closely related to the problem of alienation is the fact that the world is ruled by necessity. We have already encountered this concept in Ellul's discussion of the fundamental character of "morality of the world." Necessity is not the same thing as fate. "I do not view either man or society mechanistically. But I have to accept the fact that there are necessities which we cannot escape."[48] These necessities are experienced by individuals in varying degrees. Their primary manifestation, however, is on the collective social level; contemporary examples are political power, money, the city, and technique. Each of these necessities constricts our freedom and determines our action to some extent.

Alienation and necessity are finally expressions of sin and the fallenness of the world. Biblically, this condition is described as bondage, which is something more than finitude. What is required, then, is emancipation, redemption. Ellul turns to God in Jesus Christ in search of the keys to freedom and emancipation. Since we will return to Ellul's use of Jesus Christ in the next chapter, it will only be noted here that, for Ellul, Jesus Christ is our primary source of the knowledge of God and of freedom in relation to bondage. In Jesus Christ we learn that "freedom is not sitting back and letting God work. Freedom is knowing God's will and doing it."[49]

The human creature is a "being booked to die" and requires outside intervention. True freedom requires the intervention of the Wholly Other. This freedom is an event in the moment and it requires new interventions and renewals.[50] The freedom granted through the Word of God does not, however, objectively suppress the necessity and determination we live with. What it does is tear away the illusions. "Our freedom ... is ... lived within and by means of the determinations."[51]

Ellul digresses briefly to consider the problem of whether Christians have a monopoly on true freedom. Ellul's answer is a qualified "Yes." In Jesus Christ all people without exception are saved and reconciled. Ellul, more than Barth, though he credits Barth for this, is a full-blown "universalist." But freedom is not a metaphysical problem primarily; rather, it is an ethical problem. Freedom is not imposed on the reconciled, *opus operatum*. Freedom is arrested, rejected, undermined; Satan is still the "prince of this world." Though it is a crushing burden (and no cause for gloating), and Christians have failed miserably (again, no cause for gloating), it is nevertheless true, in Ellul's view, that Christians alone, in virtue of their conscious relationship to Jesus Christ, have the possibility of mediating freedom.

In Part II, "The Object of Freedom and the Will of Man," Ellul further elaborates his concept of freedom. Freedom is a "situation," a "power," and a "possibility."[52] It is not a virtue, but rather the "climate of all virtues." It is spontaneous, not gradual or incremental. It is "bearing fruit" rather than "doing works." It is not a matter of independent choice.

> Merely making a choice, however, is in no way akin to freedom.... The decision of freedom, in contrast, will be creative. It does not have to begin with a given situation. It is not enclosed by solutions. It does not mean choice between pre-established facts. It will manifest openness to something different, a third way, a reading at a different level, a rephrasing of the question, a situation which allows of some other path than that of constraint by necessity.... Ethical choice is not choice between a good and an evil. In the first instance it is choice between what is possible and what is not.[53]

Freedom has been defined by Ellul as "the coming of something new into the world with a creative adherence to an inexhaustible good."[54] This new possibility is simply "what God has done." Our task is simply to "choose it, to incarnate it, to live it out."[55]

With Barth (whom he explicitly affirms here), Ellul argues that this freedom is <u>for</u> God. "To share in God's freedom is to lose individual autonomy but to gain autonomy in relation to the world."[56] Our freedom is preserved only so long as we remain continually questioned afresh by the Word of God. Prayer, confession, the holy day, and the reading of Scripture are, for Barth and Ellul, signs and expressions of this freedom from the world, and for God.

Freedom is thus <u>for</u> God. But what is freedom <u>from</u>? We do not, of course, escape out of the world of conditions and necessities. But God limits himself, his judgment, his influence and decision, and accompanies men and women on their earthly paths, introducing openings, breeches, and new possibilities for life. Ellul discusses three aspects of the "freedom from." First, we are freed in relation to our self--from our past guilt and bondage, anxiety about the future, and present self-centeredness, covetousness, impotence, the spirit of might and conquest, and so forth. Second, we are freed in relation to the "powers" (exousia), interpreted as freedom from the collective "demonic" forces of institutions and structures such as the State, money ("Mammon" in the Bible), and technique.[57] Third, we are freed in relation to revelation--freed from bondage to outmoded formulations and methods as well as more recent fashions. We shall return to the subject of revelation below.

Finally, Ellul discusses the scope and limits of freedom, by focusing on the Pauline text, "All things are lawful, but not all things edify" (I Corinthians 10:23). Ellul emphasizes first the radical and total scope of this freedom. "Any lifestyle can be the expression of freedom."[58] There is no such thing as an intrinsic right or wrong. If sanctified by the Word of God and prayer, anything and any act may, by the grace of God, be free.

However, freedom is not given without an orientation, direction, or significance. "Freedom is truly freedom when it commits us to an action which we choose, when it aims at certain objectives and marks."[59] This direction must be "expedient" (useful, serious, important) and "edifying" (constructive, upbuilding). Everything must contribute to the glory of God and be loving to our neighbor. These latter two guides are frequently given by Ellul. They recall, of course, his insistence that ethics be "apologetic" in character.

Ellul's emphasis on neighbor-love is especially important in view of his strong individualism. The ethic thus is individualistic but not "privatistic." And since only God can love the totality, we must express our love to specific, particular persons.

> The fact that freedom is a choice of acts in terms of love for others means that we are faced with a purely individualistic ethics. This freedom can only be demonstrated by individual acts in individual cases. Intrinsically and primarily it does not have any social or political dimension in the traditional sense.[60]

In a later chapter we will return to examine Ellul's "resolution" of the problem of individualism in his ethics.

In Part III, "The Assumption of Freedom," Ellul

repeats his point that God does not impose freedom on us; it is a gift that we must "assume." The first step in this assumption of freedom is "recognition" of our effective liberation in Christ--we must know this freedom (via Scripture) and live it out, and our effective alienation--a concrete grasping of our actual situation, internally and externally. This recognition is another way of stating the requirement of "realism" for which Ellul persistently lobbies. Of course, recognition must, in turn, lead to action or it is not true freedom.

Ellul warns Christians to avoid slipping back into bondage through moralism, immoralism, the pursuit of happiness (which is never to be pursued but rather received as a gift from God), and the spirit of conquest. Christians have a great responsibility to avoid bondage and assume this freedom. For while Christian freedom is individual and personal in its origin and execution, it is necessarily collective (also) in its reference and consequences.

The "positive responsibility" of Christians to assume and live out their freedom may not yield very impressive visible results, Ellul admits. God usually works in secret and uses our faithfulness and freedom in ways that are hard to measure positively. The "negative responsibility" is, by contrast, immense. That is, if we do not assume and live out our freedom, the results are ominous. This (Ellul argues) is because the coming of Jesus Christ decisively changed human history. The collective securities of the human race are no longer coherent or liveable. The incarnation of Jesus Christ was God's offer of a new order and freedom.[61] "One might say, indeed, that our Western society with its insanity and increasingly complex and frightening problems is the product of the act of Christ that Christians have not followed up and made their own."[62] This is, obviously, a rather startling proposition, and we will have to examine it in the section on Jesus Christ which follows.

Finally, in Part IV, "Implicated Freedom," Ellul begins to elaborate his approach in terms of our life as "pilgrims and strangers." There is no such thing, he argues, as "pure freedom"; Christian freedom is always lived out in relation to a situation in the world. Because of the great emphasis on the primacy of the group, with no safeguards for the force and validity of the individual, our freedom must find expression today on the individual level.[63] And it is the laity, the people at the intersection of Church and world, whose life is decisive here. The laity need the support of a community, of course; in one of his rare, affirmative comments about the church, Ellul says: "It is on the basis of a church which is a strong body and community that this is possible for the layman."[64] As suggested by this statement, the main (ethical) importance of the church is to prepare and equip the individual members.

Freedom lived out in the world has three dimensions: evangelism--carrying the gospel to non-Christians; mission--where "presence" rather than conversion is the objective; and mediation--reconciliation between persons, and between persons and God. In each of these dimensions, there is no simple or general pattern. Each person must discover the appropriate style and form of action for himself or herself.

"Pilgrimage" is a key description of the implications of freedom. "Hope, by linking us to what is permanent, evokes freedom in relation to circumstances, social structures, ideological movements, and everything that might be called history."[65] Ellul recalls the biblical stories of Cain, Abraham, and the Exodus, in contrasting pilgrimage with the vain search for rootage and security outside of God.

Pilgrimage does not, of course, imply being negative or aloof in relation to society. It is as pilgrims and strangers that we are commissioned as witnesses.[66] Ellul qualifies the concept of uprooting in two ways. First, the uprooting (for pilgrimage) is individual, not collective. At the collective level we must work for stability for life.[67] Conversion and uprooting are not even possibilities if all is in chaos already at the social level. Second, uprooting and pilgrimage do not mean having no possessions, but rather having them "as if not"--i. e., not being rooted in them.

"The radical devaluation of everything in society is accompanied by the revaluation (the only one) that everything, by the grace of God, may be able to serve the kingdom."[68] In every case, relationships of ownership, domination, and power are replaced by love and freedom without domination. The situation is transformed inwardly, and then modified externally as this becomes possible. Thus, a fourfold liberation is implied by our uprootage and pilgrimage: (1) domination of one's situation instead of being ruled by necessity, (2) the ability to be content and accept different situations and variations, (3) indifference to popular social objectives, and (4) a rejection of the current thesis that material change leads to a change of life, being, and reality.

"The freedom which is expressed in hope ... enables us to live out dialogue and encounter."[69] The first act of freedom, says Ellul, is to go out and meet others, to encounter and dialogue personally with someone else. We must take the initiative, and put ourselves in the service of others without calculation, planning or a superiority complex. Dialogue and encounter are followed by "realism and transgression."[70] Realism, as we have seen earlier, means seeing things as they really are, rejecting all idealism, spiritualization, and all systems. Realism is followed then by transgression, the "extreme act of freedom."[71] Realism discerns the limits of nature and society. There can be no freedom without some transgression of these limits. This means desacralization and iconoclasm. Obviously, any transgression is to be guided by the Spirit, not by personal caprice. The biblical miracles are examples of this kind of transgression--going beyond and against the limits of the world in order to introduce freedom.

Finally, we are led to "risk and contradiction."[72] The free individual is the one who takes risks without security or guarantee. Risk is "the culminating expression of freedom in Christ." Risk is always because of, and for, God. It is a wager on the faithfulness of God. Of course, we are not free to risk someone else but rather ourselves. Contradiction is one of the most profound aspects of risk. We are to bring contradictions between levels, systems, system and practice, the whole and the part, the individual and the group, thought and life--and thus open up the society. Jesus Christ was such a sign of contradiction.

At this point, Ellul turns to "Concrete Implications" of his ethics of freedom. We will return to a consideration of some of these concrete implications in the following chapters. In concluding this chapter, we must summarize briefly the shape of Ellul's ethics.

The major characteristic of Ellul's ethics is abundantly clear. Christian ethics is essentially and primarily a matter of a living relationship to the Wholly Other God known through his Word. The good is the will of God, and because God is living and unconditioned, his will cannot be adequately encapsulated in a system of rules. History, too, is open enough that no individual situation is an exact replication of another. Nevertheless, God is not capricious or discontinuous, but the "same yesterday, today, and forever." History and human life take place on a continuum where no event is absolutely unique. Thus, while the dynamism and contextualism of Christian ethics must be fundamental, it is both possible and necessary to formulate some kind of temporary, relative guidance for Christian life in the world.

When it comes to spelling out this "temporary," "necessary" ethics, at first glance Ellul appears to be an "intentionalist" in the sense that what qualifies any behavior as good or evil, right or wrong, acceptable or unacceptable, Christian or non-Christian, is an inward reality consisting of the hearing of the command of God and a consequent attitude of freedom. On the external level, given those two internal conditions, "All things are lawful."

Ellul wants to say more, however. Although there is some ambiguity, in the end Ellul suggests the priority rather than the exclusivity of "being" in relation to "doing." Doing ("acting") must proceed from this "being" or it is falsified; "being" is distinctly prior. In terms of the categories discussed in the first chapter, then, Ellul's primary emphasis is on the "nonmoral" good; second in importance is the modification in moral character, or "being," that flows out of the relationship with God. And only (but certainly) thirdly, decision and action must flow out of the first two areas. The status of the normative ethics of the second and third areas has been clearly and frequently described (relative, humble, temporary, etc.).

The content of the ethic has been given some definition, also. Ellul's approach frustrates any attempt to come up with a neat hierarchy of values or norms. Nevertheless, it is possible to list (somewhat unsystematically) the characteristics of this Christianly moral life Ellul proposes. In each case, the value or virtue could be translated or reworded into a norm governing decisions and action (and here, Ellul would clearly be a deontological rather than a teleological ethicist). Thus a person should cultivate a personal character that glorifies God; any action can be evaluated by the criterion of whether it manifests glory to God (or, conversely, glorifies oneself). One ought to be(come) a self-conscious individual person; any specific decision or action ought to be "individual" and "personal" in its form and content--at least if we are to identify it as "Christian" or "free." The next page lists some of Ellul's already-mentioned values descriptive of "the [nonmoral] Good" and its related (moral) "good."

## "THE GOOD" AND ITS GOOD (VS. EVIL)

### (1) Primary level

| | | |
|---|---|---|
| the will of God | vs. | the will of fallen world<br>self-will |
| The Word of God<br>incarnate the End | vs. | conform to world, "this age" |

### (2) Secondary level of mediation

| | | |
|---|---|---|
| glorify God | vs. | justify, glorify self or works of creature (idolatry) |
| love neighbor | vs. | exploit neighbor, ignore neighbor, etc. |
| hope and freedom | vs. | despair, indifference, resignation, false hope<br>bondage, necessity, alienation |
| faith and holiness<br>love and relationship | | |

### (3) Tertiary level of mediation

| | | |
|---|---|---|
| waiting and patience | vs. | impatience, productivity, "results" |
| realism | vs. | myth, idealism, superficiality |
| prayer to God | vs. | appeal and recourse to human means alone |
| individuality | vs. | mass, non-differentiation |
| personal | vs. | impersonal, abstract |
| uniqueness | vs. | predictability, normality, adjustment |
| mediation/reconciliation | vs. | depersonalization, intensifying, inflaming interpersonal tensions |
| pilgrimage/uprootage | vs. | bondage, security from the immanent and measurable |
| service | vs. | exploitation, domination, ownership, and power |
| contentment | vs. | insatiable desire for things, power, etc. |
| dialogue and encounter | vs. | propaganda, impersonal relations |
| risk and contradiction | vs. | conformity, reinforcement of forces and structures of bondage |

It is not, of course, necessary that every disposition or act have every one of these characteristics! Nor is this the end of the list, as we shall discover in examining Ellul's urban-technological and political ethics. But, provided the status of the characteristics enumerated above is clearly understood, they can be considered a description of faithful and free Christian presence and action in contemporary Western technological society. Obviously, there is one remaining step to be taken, which is the discovery of how and where to incarnate the characteristics listed. Thus, one is not told to demonstrate pilgrimage by selling one's house--although that may be one way of doing it--or quitting one's job. Nor is service defined in terms of hours per week, or acceptable and unacceptable agencies or forms of such service. The disciple is left to struggle with such applications before God and in the community of faith.

It is also true that, since we are in the world, not everything or every activity of the Christian will be "Christian." Ellul offers no resolution of this problem, but fully recognizes it. Although he does not begin as a Lutheran, Ellul often appears to end with classical Lutheran ethics: that is, one may have to sin (or choose to sin). In such cases there should be no whitewashing of the action (e.g., killing an intruder to save one's children is always sinful and wrong, but so is allowing one's children to be brutalized) but rather, repentance and humility. On the other hand, Ellul never ceases suggesting that there can be no "double-life" or separation into sacred and secular spheres. At each point and each moment the problem is how precisely to incarnate the will of God, how to incarnate the presence of the End. In the concluding chapter we will return to this problem.

## NOTES

1. To Will and to Do: An Ethical Research for Christians, trans. by C. Edward Hopkin (Philadelphia: Pilgrim, 1969); The Ethics of Freedom, trans. and edited by G. W. Bromiley (Grand Rapids, Mich.: Eerdmans, 1976). See also Jacques Ellul, "Notes en vue d'une ethique du temps et du lieu pour les Chretiens," Foi et Vie, 59.5 (Sept.-Oct. 1965): 354-374.
2. Ethics of Freedom, p. 7.
3. Ibid., p. 8.

4. "Karl Barth and Us," Sojourners (December 1978):24.
5. "Between Chaos and Paralysis," The Christian Century, 85 (June 5, 1968): 749.
6. To Will and to Do, pp. 5-38; Ellul does not discuss the "right" or differentiate the two branches of normative ethics; clearly, all normative ethical approaches are in view in this critique of ethics. Any distinction between the terms "ethics" and "morals" is likewise impossible to pinpoint in Ellul's usage.
7. James M. Gustafson, Christ and the Moral Life, (New York: Harper and Row, 1968), pp. 11-60.
8. To Will and to Do, pp. 39-58. See also Jacques Ellul, "Le rapport de l'homme à la création selon la Bible," Foi et Vie, 73. 5-6 (Dec. 1974): 137-155.
9. To Will and to Do, p. 41.
10. Ibid., p. 63.
11. In the interest of clarity and simplicity, God's (non-moral) "good" will be meant by Good (capitalized), and good (lower case) will refer to the (moral) relative, human "good."
12. This recalls the similar affirmations of Romans 12:17 and I Peter 2:12f., as well as the qualification "Obey God rather than men" in Acts 5:29.
13. Concluding Unscientific Postscript (Princeton, N.J.: Princeton University Press, 1941), p. 486. See To Will and to Do, p. 99, for Ellul's explicit affirmation of this point and of Kierkegaard's formulation (though without citing the text I have quoted).
14. The discussion which follows is based on To Will and to Do, pp. 114-198.
15. To Will and to Do, p. 114.
16. Ellul criticizes the "philosophy of values" of the existentialists and phenomenologists on the grounds that their "values" are the creation of particular philosophers and are too dependent on their experiences, despite their claims to focus on concrete human existence. On "the sacred" see Ellul's sociology of religion, The New Demons (New York: Seabury, 1975), pp. 48-87.
17. To Will and to Do, p. 154. See also Jacques Ellul, "Search for an Image," The Humanist (November/December 1973): 22-25, for an intriguing discussion of the possibility and necessity of building a revolutionary movement around the value of the individual--intriguing not least because it is Ellul speaking on the level of "morality of the world" (i.e., not as a Christian ethicist) to humanists!

18. The Ethics of Freedom, p. 239.
19. To Will and to Do, p. 202.
20. Ibid., p. 204.
21. Ellul discusses this in To Will and to Do, pp. 225-244.
22. Church Dogmatics, G. W. Bromiley and T. F. Torrance, eds., Trans. by A. T. Mackay, et al., (Edinburgh: T. and T. Clark, 1936-62), III. 4, p. 5.
23. Ibid., p. 4.
24. Ibid., pp. 10-14.
25. The Presence of the Kingdom, p. 46.
26. To Will and to Do, p. 249.
27. Ibid., p. 250.
28. Presence of the Kingdom, pp. 21-22.
29. To Will and to Do, p. 43; see also p. 278, n. 5.
30. Presence of the Kingdom, pp. 21-22.
31. For Karl Barth's similar comments on the constancy of God's command and the "formed reference" of the ethical situation, see Church Dogmatics, III. 4, pp. 17-19.
32. To Will and to Do, pp. 260-261.
33. Presence of the Kingdom, pp. 22-23.
34. Ethics of Freedom, p. 7.
35. Karl Barth, "The Gift of Freedom: Foundation of Evangelical Ethics," in The Humanity of God (Richmond, Va.: John Knox Press, 1960), pp. 69-96; see also Church Dogmatics, III. 4, pp. 13-14 and passim.
36. Hope in Time of Abandonment, trans. by C. Edward Hopkin (New York: Seabury, 1973).
37. Ibid., p. 80.
38. Presence of the Kingdom, pp. 81-82.
39. Ethics of Freedom, pp. 447-448.
40. Hope in Time of Abandonment, pp. 84ff.
41. Ibid., p. 176.
42. Ibid., p. 247.
43. Ibid., p. 239.
44. Ibid., p. 248.
45. Presence of the Kingdom, pp. 20-21.
46. Cf. Hope in Time of Abandonment, pp. 258-283, and Prayer and Modern Man, trans. by C. Edward Hopkin (New York: Seabury, 1970), pp. 110ff.
47. Ethics of Freedom, p. 27.
48. Ibid., p. 38.
49. Ibid., p. 62.
50. Cf. Kierkegaard on the significance of the "moment" as the "fullness of time" in his Philosophical Fragments and Concluding Unscientific Postscript.
51. Ethics of Freedom, p. 75.
52. Ibid., pp. 103ff.

53. Ibid., pp. 116-117.
54. Ibid., p. 11.
55. Ibid., p. 117.
56. Ibid., p. 124. See also Jacques Ellul, "Le sens de la liberté chez Saint Paul," Foi et Vie, 61.3 (Mar-Juin 1962): 3-20.
57. The Ethics of Freedom, pp. 144-160. See also The New Demons and Apocalypse: The Book of Revelation, trans. by George W. Schreiner, (New York: Seabury, 1977), especially pp. 201ff.
58. Ethics of Freedom, pp. 187ff.
59. Ibid., p. 199.
60. Ibid., p. 210.
61. Ibid., p. 277.
62. Ibid., p. 288.
63. Ibid., pp. 296-298. See also Presence of the Kingdom, pp. 12ff.
64. Ethics of Freedom, p. 298.
65. Ibid., p. 301.
66. See Presence of the Kingdom, pp. 44-49, for a vivid presentation of the concept of "ambassadorship" and foreign citizenship for Christians.
67. Ethics of Freedom, p. 308.
68. Ibid., p. 314.
69. Ibid., p. 319.
70. Ibid., pp. 332ff.
71. Ibid., p. 344.
72. Ibid., pp. 355ff.

## CHAPTER THREE ☐

# THE WORD OF GOD IN ELLUL'S THOUGHT

As indicated in the previous chapter, Jacques Ellul argues that any valid Christian ethic must derive solely from the Word of God. Christian ethics mediates that transcendent, living Word to our contemporary context. An ethics of the Word of God first of all calls its hearers into existential, personal relationship with God (the nonmoral Good, the ultimate value and source of values, to put it in ethical categories), thus decisively recasting the ethical situation. Second, the ethics of the Word of God modifies our character and being (our stance, disposition, attitude, and style). Third, an ethics of the Word of God provides what is necessary for an explicit hearing of God's command in this situation: the command of God is specific, concrete, and normative for decision and action in a given context.

The next stage of this inquiry, then, is to see how Ellul describes this Word of God. Ellul's Word of God has the two expected referents: Jesus Christ and Scripture. We will examine what he has to say about each, how they relate to each other, to an ethics of the Word of God, and to the discussions reviewed in the first chapter of this study.

## THE WORD OF GOD IN JESUS CHRIST

"I refuse to pledge my mind to anything or anyone, save Jesus Christ."[1] "The word of God is fully expressed, explained, and revealed in Jesus Christ, and only in Jesus Christ, who is himself, and in himself, the Word."[2] "If it is true that God himself has come, does this not mean necessarily that everything has changed?"[3] In these three quotations, Ellul's Christology is summarized. As revealer of

God, Jesus Christ is unique and comprehensive; God himself has come. This event changes everything on earth and in heaven.

History itself is profoundly changed by the coming of Jesus Christ.

> The first truth that one has to accept--and it was felt very strongly by the first generation of Christians, much less so today--is that the incarnation of Christ, his coming to earth, has effectively changed human history. It is not just a spiritual event. It has effectively changed human history.... What I have in view is that Jesus Christ has set up a new relation between man and society and also between man and nature, which has been implanted in the world and cannot be taken out of it, since he was the Son of God....
>
> What has caused the mutation is the momentous event of God on earth, ... the historical fact of the breaking of the barrier between God and man. A bridge has been built between the absolute and the relative, the eternal and temporal.... God in his totality has localized himself in flesh--an incredible mystery.... This fact alone, as a fact and not just a belief, has cut history in two, launched man on an endless venture, and definitely exposed his situation.
>
> The incarnation has shone a ruthless light on the artificial unity that man has established, or tried to establish, in compensation for his break with God.[4]

This interpretation of history and of the significance of Jesus Christ for history is crucial for Ellul's proposals for Christian ethics.[5] We have seen earlier that the fall resulted in a universe of necessity--a world and a history strictly governed and delimited by a web of conditions and sociological requirements. This unity is essential and makes life possible, although it is nevertheless characterized by a fundamental rebellion against God.

The nation of Israel set the stage for the incarnation of Christ by negating the unity of the world of necessity. Israel announced that this artificial unity was destined to break up because it was not the world to which God has called mankind.

> What the Old Testament declares is that equilibrium, continuity, and happiness are an expression of man's basic slavery and profound and hopeless alienation. Now what the Old Testament declares has been accomplished, actualized, and lived out once and for all by Christ....
>
> Christ carries freedom to its limit by affirming in the world, among men and for men, the radical transcendence of truth, carried to its limit by Jesus, and also a perfectly clear and realistic recognition, with no false appearances, of the human reality called sin, poverty, and suffering, carried to its limit by Christ.[6]

The old unity is irretrievably destroyed and a new unity is offered. With the incarnation of Christ the world and society are plunged into chaos. At the same time, a radical new possibility is now present.

> For the old relations, foundations, and habits, however, Christ substitutes new ones, those of love and freedom....
>
> That new order, that of the Beatitudes, makes life perfectly livable and possible. It is not even necessary ... that all men without exception should live according to love and freedom. But this freedom has to be present and incarnate.[7]

The incarnation of God in Jesus Christ is *the* miracle, in light of which all other miracles, before and after Jesus Christ, receive their significance.[8] It is *the* act of freedom, shattering the forces of bondage and necessity. It is *the* historical event. The Wholly Other God has come into our history and has died and been resurrected.

> Everything is oriented around the terrestrial crucifixion and resurrection upon earth. Jesus is the one who in his life, told by the Gospels, determines what happens in the world of God.[9]

The "terrestrial event provokes the celestial event."[10] Not only the historical but the eternal, not only the immanent but the transcendent revolves around the incarnation, death, and resurrection of Christ.

There is a distinctively eschatological character to the incarnation. "The promise of the glorious return of Jesus

Christ, the Parousia" means that Christians are not to cling to the past but rather to live in expectation of the eschaton, of the "coming break with this present world."[11] Jesus Christ is the first "man of the future." His work guarantees the defeat of the rebellious "powers" (exousia) and the final salvation of every man and woman.[12] Thus, "all facts acquire their value in light of the coming Kingdom of God, in light of the Judgment, and the Victory of God."[13] Jesus Christ brings the future into the present; this task is also given to his followers.

According to Ellul, ethics "flows out of the relationship with Christ."[14] The ethics of freedom is rooted in Christ as the free man.

> We know God fully only in Jesus Christ.... The Gospels clearly show that Christ is the only free man. Free, he chose to keep the law. Free, he chose to live out the will of God. Free, he chose incarnation. Free, he chose to die.[15]

Jesus Christ's freedom is not that of the sovereign God, for he chooses to be limited to our human situation. His freedom is expressed in relation to his situation. He faces all the temptations and tests that we do.[16] Thus, his "temptations" in the wilderness are signposts and pointers toward true freedom. He faces the temptation of food, which Ellul interprets as representative of all natural necessity (food, sex, material things, etc.), and refuses it although he is hungry. He faces the temptation of power, which Ellul interprets as all types of domination (political, economic, etc.), and refuses it in favor of servanthood. The third temptation is "spiritual"--to give a proof of his divinity. It is the temptation to be religious, self-assertive, self-righteous, self-saving. A part of the temptation is Satan's use of the scriptural text against God. Again, Jesus refuses to yield. Ellul argues that Jesus' later temptations and struggles are but variations on these three. The "temptation of Christ" episode is a paradigm for Christian ethics of freedom.

Ellul's discussion of violence further illuminates his understanding of Jesus Christ and his implications for Christian ethics. Nonviolence appears to be the orientation which Jesus held.

> It seems to witness to the teaching of Jesus on the

> level of personal relations--Love your enemy, turn the other cheek. Jesus carried the commandment "Thou shalt not kill" to the extreme limit, and in his person manifested nonviolence and even nonresistence to evil.[17]

The teaching of Jesus in the Sermon on the Mount and of Paul in Romans 12 describe this orientation of overcoming evil with good, of violence with nonviolence.[18]

Yet, there is a more fundamental explanation for nonviolence. What Christ does is make us free--free to struggle against necessity. Violence, above all, is an expression of the "order of necessity." We accept either the order of necessity or the order of freedom in Christ. Acceptance of the latter means that violence must be rejected root and branch. "Because Christianity is the revelation of the Wholly Other, that action must be different, specific, singular, incommensurable with political or corporate methods of action."[19] Jesus Christ requires action in the face of violence (or any other expression of necessity) but action of a different kind.

A second example of Ellul's Christocentric ethics is law. The resolution of the tension between human justice and divine righteousness is only in Jesus Christ, he argues.

> All the characteristics of God's righteousness are united and embodied in the life, the death, and the resurrection of Jesus Christ. Jesus Christ has become the righteousness of God. There can be no justice whatsoever, even relative, outside Jesus Christ.[20]

Jesus Christ is the meeting point of the righteousness of God and the justice of man.

> What is important at this point, in the discussion of the problem of justice, including legal justice, is the absolute centrality of the person of Jesus Christ. In him the different lines of thought converge: the foundation of human law resides in him, the realization of human law is accomplished by him, the qualification of human law is given by him.[21]

Thus, Ellul argues against any autonomous concept of law

(created, natural, etc.). Rather, human law is grounded in the cross of Christ in a "substitutionary" and eschatological fashion. Human rights and human institutions have meaning only in light of the incarnation, redemption, and the eschaton. As we shall see in the next chapter, this same pattern of interpretation is employed in relation to the city.

Jesus' teachings are given a high significance by Ellul.

> There can be no doubt for those who accept Jesus as the Christ, that he knew "what is in man, and all that is necessary for man's salvation." As soon as we begin dealing with truth, what the Son of God says is valid as truth.[22]

"The voice of Jesus Christ is the voice of the holy God himself."[23] Jesus' teachings reveal the true meaning and significance of people, things, and events. They provide a description of life and freedom in the face of death and necessity. But the specific teachings are not for the purpose of creating an independent, objective, or eternal description of the Law. No philosophical or ethical system is proposed. Rather, the teachings are indications of a style of "being" which flows out of a personal relationship with God in Christ.

To Will and to Do gives a summary of Ellul's view of Jesus Christ and ethics:

> The good is that which God speaks in his word; it is, in consequence, a certain attitude of man toward God, as a result and as a function of that word; again, it is a certain attitude of man toward man, as a result and as a function of the relationship with God. But on the one hand, the word of God is fully expressed, explained, and revealed in Jesus Christ, and only in Jesus Christ, who is himself, and in himself the Word. Thus Jesus Christ is truly the good. On the other hand, the attitude toward God and toward man is put forth as a requirement, a call, and a promise in the Old Testament, while in Jesus Christ this good is totally and fully incarnate and fulfilled. The good, then, is something already accomplished into which we are to enter, but which does not on that account do away with the call and the demand addressed to each one individually.... The word of God which spells out the good is pronounced in Jesus Christ, and nowhere else.[24]

Thus, there is no possible knowledge of the good apart from a personal relationship with Jesus Christ.

* * *

In terms of James Gustafson's five styles of relating Christ to the moral life, where, finally, does Jacques Ellul fit in? The heaviest emphasis is placed on Gustafson's first category, i.e., the "nonmoral" Good which stands over and beyond our ethical systems. For Ellul, the Good is the living God, known in the Word of God in Christ. We are called to a personal and living relationship with this Jesus Christ who is Lord. The Good is not reducible to a system, but is the Person of Christ.

Gustafson's second and third categories have Jesus Christ affecting the moral self in his capacity as Sanctifier and Judge. Jesus Christ as Sanctifier makes one holy; as Judge he makes one free. At first glance, Ellul would seem to have more affinity for the latter, e.g., in his emphasis on freedom. This freedom is, however, bound up with holiness. Christians are either slaves to the old order of necessity or they are free, singular, incommensurate, "foreign." In either case, the objectivity of this transformation of the moral self is achieved by Jesus Christ's incarnation, death, and resurrection, but is profoundly eschatological. That is, freedom and holiness are not imposed *opus operatum* by God. They must be seized, incarnated, and lived out in constant renewal.

Finally, Gustafson's fourth and fifth categories have Jesus Christ providing specific guidance for decision and action through his roles as Pattern and Teacher. Ellul refers to Jesus' teaching and example in the Gospels and gives it a central place in the formulation of ethical responses to violence, politics and the state, money, interpersonal relations, and the city. Jesus provides guidance by way of teaching and example in relation to specific issues as well as general questions about life in the world. The unifying theme in Jesus' teaching and example, according to Ellul, is the introduction of the Wholly Other into the world of necessity. This, as we have seen, is variously expressed in terms of freedom, holiness, and love.

The problem of Jesus' eschatology has been a stumbling block for many Christian ethicists (as Hiers' studies illustrated above). Ellul is rather disdainful of the "demythologizers" who are embarrassed by the language of the parousia and the eschaton. Thus, he frequently uses the traditional language of Scripture and Church in referring to the "glorious return of our Lord." He disparages those who view our era with pride, and earlier eras with contempt for their presumed naivete. However, in contrast with fundamentalism, he suggests that the eschatological future is not merely or mainly a "temporal or logical future."[25] The eschaton is a "meta-historical fact" with current historical implications.[26] In his Apocalypse: The Book of Revelation (1975) this emphasis is elaborated:

> Undoubtedly, the Apocalypse is concerned only with the "last things" but it is certainly right to consider that this does not mean the last moments of our galaxy.... The apocalypse does not describe a moment of history but reveals for us the permanent depth of the historical: it is then, one could say, a discernment of the Eternal in Time, of the action of the End in the Present, the discovery of the New Eon, not at the end of time, but in this present history, the Kingdom of God hidden in this world.[27]

In the end, Ellul maintains a "realized/future" dualistic eschatology. But his emphasis is less on a real, temporal future, than a transcendent "beyond." The End does intervene in our history, of course, but these interventions are largely individual, incomplete, and temporary.

In summary, Ellul displays the same kind of robust Christology as Karl Barth and others in the orthodox and neo-orthodox theological tradition. And like Barth again, he is not troubled with the metaphysical, ontological, and epistemological problems surrounding discussion of a supernatural, transcendent God incarnate in Jesus Christ since the Enlightenment and the rise of modern science and historical criticism. Ellul sidesteps these issues by taking a confessional, fideist position and using it to criticize modernity, rather than allowing modern critical thought to filter out whatever in orthodoxy does not fit the contemporary scientific mind. This does not, of course, solve the problems, epistemological and otherwise, confronted by Bultmann and others. In the present discussion, however, as has been indicated earlier, the significant factor is that Ellul has leaped to a position where his Christology, and thus his ethics, are of potential service to a large body of Christians who continue to hold traditional, orthodox views of Jesus Christ.

In certain respects, Ellul's Christology argues more than was (or is) the case in orthodox tradition. That is, Jesus Christ has always been regarded as the "only begotten Son of God" and the "Savior" providing forgiveness and eternal life to those who have faith. Ellul goes beyond this to affirm (1) that God's power, love and grace will, in the end, effect universal salvation for all people; (2) that the incarnation, death and resurrection of Jesus Christ are the focal point and the critical influence on everything that was, is, and will be on earth and in heaven--all of history is modified, social relations are changed, transcendent reality is decided, all by this event; (3) that all of Scripture (see more on this in the next section) is centered on Christ and has Jesus Christ as its true reality; and (4) that Christian ethics is always centered on Jesus Christ--there is no independent or even complementary ethics of the orders of creation, etc.

To be (or become) personally related to this figure of Jesus Christ is, then, of decisive consequences for the moral agent--without saying any more than this. Ellul makes one additional step, however, which radically affects the content of all guidance from his ethics of the Word of God. This step is to affirm that Jesus Christ represents above all else the entry of the Wholly Other into the world of necessity. Jesus Christ is God-in-history and God-in-tension-with-history at the same time. Holiness in and against a sinful world, peace in a violent context, servanthood and death instead of power and domination, resurrection instead of death, forgiveness instead of condemnation, in the Evangelist John's terms "in the world but not of the world"--this is Ellul's Christ. His presence from beginning to end is "Wholly Other," singular, unique, incommensurate with the average, normal, and predictable. Especially as illustrated by the threefold "temptation of Christ," Jesus Christ becomes the general paradigm for ethics (character and action alike) and for life and freedom in general. In David Kelsey's term, this is Ellul's "discrimen"--a single, imaginative, synoptic judgment about the meaning of God, theology and ethics.

## THE WORD OF GOD IN SCRIPTURE

At the opening of To Will and to Do, Ellul says that in his ethical research:

> The criterion of my thought is the biblical revelation, the content of my thought is the biblical revelation, the point of departure is supplied by the biblical revelation, the method is the dialectic in accordance with which the biblical revelation is given to us, and the purpose is a search for the significance of the biblical revelation concerning ethics.[28]

This declaration of the fundamental importance of the Bible for his work is echoed over and over in Ellul's writings. Basic to this stance is the fact that at "around twenty-two years of age, I was ... reading the Bible, and it happened that I was converted--with a certain 'brutality.'"[29] Not the preaching of the Church, not the celebration of the Sacraments, not a mystical vision, but the individual reading of the Bible was decisive in Ellul's own experience. During the fifty tumultuous years since that conversion, it has been the reading and study of Scripture which have sustained Ellul, his family, and the small Reformed parish in which he is a lay leader. While his immersion in the biblically-oriented theology of Karl Barth certainly also pushes him in this direction, it is this ongoing personal encounter with Holy Scripture that most significantly undergirds Ellul's biblical-centeredness.

Ellul's commitment to the importance of Scripture comes through in all of his theological and ethical writings. In his major work _The Ethics of Freedom_, he stresses that freedom "implies more than knowing who Jesus Christ is. It also implies knowing the Scriptures."[30] The importance of knowing Scripture is underscored by Jesus' own recourse to Scripture in his debates with Satan. Ellul makes frequent statements on the character and interpretation of Scripture. He provides many samples of his biblical interpretation, in articles, passages of various books, as well as the four book-length studies: _The Judgment of Jonah_, _The Meaning of the City_, _The Politics of God and the Politics of Man_, and _Apocalypse: The Book of Revelation_. A book on Ecclesiastes in forthcoming. A good part of Ellul's importance to this subject, then, lies in his willingness to deal not only with theory and method but with specific cases and illustrations from the biblical text.

Like Karl Barth, Ellul differentiates the written text from the living word of God. In almost the same breath, however, Ellul argues that, in practice, they are virtually equivalent. The revelation in the biblical text is equivalent to the will of God.

> What one ordains and the other requires are therefore practically inseparable.... It is clear that every living word of God cannot be different from that which is attested precisely in the Bible.... It turns out that the God who spoke to men in the Bible is also our God, and directly ours, thanks to their witness.[31]

Revelation is an objective fact: at a given moment, God revealed himself to man and Scripture is witness to that revelation. "The Bible is the objectified datum both of what has been revealed and what is potentially revealed."[32] In Jesus Christ the law (objective, universal) becomes commandment (personal, individual, concrete address).

> The summons of the commandment is contained in its entirety in the Bible. But it does not cease to be a word for being "written" (hence objectified). It does not become letter, nor does the commandment become law. The word inscribed in the Bible is always living, and is continually spoken to him who reads.[33]

Nevertheless, this recognition of God personally summoning us is a decision of faith and obedience. "The word read in the Bible cannot be heard as a personal commandment except by faith."[34] With such an attitude we can "know the constant surprise of the transition from Scripture to the living word."[35] The equation works in the opposite direction as well: all "self-styled revelation of the current day" is always "subject to verification by the word revealed in the Bible."[36] Thus, revelation (the Word of God) and the biblical text are, while distinguishable, tightly related dependent phenomena.

Scripture is, of course, a book written by people in the historical forms and modes common to their ordinary affairs. This is typical of God's action in human history. He adopts human work and fills it with new significance.[37] Historical fact, myth, symbolism, prophecy, apocalyptic--God uses these and other literary genre to convey his word. In fact, Ellul argues, God uses the redactors, editors, and compilers of the Bible just as much as the authors of the "original autographs." Biblical revelation has as much to do with the shape of the whole canon and the internal relation of the parts as it does with the original historical meaning of the individual texts.

Ellul periodically distances himself from what he terms the "biblical literalist." Ellul's "literalist" represents "antiquated, outmoded, trivial attitudes."[38] Literalism

> closes its ears to the critics almost to the point of credo quia absurdum. The danger here is that of attaching faith to a record rather than to Jesus Christ. For the true reality of the book is Jesus Christ and to divert our faith from him to facts which are not so significant in themselves can be a serious mistake.[39]

The way out of the current crises is not back to the old and obsolete formulations, but forward and beyond the present situation.

Even more of Ellul's space and energy is devoted to an attack on much of contemporary biblical scholarship--nearly always on the grounds that its passion for historical and literary dissection of the text leaves nothing except a mass of dusty, isolated fragments. This complaint leads us to the heart of Ellul's understanding of Scripture. Scripture must be read and understood as a total unity, and this unity must be understood and interpreted in relation to Jesus Christ as the definitive Word of God. There is no such thing as "mere tale," "mere myth," "mere historical incident," etc., for Ellul as he reads Scripture. The original editors and canonizers were not imbeciles, and they jealously guarded the entrance to the canon. Everything has a point and a meaning. Both the literalist and the critical biblical scholar are prone to miss the "forest" in the consuming passion for analysis of individual "trees."

Thus, in The Judgment of Jonah (1946) Ellul argues that the (probably later) insertion of the "Song of Jonah" was fully intentional, and that, far from a crude patchwork, what emerges is a meaningful unity. The book of Jonah is placed, moreover, in the prophetic section of the Old Testament, not the historical section, and its interpretation is to proceed with that in mind. As prophecy, Jonah "plainly declares God's will in a given situation."[40] The prophecy is simultaneously the word of God to Israel and an intimation of Christ. We know that Jonah is, among other things, a figure and type of Christ because Jesus himself used the story in this way and because the internal details of the story make sense as references to him. Ellul disparages any interpretation of the text and its symbols by imposing "secret keys" or traditions on the text.

> We are to interpret them solely by the Bible itself. The consensus of the records of the ongoing thought which is revelation allows us to seize on what may be symbolic elements in it, but always with the realization that we must keep as much as possible to facts as facts, since revelation has always to be incarnated. Hence, there can be no single method of interpretation. As the different books fall into different categories, so there must be different categories of interpretation, though always related to the unvarying central line: Jesus Christ.[41]

Thus, Jonah must be taken as "a significative (and not just a chronological) totality. It has to be taken synthetically, with the internal connections which join the various parts."[42]

In The Politics of God and the Politics of Man (1966) Ellul repeats his argument for the Christocentric unity of the Bible. "It is impossible to ignore the fact of the unity of revelation and its movement. Everything leads to Jesus Christ, just as everything comes from him."[43] Second Kings, the subject of this volume, is a historical description of the intervention of God, especially in human politics. The problems in II Kings are, Ellul says, political in the narrow sense of that word; in fact it is, in Ellul's view, the most political book in the Bible. The connection with Jesus Christ turns on the interpretation of Elijah and Elisha as figures of John the Baptist and Jesus Christ. The superabundance of miracles in II Kings, as in the Gospels, is an indication of the unbounded presence of God's Spirit.[44] Though the problems are political, the subject is prophecy and revelation, not just principles, ethics, and political procedures. Second Kings is concerned with the interaction between God and man, and the intervention of the prophet between God's decision and human action. As in his other biblical studies, Ellul takes several passing shots at critical historians and exegetes for failing to get at this more fundamental unity and meaning of the text.[45]

Ellul's Genesis-to-Revelation study of The Meaning of the City (1970) also "takes the biblical text as it is found today, in its entirety."[46] Historical and literary critical studies can be helpful, especially in preventing gross errors. Ellul himself engages in some critical detailed study of the Hebrew words for "city" (just as, in the earlier Theological Foundation of Law, he engaged in a critical study of biblical words for justice, law, and righteousness).[47] But the compiling of the individual books and the formation of the canon as a whole is essential for a grasp of the biblical "meaning of the city." "This is why an inclusive reading of the text appears indispensable to me."[48] Ellul's inclusive style of interpretation yields an impressive result when it deals with the major themes in the biblical story of Babylon, Jerusalem, and their sister cities. The Ellulian method is much more suspect when, in the final section of the study, he speculates on the meaning of the symbols of the Apocalypse![49]

A fourth example of Ellul's understanding of Scripture is his recent Apocalypse: The Book of Revelation (1975). The now-familiar themes appear again. The Apocalypse must be related to Jesus Christ. Its symbolism is not to be feared, even though it has often provoked "delirium" in the past.[50] The Apocalypse must be read with respect for the genre of apocalyptic literature. It must be read as a unity with a specific form and an internal movement. Perceiving its meaning requires "comprehension of the structure."[51] The meaning does not reside in the antiquity of the parts but in the total, final product as it now stands. The knowledge of the original cultural milieu only partially clarifies the meaning, for the relation of the book to its milieu is as much tension as harmony, both in form and content.[52]

In Ellul's view, recent commentaries on the Apocalypse are weak because they study the text scientifically alone, abandoning the meaning; view it exclusively in historical-cultural terms, forgetting its present and future significance; and fail to develop a method appropriate to the subject and thus fail to probe the symbolic and dialectical meaning.[53]

In contrast to these recent commentaries, Ellul wishes to "discern the specificity of the Apocalypse."[54] He argues that the Apocalypse is a distinctive vehicle of revelation in Scripture, an act of God with "an internal movement."[55] It reveals the dialectic of human works (that of Politics of God and the Politics of Man was the dialectic of politics). It is the "totalization of history in one moment," and the illumination of the meaning of human works and God's work from the standpoint of the End.[56]

Already, in this brief review of four of Ellul's biblical studies, it is possible to identify certain basic assumptions or convictions which characterize Ellul's view of Scripture. First, there is "the radical unity which the thought of the Bible exhibits from end to end, over and above the diversity of authorship, schools of thought, and literary forms."[57] Thus, interpretation must search for the mutual illumination of the parts and the whole and not rest with a study of the parts. Second, this unity is rooted in Jesus Christ, the Son of God, the Incarnate Word. The interpretation of biblical revelation must be incarnational and Christocentric.[58] Third, though the Word of God and the biblical text are in practice equivalent, revelation requires the action of the Holy Spirit on the one hand and existential commitment on the part of the hearer on the other.[59] Thus, a purely scientific, objective hermeneutic may assist in the understanding of Scripture but this is clearly inferior and inadequate to the task of interpreting the revealed Word of God. Hermeneutics is properly a task for the believing community. And fourth, Ellul insists that biblical interpretation proceed in full awareness of the type of biblical literature being considered and its place in the canon (e.g., prophecy, history, apocalyptic).

A fifth conviction which Ellul's biblical interpretation evidences has to do with the relevance of the ancient Scripture for today. Ellul rejects the pretentiousness of modern critics. We have no reason for arrogance or superiority in relation to the ancients.

> No one has demonstrated that those values which one rejects--those ethical instructions, that social view, that anthropology--were _only_ assumptions of a bygone civilization. After all, even if they are _also_ to be credited to a form of traditional civilization, it is quite possible that they were nevertheless what God willed for man in the order of the fall, or in obedience to his will.[60]

The Bible, as Ellul understands it, is remarkably modern and alive. We must

> neither cover it with the trappings of tradition and theology, of moralities and rites--making a mummy

> out of it--nor expurgate it, cut it to pieces and scatter it, like the membra disjecta of Orpheus--making an experimental corpse out of it. All that is necessary is to let the explosive power of the word act, just as it is.[61]

And again:

> I fail to see the justification for accepting as legitimate all the questions about the revelation ... while at the same time refusing to question those systems, methods, and conclusions from the point of view of the revelation.[62]

Historical criticism is entirely legitimate as long as (1) it is not an end in itself which fails to move toward understanding of the whole word of God, (2) it is not a means of affirming the superiority of "man-come-of-age" at the expense of previous human beings, and (3) it is not a means of denying the inspiration and revelation of and in Scripture, that is, raising the Devil's question "yea, hath God said?" The problem is that "we can no longer read the Bible in simplicity of heart, because this theology begets suspicion.... We are in the period of 'dilution,' of watering down the expression as well as the content of revelation."[63]

In The Ethics of Freedom, Ellul stresses that we remain free only to the extent that we are "continually questioned afresh by Scripture."[64] While Scripture is thus an object which may be studied and to which questions may be brought, Ellul regards it as absolutely crucial that God be invited to question us through the Bible. It is in this sense that the "Bible becomes the Word of God."

Ellul prescribes three areas of freedom in relation to revelation.[65] First, we have freedom of interpretation. No interpretation can be definitive but neither should it be arbitrary. Freedom of interpretation (as all Christian freedom) is always bounded by and oriented toward the glory of God and love of our neighbor. Second, we have a certain freedom of deviation. The basis of our right to err, Ellul argues, is not in liberalism or sentimentality, but in the principle of "speaking the truth in love" (no coercion is permitted in establishing the truth) and the attitude of God toward man in the Bible. God often uses rebellious man and his works for his own glory, even though they are not perfect. This is not a permission to avoid combatting error but a reminder to do so in love.

Third is freedom of research. But this freedom is bounded in five ways. (1) The research method should be specified by and adequately related to the object, i.e., the Bible and the specific book or passage in view. (2) Preceding researches should consciously be taken into account and neither exalted nor rejected too radically. We must be conscious of our indebtedness to and conditioning by preceding research. (3) The goal of research should be to aid the witness and proclamation of the Church, accepting the Bible as a postulate. (4) Research must proceed from a position that is rooted in the word, located in the fellowship of the church, and ordered to the confession of the faith. (5) The ultimate limit is that one must never raise the Devil's question, "Yea, hath God said?" All Scripture must be approached in openness to God's revelation. All of Scripture is a vehicle through which God has something to say.

Judged by these criteria, Ellul finds much contemporary biblical research and interpretation wanting. He is especially critical of the public airing of research that is prematurely or poorly articulated or shocking for its own sake and thus confusing to the faithful.

If Ellul is frequently critical of the approaches taken to Scripture by both conservative and liberal interpreters, how, it may be asked, has his work been received by recent critics and reviewers? Ronald R. Ray's essay "Jacques Ellul's Innocent Notes on Hermeneutics" in _Interpretation_ credits Ellul with having "reminded biblical scholars of some basic Christian convictions that they can easily forget in preoccupation with more technical issues."[66] Vernard Eller's excellent summary of "How Jacques Ellul Reads the Bible" in _The Christian Century_ applauds Ellul's labors with a very fitting analogy:

> [T]he difference here is between a drama critic's treatment of a playwright's _script_ and his treatment of a _performance_ of the same play. Most scholarship confines itself to the original script.... Ellul evaluates its performance as _Christian Scripture._[67]

Ellul's biblical studies have also been warmly commended by Brevard Childs:

> Fortunately, creative homiletical exegesis is not confined to antiquarian volumes. Jacques Ellul's brilliant interpretation in _The Politics of God and_

> the Politics of Man can be recommended with enthusiasm to the pastor. Obviously, his interpretation is often subjective and at times even fanciful, but Ellul offers a bold and creative mode for serious exposition of Kings.
>
> . . .
>
> Jacques Ellul's short monograph on Jonah is far more akin to the genre of sermon than commentary. Probably the book will satisfy neither the left nor the right in the traditional theological spectrum, but it represents a highly creative, robust theological interpretation which cannot but stimulate serious reflection.[68]

Typical of the more negative criticism of Ellul's hermeneutic is George Landes' review of The Judgment of Jonah.[69] Landes finds this study "deeply disappointing." Ellul's Christological interpretation seems incautious, irresponsible, and untenable. Ellul has failed to deal adequately with the original meaning of the book and has misinterpreted its meaning in the Gospel allusions. A theological interpretation has been imposed "without prior, careful historical exegesis."

Gibson Winter's review of The Meaning of the City lashes out at Ellul's work for being "one-sided," "distorted," and "oversimplified."[70]

> The distortion appears in two ways: (1) in the imposition on Scripture of a condemnation-fulfillment schema that leads to Christ; (2) in the suppression of the multiple strands of biblical experience and symbol in the name of an apocalyptic interpretation appearing in the first century of our era.
>
> . . .
>
> The assimilation of the Old Testament, so-called, to this apocalyptic Christ leads to a spurious "Judeo-Christianism" . . . ; indeed, the term reflects an historical arrogance that has caused unimaginable evil in the West.

Of the same book, Walter G. Muelder says that Ellul has written a "powerful sermon," but that, finally, his foundational paradigm of a unified biblical theology is unacceptable and undemonstrated.[71]

Walter Brueggemann finds The Politics of God and the Politics of Man "significant," "powerful," "passionate," and "suggestive."[72] However, it remains "problematic" on methodological grounds. Ellul's exegesis is "risky," "without control," "historically one-dimensional," and above all too subject.

> We were offered much Ellul and only some Scripture. I have no quarrel with most of his conclusions, but I wonder whether his method can be used for some other social stance which might be more ideological and demonically-inspired.

David Alan Hubbard's review of the same book found Ellul's message "unusual," "stimulating," "penetrating," but also disturbing.[73] In particular, Hubbard complains that Ellul leans too far toward the typological hermeneutics of Wilhelm Vischer (The Witness to Christ in the Old Testament.)

The foregoing criticisms can be summarized in two points. First, there are critics who reject Ellul's program as a whole. Ellul presupposes the legitimacy and desirability of a "continuous" and "inclusive" reading of the canon of Scripture as a (the) book about Jesus Christ. This choice of perspective and agenda is deliberate and explicit. It is, prima facie, neither more nor less legitimate an enterprise than any other narrower or broader historical, scientific, or theological paradigm. Its results must be judged, first of all, in relation to its intentions.

The second criticism is of greater importance. That is, has Ellul done an adequate job in developing a unified, Christological interpretation of Scripture? As most of even his most negative critics would admit, Ellul has been stimulating, provocative, and generally illuminating. Questions remain about his sometimes speculative interpretation of types, figures and symbols. It is not the presupposition of a unified biblical theology centered on Jesus Christ that is the problem; rather, it is the sometimes fanciful, subjective, or speculative result that troubles. The saving grace of Ellul's biblical theology, on this issue, is that he invites his readers to go beyond him, to "do it better" if they can. Those who read Ellul and disagree (which means all of his readers at one point or another) are driven back into the text with new eyes and new desire to hear more clearly the word of the Lord.

Aside from more or less important specific points in Ellul's interpretation, there are two other issues raised by his approach to Scripture which are significant, especially for American Evangelicals. The first of these has to do with his understanding of "the dialectic in accordance with which the biblical revelation is given to us."[74] Ellul's sociological as well as theological thought is dialectical, through-and-through.[75] Everywhere, Ellul sees paradox, tension and contradiction. On many levels, there will be broad agreement with his views, e.g., the conflict between sin and grace, between this age and the age-to-come, the paradox of human freedom/responsibility and divine sovereignty, and so on. The difficulty with this dialectic has to do with the fact that "contradictions, or opposite trends of inspiration, are possible in the Bible," and these must not be brushed aside, twisted into harmony, or ignored.[76] Ellul is temperamentally prepared to live with this sort of contradiction and paradox (at some levels) while others will prefer a casuistic resolution of such tensions.

Finally, however, Ellul always argues that "the harmony of the biblical texts is essential."

> Each text should be interpreted by the consensus of the others, and no text carries decisive weight wrested from its theological and historical context.[77]

Ellul doubts that contradictions will be found in the same biblical writer and almost certainly not within one biblical book. Any "contradiction" (e.g., in ethical guidance on war, marriage, etc.) would appear on a broader level in the canon. In the end, he is convinced, even these "contradictions" can be resolved into a larger unity. God is not capricious!

> The very revelation which he grants us shows us a remarkable continuity in his decisions.
>
> ...
>
> Neither are there conflicts between the successive stages of the revelation.
>
> ...
>
> Therefore when we refer back to the revealed word, to the objective testimony contained in the Bible of the living revelation which took place once for all, there is no contradiction.... Thus it is legitimate, even ordained, that we should

> lay hold of that past revelation and seek in it an ethical instruction for today. And for that reason we should be well assured that there is no conflict between the objective revelation and the revelation *hic et nunc*, between Scripture and the Holy Spirit, between the permanent will of God and his *hic et nunc* for each one.[78]

The problem of contradiction, then, is answered by Ellul's insistence on the unity of biblical revelation itself and the constancy of God in our times as well as biblical times.

The second, and ultimately thornier, problem with Ellul's approach to Scripture is what Ronald Ray calls his "moderate approach to facticity."[79] In current Evangelical parlance, it is the question of inerrancy. The question is not raised because Ellul is in the habit of pointing out various errors in the Bible! The problem is simply that he does not seem concerned to link theological truth assertions to historical or scientific assertions of truth in Scripture. In the case of Jonah, for example:

> Whether or not the book is historical is of secondary importance, for the story finds its true value not in itself, in what it is, but in what it denotes. Its relevance derives from the truth which it embodies, from the one who fulfills the prophecy.
> . . .
> God brings a great fish. It is idle to seek its name or to consider zoological possibilities with a view to identifying the species. It is idle to ask whether the Mediterranean could have contained such a monster. That is not the question. The real question is: Of what is this fish the sign?[80]

Ellul has no interest in arguing that Jonah is nonhistorical or that the fish story is impossible. Quite the contrary, Ellul argues that with God all things, including quite miraculous things, are possible. The traditional apologist argues that the truth of Jesus Christ *depends* on a kind of historical (and demonstrable) facticity here, for our Lord said, "As Jonah was three days and three nights in the belly of a huge fish, so the Son of Man will be three days and three nights in the heart of the earth."[81] To this, an Ellulian response says that (1) the truth of Jonah derives from the truth and the facticity of Jesus Christ, crucified, dead, buried, and resurrected, and not vice versa; (2) Jonah is deliberately placed in the "Book of the Twelve"--the prophetic not the historical books, and its historicity should not be pressed so hard for that reason; and (3) how far should the comparative "as" (in Matthew 12) be pressed? "As" Jonah was asleep in the fish (not dead)? Is the truth of the parable of the treasure in the field or the pearl of great price or the Good Samaritan undermined if these were not references to historical incidents? None of this is to say that historicity or errancy is unimportant, but rather that the truth and the fact which authenticates all biblical revelation is the Word of God in Jesus Christ.

What Ellul is arguing for, finally, is careful attention to the revelation of God himself. The creation story, for example, is intended

> to show us who is the God of creation, the God of Israel. It is not the description of the process. Consequently, whether the days might be days or not, whether the stages of creation correspond to the scientific model or to the criteria of science--this is not the question. The bible makes no mistakes when it comes to the revelation of God himself, or about man himself.... The important thing is to ask ourselves what is the most essential thing: to know who God is, the God who liberates and pardons me ... or rather to know how long it took the creation to occur.
>
> ...
>
> When God speaks, he cannot lie. He does not lie about himself. The purpose of the Bible is to reveal God to us, and in this purpose God is successful and without error.[82]

Ellul argues that scientific and historical criteria for truth and error are not permanent themselves and, thus, to base our belief in God's truthfulness on a scientific or historical "proof" is, in itself, an uncertain foundation.

Having examined Ellul's general stance with respect to Scripture and its interpretation, we must now turn to the question of how Scripture functions in Christian ethics. Biblical revelation is decisive in Christian ethics, not least because there is no possible natural knowledge of God. "Whatever of the imageo dei may remain, it is certainly not a 'moral sense.'"[83] In contrast, the Christian Gospel is radical and decisive for ethics. Christianity "must be accepted in its revealed totality--accepted absolutely, intransigently, without cultural or philosophical or any other kind of accommodation or adaptation."[84] This "revealed totality" in Scripture is not to serve as justification of our opinions or cannon fodder for our battles. Rather it judges and condemns us first and then shows us salvation through the grace of God. And, as in the case of Jonah the Prophet, everything begins from the moment God speaks his Word. "And the Word of the Lord came to Jonah, saying...." The Word of God is power and not just information or discourse. It transforms what it touches, changes situations, and the one addressed, whether it is obeyed or not.[85]

Ellul keeps alive a profound tension between the dynamic and constant aspects of biblical revelation. The living Word cannot be formulated directly into an ethic, but it can and should "give rise to an ethical requirement."[86] Recognizing the temporary nature of any ethics, it is nevertheless possible to have a "coming together of the _hic et nunc_ of the word of God and the _hic et nunc_ of a valid and true ethic for man."[87]

On the one hand, Ellul says that there are "many moralities" possible in Christ and Scripture. We cannot seize on any one center, such as the Sermon on the Mount, from which to build a conflict-free system of Christian ethics. As an example of the importance of not fixing God or ourselves to one abstract, eternal ethical system, Ellul refers to the story of God's command to Abraham to sacrifice Isaac, his son. With Søren Kierkegaard, Ellul ascribes the Abraham and Isaac episode (as well as the _herem_ of Israel) to a "teleological suspension of the ethical."[88] Thus, Ellul wishes to affirm as strongly as possible the practical unity of Scripture for Christian ethics, while leaving an "out" for the exceptional case attributable to God's sovereign freedom in unique circumstances.

Scripture should be read by all Christians in search of ethical guidance. Indeed, the first act of freedom is "to know and understand and scrutinize all that scripture has to say about this freedom which is now mine."[89] God's Word in Scripture frees us from the world, enlightens us and engages us in a precise action.[90] We need not demythologize or dissect, but simply read Scripture, for it conveys the Word of God, the truth, "through an actualized decision of God."[91]

Once the Word of God in Scripture addresses us, "it must be my foundation on which I try to find out what can fulfill it and accomplish it among my acts and decisions."[92] Two kinds of guidance will be discovered in our reading of Scripture:

> In this one Word of God we do in fact find two types of eternal decisions regarding man. Some decisions concern his concrete life on earth.... Then we have God's judgment on the inner core of the problem, on the final relation between this man and God.[93]

The latter judgment gives the eschatological character to our acts and decisions as we try to incarnate that End. A decision concerning concrete life will serve that End though "a priori it necessarily seems to be absurd, for it is of a different order."[94] Christian action will often appear absurd and ineffective--but so also appeared the death of Christ!

But cannot we go further than this affirmation? We have observed already that Jesus Christ is the definitive Word of God and the interpretive center of all biblical revelation. The mode of Jesus Christ's presence in the world (recall the temptation discussion) provides guidance. Though Scripture yields no philosophical system of ethics, it does contain a history of God's action and intervention in the world. This leads us to the method of analogy.

> What God reveals to us ... by the Scriptures, is not a doctrine or principles--it is judgment and action, wholly directed towards the accomplishment of the work of God.... The Bible shows us a God at work in political and civil history, using the works of men and bringing them into his action for his promised kingdom. From what the Scripture reveals to us about this action we can draw similar analogies, we can conceive the essential direction which our action should take.[95]
>
> It is clear that every living word of God cannot be different from that which is attested precisely in the Bible. It follows from this that we are not only called to act by analogy with biblical circumstances, but it turns out that the God who spoke to men in the Bible is also our God, and directly ours, thanks to their witness. The good revealed

> to them is also ours. We must act, then, as though living out a repetition and a confirmation of that which was confided to them.[96]

A truly Christian ethic will provide us with real guidance from God in relation to the world in which we live. As we have seen, Scripture yields guidance, often by way of analogy, for our decision and action. It provides a view of the absolute End which both judges and informs our relative efforts. Integral to the whole process is the way in which biblical revelation provides essential illumination and understanding of the very situation and context for which we seek ethical guidance. Taking urban ethics as an example, Ellul argues:

> The reality of the city ... can be understood only in light of revelation. And this revelation provides us with both a means of understanding the problem and a synthesis of its aspects as found in the raw data of history and sociology....
>
> Revelation ... enlightens, brings together, and explains what our reason and experience discover. Without revelation all our reasoning is doubtlessly useful, but does not view reality in true perspective.[97]

Thus, biblical revelation plays a major role in Ellul's proposals for Christian ethics. Now we must ask where this view of Scripture fits in relation to the categories and questions raised by Birch and Rasmussen and by Kelsey. It should be recalled that Birch and Rasmussen suggest that the Bible functions in two areas: character formation ("being") and decision/action ("doing"). It was pointed out that a third area in ethics--that of the "nonmoral" Good which stands over and above all normative ethics--was virtually ignored in their analysis. It was also observed that, in his treatment of Jesus Christ and ethics, James Gustafson dealt with this category under the title "Jesus Christ the Lord who is Creator and Redeemer." As in his use of Jesus Christ, so also with Scripture, Ellul sees the primary significance in this third area. The Bible mediates the Word of God which establishes a living relationship. It functions to put us in touch with God, the Good.

Secondly, Scripture guides us into a particular stance --a certain fundamental understanding of the reality of the world and of Jesus Christ. It is, thirdly, out of this stance that we decide and act. Ellul avoids the "genre-reductionism" and "norm-reductionism" that Birch and Rasmussen warn against. Ellul's forays into myth, history, prophecy, gospel, epistle, and apocalyptic literature of the Bible--his reliance on examples and patterns of response, on explicitly didactic sections and on mysterious symbolic materials--suggest at least that he cannot be faulted for a narrow selection of materials!

In terms of David Kelsey's categories for the use of Scripture, Ellul inserts Scripture into his arguments primarily as data and warrants. Scripture (along with the data of reason and experience) provides the data that begin the ethical argument. Scripture provides the warrant for moving from data to conclusion. The conclusion may or may not be stateable in biblical terms. The conclusion may be a very explicit, concrete command of God or it may be a guide or an indication of direction for the faithful. We will be in a better position to see this after looking at the case studies which follow. It is enough to recall Ellul's opening statement in _To Will and to Do_, that the point of departure, content, and method he employs all derive from Scripture.

As for the _discrimen_ guiding his use of Scripture, Ellul is closest to the "mode of concrete actuality" ("rendering an agent present"). That is, his basic picture catching up the complexity of God's presence is similar to that of Kierkegaard or Barth (especially the early Barth). A dialectical chasm is seen between this immanent world locked into its web of necessities and conditions and the Wholly Other God. This tension is resolved in the Incarnation of Jesus Christ. Scripture, witnessing to Jesus Christ, renders the living God present and becomes living Word to those who read in faith. This process is profoundly individual for Ellul as it was for Kierkegaard.

* * *

If it is granted that large populations in the Church today regard Jesus Christ and Scripture as authoritative sources of guidance for Christian ethics, Jacques Ellul's proposals for a biblical, Christocentric ethics would seem to deserve a careful hearing. He has not suggested going back to naive and outmoded formulations, despite the premature judgments to that effect by some critics who have only sampled his work. Rather, he has proposed that we go beyond the minute, technical and historical studies of the parts of Scripture to a quest for canon-wide themes and perspectives which may illuminate our situation today. Like John Howard Yoder (in this respect), Ellul comes to Scripture looking for resolution and harmony, rather than deliberately highlighting contradiction and conflict. If the latter are discovered, he would have us seek a broader (developmental, dialectical, etc.) perspective which can "contain" those problems.

Ellul takes the promising path of subordinating all interpretation of Scripture as Word of God to Jesus Christ as definitive Word of God. This is both biblically accurate, I would argue, and practically promising and helpful in ethical instruction for the faithful. The fact that his approach has led him into some questionable interpretations (of symbols, of particular stories) need not disqualify his general approach. But the only way to pass judgment on that issue is to turn from theory to application.

## NOTES

1. "Mirror of These Ten Years," The Christian Century 87 (18 February 1970) p. 200n.
2. To Will and to Do, p. 27.
3. Ethics of Freedom, p. 278.
4. Ibid., pp. 274-275.
5. See David W. Gill, "Jacques Ellul and Francis Schaeffer: Two Views of Western Civilization" Fides et Historia XIII. 2 (Spring-Summer 1981): 23-37.
6. Ethics of Freedom, p. 276.
7. Ibid., p. 278.
8. Politics of God and Politics of Man, pp. 186-187.
9. Apocalypse, p. 48.
10. Ibid., p. 47.
11. Presence of the Kingdom, p. 49.
12. On the exousia, cf. Ethics of Freedom, pp. 144ff.; on "universalism" cf. Apocalypse, p. 88; also "Karl Barth and Us," Sojourners (December 1978): 24.
13. Presence of the Kingdom, p. 49.
14. Ethics of Freedom, p. 7.
15. Ibid., p. 51.
16. Ibid., pp. 52ff.
17. Violence: Reflections from a Christian Perspective, p. 9.
18. Ibid., p. 172.

19. Ibid., pp. 148, 157; cf. Hope in Time of Abandonment, pp. 148ff.
20. The Theological Foundation of Law, p. 42.
21. Ibid., p. 44.
22. Meaning of the City, p. 116.
23. To Will and to Do, p. 28.
24. Ibid., p. 27.
25. Presence of the Kingdom, p. 49.
26. Ibid., p. 51.
27. Apocalypse, p. 24.
28. To Will and to Do, p. 1.
29. "From Jacques Ellul," Introducing Jacques Ellul (Grand Rapids, Mich.: Eerdmans, 1970), p. 5.
30. Ethics of Freedom, p. 87.
31. To Will and to Do, p. 274n.
32. Ethics of Freedom, p. 161.
33. Prayer and Modern Man, p. 104.
34. Ibid., p. 116. See also Ellul's Preface to Psaumes, p. xv. There, he describes the Bible as "un livre qui, pour les croyants, contient la parole de Dieu. Dans ce livre, c'est Dieu qui parle" (emphasis added).
35. Ethics of Freedom, p. 125.
36. To Will and to Do, p. 264.
37. Meaning of the City, p. 176.
38. Hope in Time of Abandonment, p. 138n.
39. Judgment of Jonah, p. 10.
40. Ibid., p. 11.
41. Ibid., p. 46.
42. Ibid., p. 101.
43. Politics of God and the Politics of Man, p. 9.
44. Ibid., p. 11.
45. Ibid., p. 80.
46. Meaning of the City, p. xvii.
47. Ibid., pp. 9-10n; cf. Theological Foundation of Law, pp. 37ff., 88ff.
48. Meaning of the City, p. xviii.
49. Ibid., pp. 196ff.
50. Apocalypse, pp. 9-10.
51. Ibid., p. 257.
52. Ibid., pp. 29, 137-138, 266-267n.
53. Ibid., pp. 259ff.
54. Ibid., p. 11.
55. Ibid., p. 12.
56. Ibid., pp. 24, 156.
57. Hope in Time of Abandonment, p. 142. Cf. To Will and to Do, pp. 47-48.
58. Hope in Time of Abandonment, pp. 172ff.

59. Ibid., p. 221.
60. False Presence of the Kingdom, p. 56.
61. The New Demons, p. 224.
62. Hope in Time of Abandonment, p. 145.
63. "Mirror of These Ten Years," p. 203.
64. Ethics of Freedom, p. 125.
65. Ibid., pp. 162-184.
66. Ronald R. Ray, "Jacques Ellul's Innocent Notes on Hermeneutics," Interpretation XXXIII. 3 (July 1979): 282.
67. Vernard Eller, "How Jacques Ellul Reads the Bible," The Christian Century 89 (November 29, 1972): 1214.
68. Brevard Childs, Old Testament Books for Pastor and Teacher (Philadelphia: Westminster, 1977), pp. 52, 86.
69. George Landes, Interpretation, 26 (Jan. 1972): 98-99.
70. Gibson Winter, JAAR, 40 (March 1972): 118-122.
71. Walter G. Muelder, Christian Century, 88 (March 3, 1971): 299.
72. Walter Brueggemann, JBL, 92 (Sept. 1973): 470-471.
73. David Allan Hubbard, Christian Scholar's Review, 3. 2 (1972): 172-173.
74. To Will and to Do, p. 1.
75. Cf. Jacques Ellul, "On Dialectic," in Christians & Van Hook, op. cit.; also John Boli-Bennett, "The Absolute Dialectics of Jacques Ellul," in Research in Philosophy and Technology III (1980): 171-201.
76. To Will and to Do, pp. 47-48, 221-222, 300n.
77. Ibid., pp. 47-48.
78. Ibid., pp. 263-264.
79. Ronald R. Ray, op. cit., pp. 278-280.
80. The Judgment of Jonah, pp. 17, 43.
81. Matthew 12:40.
82. Interview with the author, Bordeaux, June 23, 1982; translated by Lucia and David Gill.
83. To Will and to Do, p. 42. See also "Le rapport de l'homme à la création selon la Bible," Foi et Vie 73. 5-6 (Dec. 1974): 137-155.
84. Violence, p. 145n.
85. Judgment of Jonah, pp. 21-24.
86. To Will and to Do, p. 264.
87. Ibid., p. 265.
88. Ibid., pp. 206-208; cf. Violence, p. 161.
89. Ethics of Freedom, p. 229.
90. Judgment of Jonah, pp. 22-23.
91. New Demons, p. 223.
92. Politics of God and Politics of Man, p. 71.

93. Ibid., p. 54.
94. Ibid., p. 30.
95. *Presence of the Kingdom*, p. 53.
96. *To Will and to Do*, p. 274n.
97. *Meaning of the City*, p. 153.

## CHAPTER FOUR □

# URBAN-TECHNOLOGICAL CIVILIZATION

In this chapter we will examine how Ellul's Christian ethic works out in relation to our urban-technological civilization. In the following chapter we will direct attention in the same fashion to politics and the nation-state. Although other cases might have been chosen (e.g., violence, money), the choice of these two is not accidental. Never has human life been so urbanized; never has it been so politicized; and never has the rule of "technique" (to be defined below) been so pervasive. In fact, Ellul argues, these two realities constitute the new "sacred" around which our existence is ordered.[1]

The pattern to be followed in this and the following chapter is to begin with a brief review of Ellul's sociological-historical perspective on the subject. Some justification for this approach can be found in Ellul's own remark (quoted earlier):

> The reality of the city ... can be understood only in light of revelation. And this revelation provides us with both a means of understanding the problem and a synthesis of its aspects as found in the raw data of history and sociology....
>
> Revelation ... enlightens, brings together, and explains what our reason and experience discover. Without revelation all our reasoning is doubtlessly useful, but does not view reality in true perspective.[2]

Thus, we shall examine first the results of Ellul's sociological "reason and experience" in regard to urban-technological civilization and politics and the nation-state. Second, we will turn with Ellul to Scripture and Jesus Christ in search of illumination of these realities. Finally we will examine what sort of Christian ethic comes out of this process, and evaluate it in terms of the promise of the method described earlier.

The method of these two case studies is further warranted by Ellul's own explanation of the pattern of his work:

> The writing I had undertaken in a tentative frame of mind assumed a progressively better structure. The whole of it is a composition in counterpoint. Every sociological analysis of mine is answered (not in the sense of replying, but in that of noting the other dialectical pole) by a biblical or theological analysis. For example, to my book _The Political Illusion_, a study of politics as actually practiced in a modern state, corresponds my _Politics of God, Politics of Man_, a biblical study of the Second Book of Kings. To my book on technology corresponds my theologically based study of the great city as the supreme achievement of man's technology.[3]

It is out of this confrontation that progress is possible. It is the individual who lives at the intersection of the world as it really is and the Word of God in all of its radical power who will resolve this dialectical tension in his or her life and decision. Without discounting this profoundly individual and existential character of Christian ethics it is nevertheless possible to seek (and find) a "temporary" Christian ethics that will provide some indications of the general direction of Christian life today.

## SOCIOLOGY OF THE CITY AND TECHNIQUE

Although Ellul's sociological method is not of primary concern in this study, it is important to understand his basic approach. Ellul likes to term his approach "realism." Realism "is the fundamental attitude of the Christian toward the world, and ... its intellectual role is one of the foundations of ethics."[4] The reality of the world and of life can be and must be "grasped and experienced directly."

> There can be no sociology or psychology without a personal experience of the fact, which one first tries to grasp and afterward to explain....

> Yet this realism cannot be reduced to the purely individual experience of the moment.... Any genuine and usable realism, the kind which will always remain the necessary condition for hope, has to be defined in its sociological dimension.[5]

There are three possible levels at which the social group and its history may be analyzed. On the most superficial level one analyzes current events, personalities, happenings, photographs, speeches, slogans, elections, and so forth. At the opposite extreme one deals with reality at its most abstract and general level: all people have to eat, all groups need power, etc., the deepest constants of human and social life.

> But between those two levels there is an intermediate territory. Underneath the events and above the fundamental constants, there are the structures, the movements and the temporary regularities which go to make up the actual history, and which produce an epoch or a regime with its characteristic features.... The differences are secondary compared with the phenomenon itself, which is determinative for our epoch.
>
> As an analogy, consider the ocean. On the surface are the waves and the splash brought about by the wind. To be sure, they could be substantial and cause shipwrecks, but those are surface phenomena. In the depths there is sepulchral stillness. Between the two are the currents, the tides, modifications in the ocean floor, the formation and the shifting of sand bars. My contention is that it is in this in-between that one should apply Christian realism. I have tried to show elsewhere that from the sociological, political, and economic points of view, it is this in-between area which is decisive and the most interesting.[6]

Ellul's objective being clear, what precisely does he identify as the major components of this "in-between" region of the currents that are determinative for human existence today? Two summary statements, the first made in 1948, the second in 1968, indicate his answer:

> In point of fact there are a certain number of values and of forces which are of decisive importance in our world civilization: the primacy of production,

> the continual growth of the power of the State and the formation of the National State, the autonomous development of technics, etc. These, among others, ... are the constitutive elements of the modern world.[7]

> Technological mechanisms, the demand for economic growth, the primacy of science, bureaucratization, manipulation of man to adapt him at whatever cost to the lite others make for him, the development of the "society of spectacle," urbanization, the collectivization of life (whether in the shape of American conformism or of communist integration)--these are the real forces at work in our world.[8]

The modern city is, in Ellul's words quoted earlier, "the supreme achievement of man's technology." The urbanization of modern civilization is, to a great degree, the product of technique. Its character and operations are radically "technicized." Reciprocally, the city hosts, nurtures, and stimulates the further growth of technique. In view of this intimate relationship, this case study is focused on urban-technological civilization and on urban-technological ethics.

"No social, human, or spiritual fact is so important as the fact of technique in the modern world."[9] Ellul, who is a master of hyperbole and unqualified generalization, really means this. The most important reality of our urban civilization is technique. The French title of his most famous and influential book, The Technological Society, ought literally to be translated "Technique: The Stake of the Century."[10] In fact, the use of the term "technological" (rather than Ellul's "technique") is also a major source of confusion. By "technique" Ellul means something much broader than machine technology or computers.

> Technique is the totality of methods, rationally arrived at and having absolute efficiency (for a given stage of development) in every field of human activity.[11]

> Technique is nothing more than means and the ensemble of means.... Our civilization is first and foremost a civilization of means; in the reality of modern life, the means, it would seem, are more important than the ends.[12]

> Technique is the translation into action of man's concern to master things by means of reason, to account for what is subconscious, make quantitative what is qualitative, make clear and precise the outlines of nature, take hold of chaos and put order into it.[13]

The technical phenomenon is the quest for the "one best means in every field," and it is the aggregate of these means which produces technical civilization.[14] The principal divisions of technique are mechanical, intellectual, economic, organizational (including politics), and human (including education and propaganda). The primary characteristics of technique are rationality, artificiality, and efficiency; it is the rule of a "raving rationalism" in every area of life.

Ellul's commitment to this thesis about the centrality of technique pervades all of his sociological work, through his recent "up-dating" of the thesis in The Technological System (1977).[15] The beginnings of this commitment were described by Ellul in conversation with David Menninger:

> Marx showed me the dialectical nature of social phenomena, and also oriented me strongly toward the study of technique. I was actually a Marxist in 1933-34, and I asked myself then: If Marx were alive today, would he be so disposed to cite as the crucial social phenomenon of history the ownership of property? What would he cite as crucial? And I decided that it would be the phenomenon of technique. Of course, this is something that many followers of Marx today would not propose.[16]

A 1935 article on technique was only the beginning for Ellul. His 1948 Presence of the Kingdom devoted a chapter to the problem of "The End and the Means" and presented in germinal form his critique. In 1954 his La Technique ou L'Enjeu du siècle presented a massive analysis of the subject. This is the book of which Aldous Huxley said he was jealous of its penetrating insight and that it made the case he had tried to make in Brave New World.[17] It was translated and published in English in 1964 and has provoked widespread reaction ever since.

Obviously, people have always employed techniques of various kinds in their labor, in primitive magic, etc. The contemporary problem is emphatically not with any single technique; Ellul is not a Luddite wishing to smash all machines! The problem is the ensemble of techniques, the triumph of Technique as a sacred all-encompassing theme and guide, to the exclusion of moral judgment, true democracy, spontaneity, spiritual awareness, gratuitous or ineffective areas of life, passion, and human personality. Obviously these phenomena continue to exist on an individual level here and there. But technique, as a main current underneath the surface, is inexorably circumscribing and penetrating these and all other areas of life.

Ancient Greece developed intellectual technique to a high point, as Rome did with social and political techniques. In both cases, Ellul suggests, Eros (the will to power and domination) was the dominant instinct behind the development of these techniques. Nevertheless, there was a degree of "self-control" in the application of these techniques. And with the entry of Christianity into this Greco-Roman world, Agape (the will to love and serve) mounted a sustained contest against Eros. The history of the West is marked by this tension and conflict between Eros and Agape.[18]

From the fourth to the tenth centuries, during the development of Christendom, there was a breakdown and regression of all techniques, including Roman political technique. A vital civilization without extensive techniques was restored during the tenth to fourteenth centuries, although this Christendom is not to be glorified and, in fact, enthusiastically betrayed Christianity into a religion (a trend which began much earlier, of course).[19]

The fifteenth century saw a brief rise of technique, especially in the authoritarian state. The period from the sixteenth to mid-eighteenth century was characterized by a distinct lack of technique in all areas except the mechanical. There was a rejection of specialization by intellectuals and theologians. The period of the mid- to late-eighteenth century saw the emergence of autonomous technique in the self-serving state, and in military, economic, and legal affairs. Systematization, classification, unification, and clarification were carried out everywhere.

The fruition of this technical development occurred in the nineteenth century. The slow development of the "ingredients" of the technical complex between 1000 and 1750 culminated at this time. Population growth and urbanization created needs that could only be met by developing various techniques. The economic environment was stable at base but flexible enough to absorb technical innovation. The social milieu showed a good deal of plasticity as social taboos disappeared, natural groups were uprooted or disappeared, and the rise of the individual began.

By the nineteenth century the bourgeoisie had a "clear technical intention" and commercial and industrial entrepreneurs grew in power and influence through rigorous application of techniques. The State could only respond in kind by developing its own technique. Marx, among other things, rehabilitated technique and work for the proletariat. Between 1850 and 1914 the working class began to reap some of the benefits of technology and, thus, joined the trend quite willingly.

The technical complex that emerged during the nineteenth century has become a monster in the urbanized twentieth century. Not only the West, but the whole globe is now ruled by Technique--bringing its benefits and problems everywhere. As Russia, China, and now the countries of the Third World have undergone their "revolutions," they have joined the world of Technique. The irony of various colonial peoples throwing out their European oppressors only to leap on the technical bandwagon of the West has not escaped Ellul.[20]

The two traditional characteristics of techniques are rationality (the use of discourse and reason for the logical reduction of phenomena to systems) and artificiality (the subordination and destruction of nature). The new additional characteristics of Technique, as identified by Ellul, are automatism (the "one best way" automatically asserts itself), self-augmentation (the human role is reduced; technical developments create new technical problems for which technical solutions must be sought), monism (techniques link together; there is no distinction between good and bad techniques), universalism (geographic expansion around the globe; totalitarian absorption of all areas of life), and autonomy (the new "prime mover," insubordinate to economics, politics, morality, and spirituality, which dominates and exploits nature and humanity; Technique now has its own "specific weight").[21]

Ellul suggests that Technique is the new "sacred" in our civilization (along with the nation-state).[22] The sacred functions now, as always, in a hostile, threatening world, as that which both threatens and protects. It puts one in tune with the universe, establishes on order of time and space, integrates the individual and the group, and bestows meaning and orientation for life. In an intriguing argument, Ellul suggests that sex is the other pole of Technique, the means of profaning and violating the sacred Technique. The rigor of Technique is profaned by unbridled free expression of sexual impulse. In a strange, ironic, but necessary inversion, sex itself becomes a kind of sacred. The "sexualization of the technical object" (the automobile as sex symbol, etc.) and the "technicalization of the sexual object" (sex manuals, impersonal sex, etc.) attest to this trend.

Ellul's 1954 volume deserves credit as one of the first and most exhaustive discussions of Technique in our generation. However, it is also important to note the affinities of his critique with those of Friedrich Schiller, Thomas Carlyle, and the Romanticists of the Industrial Revolution period who raised warnings about the ominous threat of a generally mechanistic, rationalistic view of life and the world.[23] Schiller, for example, railed against the degenerative effects of the growth of machines on European culture. The machine was leading to "The Machine" as a social system. Thomas Carlyle (who, not incidentally, published a "Life" of Schiller in 1823-24) developed this argument by suggesting that the Age of the Machine had not only an "outward sense," referring to machine technology, but also an "inward sense," that is, an internal, spiritual patterning of art, religion, and other human activities, on the model of the machine. In 1829 Carlyle wrote that "it is the Age of Machinery in every outward and inward sense of that word." Many apologists for industrialization countered these charges on Newtonian and Enlightenment grounds: opposing Nature to Machine is false, for the universe itself is a great machine, like a great clock designed and set in motion by the great clockmaker in the sky!

The list of important predecessors of Ellul must also include the pioneer sociologists of the later nineteenth century. Karl Marx has been mentioned earlier. Emile Durkheim, who created the first course in sociology to be offered at a French university while a professor at the University of Bordeaux (1887-1902), perceived the pivotal significance of the division of labor, the breakdown of traditional groups and values, and the impact of all this on social solidarity, in a way that anticipates Ellul's analysis at several points, although

Ellul's differences from Durkheim are perhaps even more striking. Max Weber's work on rationalization and bureaucracy is echoed loudly in Ellul's work. Weber's fear that the encroachment of zweckrational forms of action on all phases and areas of individual and social life was yielding an "iron cage, a nullity without heart" for a society is fully shared by Ellul.[24]

More recently, Lewis Mumford's history of technics corresponds at many points with that of Ellul, as does his fear about the invidious effects of the "Megamachine." And although their evaluations and prescriptions differ, Herbert Marcuse, John Kenneth Galbraith, Rene Dubos, C. Wright Mills, Theodore Roszak, Alvin Toffler, and many others agree substantially with Ellul's analysis.[25] Of course, there has also been vigorous dissent from Ellul's analysis. Some of this dissent is due to a common misunderstanding of what Ellul is describing. Some reviewers persist in thinking that Ellul opposes all machines, computer technology, or even modern advances in medical technology and "would not hesitate to plunge himself and all mankind backward in time."[26] Others scoff that various events as well as personal experience belie any assertion of technical determinism, forgetting that Ellul allows for a sector of "free choice" but argues that it is increasingly circumscribed and affected by the undercurrent of technique. A much more interesting question concerns the autonomy of technique. Victor Ferkiss, for example, writes:

> Technologies are created and used by men. Those who, like the French social critic Jacques Ellul, hold that we are becoming a technological society defined by the fact that technology has become an end in itself, subject to no external controls, are plainly mistaken....
>
> Indeed, the central danger facing humankind in the latter part of the twentieth century lies not in the autonomy of technology or in the triumph of technological values but in the subordination of technology to the values of earlier historical eras and its exploitation by those who do not understand its implications and consequences but seek only their own selfish personal or group purposes.[27]

Of course, Ellul says, he would be delighted to be proven wrong, but on the general sociological level he sees no significant countertrends to the rise of technique. This brings us to a final criticism of Ellul's sociological analysis. That is, why has he been so deficient in suggestions of ways to counter technique? He has actually given more suggestions than many critics realize, but much more could be expected. His excuse that such solutions "would necessarily be theoretical and abstract" is finally unacceptable, for his analysis itself is a "theoretical abstract" reflection of life, which does not prevent it from being helpful.

## TECHNIQUE, THE CITY, AND THE WORD OF GOD

The theological counterpoint to The Technological Society is Ellul's The Meaning of the City. His recent study, Apocalypse: The Book of Revelation, is also of importance.

> And just as, in writing The Politics of God and the Politics of Man I have attempted to explicate the dialectical position I have in regard to politics, between the modern concrete political reality and the reading of an example (not at all a doctrine of the Old Testament), in the same way here I attempt to set forth the dialectical position I can have in regard to society, human works, and especially technique, for the confrontation between the sociological reality and the reading of an example: here again because the Apocalypse is the unique example (and not the doctrine) of the meaning of the work of humanity and, equally, of its non-meaning.[28]

The Apocalypse provides illumination of the present from the standpoint of the End, in an explicit fashion. The entire biblical revelation about the city, from Genesis to the Apocalypse, "concerns man's essential work--the culture of man in history and eternity."[29] The two quotations in this paragraph help to explain the fact that Ellul's sociology is focused primarily on technique while the biblical theology in counterpoint focuses on the city. The city is, both in Scripture and the contemporary world, the focal point of human society and culture, the symbol as well as the real product of human work. Today's city is characterized above all, in Ellul's view, by the rule of technique. Technique defines the essence of contemporary urban civilization.

Whatever the factual history of the city may be, the biblical stories and examples give us God's perspective on the attitudes and activities of mankind. In biblical perspective, then, the origin of the city is bound up with the story of Cain.[30] Cain shattered the serenity of the world by murdering his brother, thus introducing insecurity and vengeance. Cain then rejected God's protection (the "mark of Cain") as a wanderer--in favor of a self-made security "struggling against hostile forces, dominating men and nature, taking guarantees that are within his reach, guarantees that appear to him to be genuine, but which in fact protect him from nothing."[31]

Cain builds a city and fathers a child--both to try to make life bearable. But the "land of Nod, east of Eden" is also "away from the presence of God"; it is a false and self-made security. Both the child and the city are called Enoch, which means "initiation" or "dedication"--a new counter-creation. Even the Hebrew root word for city (`iyr or `iyr re´em), closely related to the meaning of "Watching Angel," "Vengeance," and "Terror," implies that the city is fundamentally not just a collection of houses but a spiritual power capable of directing or changing human spiritual life.[32]

Nimrod, the first of the earth's "mighty men," the son of Ham, the impure and cursed son of Noah, is the next great builder of cities in biblical revelation.[33] Once again, Ellul argues, the building of cities arises out of a hardened heart toward God, an attempt to escape the curse by making oneself strong, by building and conquering. Thus, Nimrod is a "plunderer and conqueror" as well as a builder of cities; the city is the base from which he wages war. Nimrod settles in the land of Shinar ("shaker," "fury," "roaring"), the place of opposition to Abraham and Melchizedek. Among Nimrod's cities is Resen ("bridle," "bit"), which Ellul views as the city of technique, invention, and domination of nature.

Babel/Babylon is particularly significant in this search for biblical perspective on the meaning of the city.[34] The story of the tower indicates that the essential purpose of this city is to "build a city and make a name for ourselves." Given the significance of names in Israel, this act expressed a fundamental desire for independence. God responds by confusing their language; the city comes to mean "lack of communication." There is a very real irony in this. The city has become the place of separation from God, but after Babel it is no longer a place of human unity or a proof of human spiritual power. Its meaning is lost. To preserve the possibility of life God has providentially and necessarily confused the languages. Human truth will henceforth be partial and contested, not valid for all. The city is not destroyed but construction of the tower is halted.

Babylon, built on this foundation, is the city in Scripture, the synthesis and symbol of all cities and all civilization. Ninevah plays an important, if secondary role, in being the city of bloody violence and lies, the synthesis of war --and later on, with Jonah, the example of the extreme possibility of an entire city in repentance. Babylon and Ninevah represent the two basic forms of man's spirit of power: civilization and war.

In contrast to all of this, Israel's first act of building anything at all is a heap of stones for an altar at Galeed (Mizpah).[35] When the people of God, originally nomads and shepherds, first encounter cities it is merely to "dwell in them." That is, they relate to cities as mere objects and not as spiritual powers. Before long, of course, Israel is in bondage and forced to build the storehouse cities of Egypt --including Mizraim (N. B.: the son of Cain with the same name! Genesis 9:25, 10:13)--showing the linking of economic power with the city. Israel is caught in the trap of doing work which aids the enemy. But "God's constant effort is to denude this act of the meaning given to it by men." "God takes upon himself the act and gives it new meaning."[36]

In Canaan, after the Exodus and journey through the wilderness, Israel is ordered to destroy the pagan cities because of their religious and other corruption. Joshua, for example, pronounces a curse on anyone who ever rebuilds Jericho. Four hundred years later Hiel yields to the seduction of the city and, willing to sacrifice self, family, and all else, ignores the curse. Solomon is the first great building king of Israel. Ellul argues that Solomon's error is to build cities in slavery for the purpose of power. He is abandoned by God not at the end of his life but rather at the moment he builds the Millo (I Kings 11:26f. ).[37] Solomon's construction of the temple and his later construction of cities shows that the important thing is the spiritual meaning and quality of our acts. Solomon goes after "other gods" as he builds other cities. As Jeremiah later laments, Israel's false gods are as many as her cities.[38]

Rehoboam, like his father, Solomon, is a great builder of cities (II Chronicles 11-12). After losing ten tribes Rehoboam relies on his own means and builds cities to compensate for the loss of the chosen people. Asa and Jehoshaphat, in contrast, are godly kings who build cities but subordinate them to God and refuse them spiritual significance. Nevertheless, the city retains its power to sting and tempt; as Shishak of Egypt defeated Rehoboam, so Asa is later caught in an unfortunate alliance with Syria.

Of all the historical books only Chronicles gives an extended account of the building of cities. The prophets condemn the cities not out of a nostalgia for a lost, ideal past but because they see with their own eyes the corruption of urban man. "The Chronicles considers the city as one of the predominant forms of man's opposition to God."[39] Sin and holiness are viewed primarily as sociopolitical phenomena in the Chronicles. The problem of the city is partly the problem of necessity. Necessity can never be totally escaped or set aside. The spiritual power of the city clashes with the spiritual power of God. A struggle is inevitable, for the city displays a constant, unswerving resentment against God. God has cursed the city, not because of its human origins, but because of its collective spiritual reality. The city dweller is alienated--becomes someone else--by the city's power. But to that city dweller God addresses both a Yes and a No. To the city itself, as an entity, as a power, he has only a No.

The curse is stated most precisely in reference to Babylon--"The City" from Genesis to Revelation.[40] It is because of what the city represents that she is cursed. She is constantly in revolt against God; immersed in war, bloodshed, oppression; the bearer of corrupt moral attitudes; filled with pride, exalting herself and her works; pushing sin to its limits. Humanity has constructed something stronger than itself.

The city always tends to exclude God and pervert its inhabitants, kings, and merchants.

> Such valid human activities as political involvement and business become works of death and sin when they are shut into a world which has excluded God in order to glorify, to force, to seduce man.... The city has chosen her special role by specifically

> and voluntarily shutting herself off from any divine intervention.[41]

She does this by creating idols and by seducing people from carrying out the search for God implanted in their hearts. The end is complete slavery, the reduction of people to merchandise.

Has Ellul overspiritualized the biblical message? No, he protests: the city both symbolized and mediated sin and evil. The city is specifically and appropriately chosen as the spiritual symbol of human building in independence and rebellion against God. The city is condemned to destruction, to lose what made up its being. It drags its inhabitants to ruin, although it began as a quest for protection! The city is also a sign, "an event by which spiritual and even eschatological realities become no longer abstract, but actual. They are presented figuratively, but concretely and effectively; that is, they have an effect."[42] The city is a sign of the world's response to God and is subject not only to the judgment of the prophets but to the Last Judgment in Revelation. The marks of the curse are present in abundance even today --slavery, corruption, insecurity, the city as the target of modern warfare.

The judgment of God on the city as a spiritual entity is inevitable. A way of escape is, however, left open to the city dweller:

> What he wants is for man to separate himself from the city.... Man can, then, choose to include himself in the condemnation of the city, or he can avert the destruction of the city by removing it from the great whole which cities make up and making it into a community of men on the order of other human groups, acceptably gathered together before God.[43]

The way of escape is only that of Sodom or Ninevah. Sodom shows the possibility of a city being spared because of a pocket of righteousness. Ninevah is the counterpart of Sodom in terms of its lies, violence, and corruption--but it is spared because it demonstrates the remote possibility of a whole population and government being repentant and converted.

If Ellul is anything he is the consistent dialectician!

Though the city is condemned, though the city is fundamentally Babylon, it is precisely in this arena that we must live. Thus, Jeremiah the prophet urges the captive people of God to seek the welfare of the cities wherein they dwell as exiles (Jeremiah 29:2-7, 10). Though the church is in captivity in Babylon, she is not told to escape or to destroy, but to preserve her alive. The judgment of God is not a separation of good and evil elements, but annihilation and re-creation.[44] Our role is not to play God as Judge and Executioner, but to participate. We are not to build up the essentially rebellious nature of the city, but to participate in its life, pray for its good, and ask God to remove the condemnation (as Lot prayed for Sodom, as the repentant Ninevites prayed for their city).

We are physically captives of the city; we must not, however, be its spiritual captives. We must proclaim God's curse and condemnation, but pray that it will not be applied. The presence of God and the Word preserve the city. "Come out from Babylon, my people" is thus only a final and extreme order when there is no hope left and judgment has begun. Only God determines when this extreme possibility occurs. Our role is to go to the cities where the people of God are enslaved, to the places of man's rebellion against God. "Shake the dust off of your feet" is only the final, extreme possibility; to go there is Jesus' first word to his disciples.

Like the state, the city occasionally appears as the instrument of God, e.g., as Babylon punishes the people of God. The "cities of refuge" also indicate the possibility of a productive relationship between the people of God and the city. The important thing to notice in this, however, is that these cities of refuge are elected by God to be different from the ordinary city. They are, in Ellul's words, "the first fruits of what God wants to make of the city."[45] But it is Jerusalem which is the primary symbol of what God will do with man's urban history.[46] Jerusalem already exists, in the hands of the Jebusites, when Israel enters the promised land. What transforms the city is David's act. In the name of the Lord he makes with her a pact of love and makes her the home of the Ark of the Presence of God. This, Ellul suggests, shows the miracle of God submitting to an act of man. In this God chooses and elects the city.

Jerusalem is a holy city, though it remains a bloody city, a city of idolatry, a city with all the marks of the fall.

God's love and grace reside in Jerusalem simultaneously with her sin. The curse coexists with the covenant and promise. The other cities are to become "daughters of Jerusalem." Jerusalem may evidence little promise, but God has gotten a foothold in man's world. He has intervened in precisely the place constructed to exclude him. This is God's loving humility, to enter into the very heart of human refusal and revolt, on the level of human and spiritual powers. God comes where he is not wanted, where his creatures are hiding behind their walls. Even more remarkably, God adopts our environment and our work as he saves us. The curse is, after all, the "next-to-last" act; God's redemption and adoption are the last word.

Indeed, God now becomes a builder: the returning exiles are commanded to build Jerusalem again. Jerusalem is elected to become a witness city, an example of what God's action and desire for the city really are. Jerusalem is to witness both to judgment and grace, both to condemnation and adoption of the city. The bond between Jerusalem and the Word of God indicates God's intention to reverse the process of Babel. It is in this city that the Word must resound. God's sovereignty removes and replaces human sovereignty over human works. By human standards Jerusalem is mediocre and unimpressive. Her significance is as a witness announcing the New Jerusalem which will replace her. Jerusalem's last task is to witness and wait for Jesus Christ her Lord.

The incarnation of God in Jesus Christ brings into sharp focus the Word of God to the city.[47] Jesus Christ fulfills but does not modify the message of the Old Testament with respect to the city. For the people of the city he brings both judgment and pardon; but for the city as a spiritual entity he has only rejection and condemnation. The temptation of Jesus takes place both in the desert and on the pinnacle of the temple in the holy city. Is this, Ellul asks, Jesus' first encounter with the city--as the place of temptation? Following his temptation comes the pronouncement of "woes" on Chorazin, Bethsaida, and Capernaum--again, not on the inhabitants per se, but on the city. These woes are directed against the placing of confidence in something other than God, the failure to respond to the miracles with trust in God's Spirit (rather than their own walls).

Jesus had no home. His entire life was one of wandering. In fact, Ellul's original French title for <u>The Mean-</u>

ing of the City was Sans Feu ni Lieu: "Neither Hearth nor Home." At his birth the city closed up to him; only shepherds and travellers visited his birth. Those who follow him must be prepared to walk a lot! Jesus accepts only God's protection and rejects the security of the city, its money, etc. Even his death takes place outside the gates of the city. Jesus' call and ministry have the effect of separating the multitude from the city which seduces and enslaves them. He differentiates them as real and valuable individuals, while the city reduces them to an anonymous urban mass. Jesus feels compassion for the miserable searching flock without a shepherd. His very presence in a crowd explodes it, restoring individuality to its members. Jesus does not become the leader of a mass movement to build the ideal city. Rather, he leads the people into the desert, the place of honesty and trial. He brings about a break between the people and the city. The break is followed, however, by sending the crowds back into the city, this time freed from the spiritual domination of the city and its work.

Jesus is not only teacher and pattern here. With his arrival the "sign of Jerusalem" is fulfilled.[48] Jesus replaces Jerusalem as the cornerstone of the coming Kingdom, the scandal to cities and nations. The specific, delimited place is replaced by the Incarnate Word. Jesus not only fulfills, he is the substitute, taking on God's judgment and fulfilling God's promise. "Both man and his work are completely adopted."[49] Jesus prophesies and then enacts the destruction and rebuilding of the temple, in his own person. In so doing, he desacralizes the city, taking away Jerusalem's sacred role.

The promises to Jerusalem are not revoked. Typical of God's work in the world, however, those promises are fulfilled in ways different from what we might expect. With the coming of Jesus Christ, Jerusalem desacralized becomes just like all other cities. Jerusalem rejected the true temple of God in rejecting Jesus Christ and now symbolizes all cities. The requirement to leave the city is now in force--but in the sense of leaving the attitudes, values, and spirit she represents, leaving her brand of security. This implies a judgment on work, money, technique, indeed, on all human works insofar as they are a bulwark against God and an attempt to build a godless security.

Just as Jesus Christ is God's greatest work, so,

Ellul argues, the city is humanity's greatest work. The city is assumed, never called in question per se, by modern scholars. Even decentralization does not represent a questioning of the city per se. Civilization assumes the concrete form of the city; without cities there is no civilization. Ellul describes the "specific atmosphere of the city" in strong terms:

> [it is] made of anonymity, seedy luxury, vast organization, definitive truth, a share in the world's folly and diversity, the constitution of a community vibrating intensely by the fake shocks of an illusory current.[50]

Industry and politics are its hub; masses of people are the material. The city is a parasite drawing all life and work into its orbit. It produces things without value or meaning except to itself, especially in the intellectual realm. The city is a condition for ideological development. It is an urbanist and sociologist illusion, Ellul argues, to think that the city (as an entity) can be reformed or change course.

But the "true history" of the city is made by Jesus Christ. The irony of the situation is that the future of the world, the coming kingdom is precisely a city, the New Jerusalem. Ezekiel, the prophets, and the Apocalypse all picture the future as a city--a step forward from our cities, certainly not a retreat to a golden age in the past or a renewed Garden of Eden. This step forward is, of course, solely God's act and not a developmental evolution of our present efforts. This dialectical paradox, that Christ both judges and establishes the city, is most clearly seen from the standpoint of the End (described in the Apocalypse, for example). Jesus' relationship to the city-as-spiritual-power and to the city-as-dwelling-of-the-people provides us with clues in our discernment of this decision of God. Desacralized by the death and resurrection of Jesus Christ as the new Temple of God, the positive pole of the dialectic concerning the city is firmly established. "The radical devaluation of everything in society is accompanied by the revelation (the only one) that everything, by the grace of God, may be able to serve the kingdom."[51]

Ellul summarizes this movement in two basic directions--from Cain to Jerusalem and from Eden to Jerusalem--each of which expresses one form of the saving and kingly act of God in Jesus Christ.[52] From Cain to

Jerusalem, God dissociates human work from its spiritual power through the act of Jesus Christ. The exousia, among which is the city, have been defeated but not yet eliminated. In their death throes these powers remain in violent rebellion. It is folly to think that we can control a demonic situation when there are powers at work in it. Nevertheless, the city is a mixture of what humanity does and what the powers do. God's act has made the city a neutral field where new possibilities exist. People may cease to be a plaything of the powers and can struggle to bring God's truth into the reality of the urban world. Certainly, Ellul says, the idealists should be saluted for their attempts at reform, even if they do not succeed entirely. There is some agreement between what urbanologists do and what God wills. Ellul advocates realism but not cynicism or apathy.

From Eden to Jerusalem, God changes his mind when humanity chooses the city instead of the garden. The one desire that God would not allow humanity was its desire to be rid of God. Human action provoked God's intervention. Thus, God's love and patience are undefeated, for God takes over and assimilates human choices and human works into his own plans. The city is one example of this process; language (in the case of Scripture) is another.[53] This work is adopted in Jesus Christ, the great recapitulator of all things. In him all things are completed (Ephesians 1:10).

As individuals today we are in primary contact with the condemned city, not the New Jerusalem. Only by faith are we aware of the revelation of the final truth of the city. But, because God forgives, we must forgive and participate in the life of the city, even while understanding the relativity or even vanity of our work. We must rely on God's Spirit for discernment and forgiveness. As participants in the work of the city, Ellul suggests, we must perform at least two tasks: (1) we should inject humor into our situation, thus combatting idolatry and evidencing the irony of faith, and (2) we must represent Christ in the heart of the city, whether this leads to our rejection or not.

The eschatological expectation of the Heavenly City provides the perspective of the End from which the present is to be judged and our action guided. In Ezekiel's apocalyptic visions, he sees a city but speaks interminably of the temple. In the Revelation of John no temple is mentioned and the city is everything. Ellul's explanation is that in biblical apocalyptic expectation there is a development. The temple is the shadow and pledge of God's presence. In the Revelation of John the city is the temple where God's presence is all in all. "Yahweh-Shammah" ("The Lord is here," Ezekiel 48:35) replaces Jerusalem as the name of the city. It is the exact counterpart of Immanuel ("God with us"). When he builds, God comes from the East, just like Cain (Ezekiel 43:2, Zechariah 14:14). The New Jerusalem both parallels and contradicts Babylon: the prostitute is replaced by a bride. It is on a high mountain. All of creation is reconciled and renewed, but people will live only in a city, a limited place, like Eden in this respect. The city is the center of the nations as well as the new creation--an "open city" at last. It is a center for all peoples united by grace, not constraint. God offers the city, the sum of all human desires and efforts, in righteousness and communion with Himself. The counter-creation is recreated in freedom, knowledge, and unity. It replaces the Church.

Ellul's recent book Apocalypse: The Book of Revelation elaborates this eschatological perspective in greater detail.

> The Apocalypse does not describe a moment of history but reveals for us the permanent depth of the historical: it is then, one could say, a discernment of the Eternal in Time, of the action of the End in the Present, the discovery of the New Eon, not at the end of time, but in this present history, the Kingdom of God hidden in this world.[54]

The Apocalypse reveals history for what it is in essence. Of particular interest here is Ellul's discussion of the "powers" (exousia). The well-known scroll with its seven seals is interpreted by Ellul as the "book of man and of history." The first six of the seven seals give the components of history.

> History is not the result of chance, of an ensemble of automatisms, but the result of the interplay between the will of God (which is the love of God and not his imperative power), the will of men, and a certain number of abstract forces.[55]

The fifth seal is the prayer of the witnesses and the sixth is the cataclysm and the appearance of the people of God. The first four seals are the four horsemen, the chief components of history. The white horse represents the Word of God sent into the world bearing life and salvation. The three others are immaterial, abstract forces--*exousia.* The red horse is the power of war and bearer of the sword of justice, i.e., the *exousia* of the State. The black horse represents the *exousia* of the economy and the economic scourge. The pale horse is the *exousia* of death.

In addition to the power of the Word of God, these three horsemen/powers are the primary components of history, according to Ellul. Ellul follows Oscar Cullman, Karl Barth, Hendrik Berkhof, and others, who have argued that this biblical cosmology with its angelic/demonic "principalities and powers" is not an outmoded, superstitious remnant of a bygone culture.[56] Rather, the language quite fittingly describes the existence and character of various forces at work in our history. The powers language need not be restricted to the three horsemen of the Apocalypse, even if those three deserve (as Ellul argues) some kind of priority. Money, described as Mammon in the New Testament, can function as demonic power. Technique has, not surprisingly, been denoted a power by Ellul.

Ellul's definition of the *exousia* leaves something to be desired in terms of rigor and clarity.[57] However, the powers are at least "abstract forces" which work in "concrete experience," if we may summarize Ellul's view this way. These powers "have an existence, reality, and ... objectivity of their own" but are also partially dependent for their constitution and effectiveness on the disposition of the people to exalt them as such. The *exousia* are "supra-individual" and, perhaps, "supernatural." Unlike Barth and Cullmann, Ellul gives no hint of the possible participation of the *exousia* in God's redemptive order. Rather, they appear invariably as enemies and are destined for damnation. Jesus Christ has won the victory over the powers, however, detaching them from human works. Although their final defeat and damnation is assured, living this side of the *eschaton* means that we must continue to struggle against the *exousia,* making real the presence of the End in the *hic et nunc.*

For the purpose of the discussion in this chapter, we must note that the city and technique are described as powers. Indeed, the great city, Babylon, is the meeting place of the various powers. If Ellul's interpretation of the Apocalypse is correct, and the three horsemen represent the State, the Economy, and Death, it must be noted that Technique is the premier characteristic of each.[58] Our calling is to make present and actual the victory of Christ and the presence of the coming Kingdom. Specifically, that means desacralizing the city and technique--relativizing them but then attributing to these realities an appropriate, relative significance and a humble place in service of the glory of God and love of our neighbor.

Finally, we must recall Ellul's repeated references to necessity as the converse of freedom and the primary characteristic of a fallen world.[59] Necessity is both a sociological and a theological concept for Ellul. Technique appears in germinal form as an element in necessity from the fall onward. Today, however, technique has become the all-encompassing primary form of necessity. Fallen and closed off from the Wholly Other God, human life is ruled by conditions and determinations.

> I do not maintain that the individual is more determined today than he has been in the past; rather, that he is differently determined. Primitive man, hemmed in by prohibitions, taboos, and rites, was, of course, socially determined. But it is an illusion--unfortunately very widespread--to think that because we have broken through the prohibitions, taboos, and rites that bound primitive man, we have become free. We are conditioned by something new: technological civilization.[60]

Nature (the need for food, the fight against disease, etc.) has also been a major force of necessity until recently.

> All men are constrained by means external to them to ends equally external. The further the technical mechanism develops which allows us to escape natural necessity, the more we are subjected to artificial technical necessities.[61]

* * *

Before summarizing and analyzing the urban-technological ethic for Christians that emerges from this hearing of the sociological data and biblical revelation of the Word of God, we must briefly consider the critical reaction which Ellul's work has generated. The reaction from the Committee of Southern Churchmen, John Wilkinson, Martin Marty, and many others has been generally enthusiastic.

More interesting, from the present standpoint, is the negative criticism. For example, Jeffrey K. Hadden asks, "Can any serious scholar view this work [The Meaning of the City] as anything other than a diatribe by an angry and disillusioned man whose mind and soul belong to another era?"[62] Hadden suggests that Ellul's positions will only "reassure those professing benign neglect as an appropriate policy for dealing with urban problems." Hadden's real quarrel is with "the Bible's pervasive negative sentiment toward cities." He appreciates Ellul's work in bringing this source of antiurbanity into clear focus--although his disgust with both the Bible and Ellul is unconcealed.

Gibson Winter, like Jeffrey Hadden, has written a very angry rejection of The Meaning of the City.[63] Unlike Hadden, however, Winter contests Ellul's thesis partly on biblical grounds. He refuses to admit that Ellul's interpretation is possible. "It is true to neo-orthodox thinking, if not the biblical realities." Winter's major complaint is that Ellul's apocalyptic, eschatological, "transhistorical Christianity displaces man's history with a divine triumph--the earthly city contributes nothing to the positive meaning of the heavenly city." Winter cites several biblical affirmations of the city, its people, and its work as counter-evidence.

By far the best and most complete critical review of Ellul's major work on the city is Harvey Cox's "The Ungodly City: A Theological Response to Jacques Ellul."[64] Cox affirms most of what Ellul has to say about the city as a demonic "power." "Ellul's radically corporate and stubbornly theological view of human evil is his most important insight." The problem, Cox says, is that "Ellul's grace doesn't quite reach.... My argument with him is that he hoists grace to such a removed and transcendent sphere that the result for man turns out to be something akin to inertia if not resignation." Cox continues,

> Although his recognition of the irreducibly structural quality of evil is both theologically and politically accurate, he has been led astray by a flabby doctrine of grace and a serious misreading of the Biblical evidence on the positive possibilities of the exousia, the mystiques suffusing the corporate structures of human life.[65]

What are we to make of these criticisms? Cox's complaint that Ellul's doctrine of grace is "flabby" is not nearly so telling a criticism as his other remark that it "doesn't quite reach." Ellul argues that the city as a "power" is condemned, but the city as human work, is adopted by God and given new meaning. Ellul's writing could stand some clarification; it is true that the negative pole in the dialectic is so insistently presented that the positive pole gets somewhat lost at the end. But both poles are certainly noted; and God's grace wins the decisive triumph in the end. This "end" is not as clearly identified in The Meaning of the City as in Apocalypse--as a nontemporal transcendent reality. In the final analysis, all of the criticisms of Hadden, Winter, and Cox could have been met by Ellul with a more careful and thorough presentation of the "Grace" alongside the "Judgment" of God, even beginning with Melchizedek at Salem (Genesis 14)--an episode that pushes the "gracing" of the city of Jerusalem back much earlier.[66] The other shortcoming of The Meaning of the City is its lack of a forceful or systematic presentation of suggestions on how this transhistorical combat between Grace and Judgment gets worked out, especially in a positive sense, in our empirical history.

## URBAN-TECHNOLOGICAL ETHICS

Having examined the world of technique and the city, and having explored the Word of God in Jesus Christ and Scripture concerning these phenomena, some questions must be raised: What urban-technological ethic emerges? What are we to do or be in our situation? What guidance do we have in formulating an agenda? These queries have, of course, already been hinted at or briefly touched on in the preceding pages. But we have observed Ellul's reticence to spell out "solutions" since, he says, they would necessarily be theoretical and abstract. We may recall his strong insistence on the impossibility of a systematic formulation of a Christian ethic.

Nevertheless, Ellul finally admits that a Christian ethic is a necessity and a possibility, provided that it is properly qualified as temporary. In searching for a more or less comprehensive temporary ethic from Ellul, one is forced to draw together elements from many of his various writings. Even his most "systematic" volumes on ethics do not bring together all that he has to say on a particular subject. Again, one reason for this is Ellul's determination "to provide Christians with the means of thinking out for themselves the meaning of their involvement in the modern world."[67] Thus, Ellul's books are all partial in intention, and not complete syntheses. To the extent that he does have an agenda: "The system and the conclusions to be drawn therefrom will appear only at the end of my work, if God permits me to arrive at the end."[68] Although the end of Ellul's production is not in sight, enough of his work is now available to be able to identify the main contours of his normative ethics.

The first point that must be made about Ellul's ethics is that Christians are commanded to be in the world, but not of the world. Ellul never counsels withdrawal or acquiescence --always presence and challenge. All of his work grows out of the convictions he powerfully stated in his programatic Presence of the Kingdom (1948):

> The Bible tells us that the Christian is in the world, and that there he must remain. The Christian has not been created in order to separate himself from, or live aloof from the world.... If the Christian is necessarily in the world, he is not of it. This means that his thought, his life, and his heart are not controlled by the world, and do not depend upon the world, for they belong to another Master. Thus, since he belongs to another Master, the Christian has been sent into this world by this Master, and his communion with his Master remains unbroken, in spite of the "world" in which he has to live.[69]

> Thus we seem to be caught between two necessities, which nothing can alter: on the one hand it is impossible for us to make this world less sinful; on the other hand it is impossible for us to accept it as it is.... We must accept this tension, and live in it.[70]

> Now the situation of the Christian in the world is a revolutionary situation. His share in the preservation of the world is to be an inexhaustible revolutionary force in the midst of the world.[71]

These ideas are reemphasized in many of Ellul's writings,

and it is important at the outset to recall them, as well as their grounding in Jesus' teaching (John 17). Ellul's work can have a withering effect on much of our activist bent. But this is not its intention finally.

Although we are impatient to find out what we should do, Ellul argues that the "first duty" for Christians is the cultivation of awareness, i.e., to know.[72] This awareness is first of all a matter of becoming aware of the Word of God in Jesus Christ and Scripture, a process which has been described earlier. Putting time and energy into this is indispensable on Ellul's agenda.

The second aspect of awareness is awareness of the world. This means, as discussed earlier, understanding the reality of the world at the level of its major constitutive forces. This is not an easy task because of the complexity of the modern world, the blizzard of information, the speed and distraction of life, the impersonal and selective media of information, the abundance of explanatory myths.[73] Thus, awareness of the world will depend on a determined effort to reject all idealisms, myths, commonplaces, orthodoxies, and propaganda, and a will to analyze in some depth the forces that are determinative of life. This whole quest is grounded generally in the fact that the Bible gives major attention to this level of powers and forces. One of Ellul's favorite texts is Ezekiel's description of the "watchman on the wall" (Ezekiel 3) who foresees coming events and trends and thus will be able to affect life while situations are still fluid.[74]

The other side to awareness of the world is to know it in the form of one's neighbor. Our awareness of people tends to be filtered through statistics, abstractions, fleeting news stories, and images on a screen. Life in the modern city tends to be anonymous and impersonal. The speed of life, the mobility of the population, and other distractions can easily lead to a rather unrealistic understanding of the life and struggles of our neighbors. And yet it is with that flesh and blood reality which, as Christians, we must reacquaint ourselves.

It is on the basis of this kind of awareness, which may well require us to pull back from our frenetic activities at times, that we are to make a "resolute committal in words and deeds."[75] The Christian faith must be incarnated in daily life or it means nothing. The "Word became flesh and lived among us." The basic theme or qualification of Christian action is stated most succinctly in Violence:

> The idea that Christian radicalism inhibits action is utterly false. It calls for action--but of another kind. Certainly it inhibits the action of the capitalist bent on conquering new markets, the action of guerrillas, etc. But it does require action. However, because Christianity is the revelation of the Wholly Other, that action must be different, specific, singular, incommensurable with political or corporate methods of action. Those who think that technological or political action is the only kind there is are, of course, free to go on thinking so. The worse for them. In any case, it is not by aligning Christianity with those sociological forms that the specific form Christian action should take today will be discovered.[76]

Thus, one can say that to qualify as Christian, an action should be a making present of the "Wholly Other." It is a matter of making present the End, the coming Kingdom of God. Ellul suggests that biblically, three descriptions are of central importance. These are the "salt of the earth" (a visible sign of the new covenant, a preservative), the "light of the world" (eliminating darkness, explaining the meaning and direction of history), and "sheep among wolves" (sacrifice and servanthood in a world where too many want to be wolves).[77]

The question is how to work this out in the contemporary urban and technical milieu. The absolute starting point, Ellul says, is the rediscovery and rebuilding of the individual, of myself. In this Kierkegaard "is the only one who can show us the way."[78] This is grounded in the biblical affirmation of the worth of the individual and the fact that God was incarnate in an individual--the root of everything. The urban and technical structures menace individuality and crush personality.

> When I speak of the individual as the source of hope I mean the individual who does not lend himself to society's game, who disputes what we accept as self-evident (for example, the consumer society), who finds an autonomous style of life, who questions even the movement of this society.[79]

This "radical subjectivity" must build on the three elemental human passions to create, to love, and to play. This means creating and inventing new ways of acting, being, loving, and celebrating which "cannot be annexed by the sociotechnological order." It will require great effort and is only possible by leaning on the Wholly Other. Thus, prayer and waiting are also central in this individual lifestyle.[80] It is impossible to overstate Ellul's commitment to this beloved "individual" (recalling Kierkegaard). The West has betrayed its long commitment to the individual.[81] In one of his most brilliant articles, Ellul has argued the importance of "a new thrust of the individual" as the hallmark of our stance toward the Third World--rather than encouraging the Third World to become the technological adjunct of the West.[82]

Ellul's discussion of the individual is well-conceived and powerfully stated. We shall return in a moment to consider the relationships of this individual to the world. If there is one great weakness in Ellul's ethics it is his failure to balance his individualism with an adequate concept of the corporate possibilities of the Church (or any other intermediate group, for that matter). Ellul's suspicion of intermediate groups is clear:

> Of course, if revolution occurs, it must oppose all attempts to integrate individuals into the totalitarian social body by means of intermediary groups and communities.[83]

> Revolution must always emanate from the diametrical opposite of the organism under attack. If that organism is truly totalitarian, its sole antithesis is the individual.[84]

In The Ethics of Freedom, Ellul differentiates individual from private, but the rejection or depreciation of any group continues:

> The fact that freedom is a choice of acts in terms of love for others means that we are faced with a purely individualistic ethics. This freedom can be demonstrated only by individual acts in individual cases.[85]

There is no social dimension "in the sense of commitment to a collective movement, a part, a union, etc.... It is not a private act. But I think we have to make a distinction between individual and private."[86] If there is a social transformation, "It will not come about ... by a collective movement.... It will come from below by the accumulation of a vast number of individual decisions."[87] Ellul, of course, has in mind political groups, labor unions, and other groups more commonly thought of as potential opposition to the State or society. Nevertheless, his indictment includes the Church, which is also an intermediate group conforming to sociological laws.[88]

Occasionally, Ellul contradicts this trend, as when he says that "It is on the basis of a church which is a strong body and community that this [living out of freedom] is possible for the layman."[89] But the usual reference to the Church is to its lack of freedom, its bureaucratization, its conformity, its institutional rigor mortis. All of this digression is merely to point out that Ellul's individualism is thoroughgoing and consistent. The individual is to love his or her neighbor; the two of them together, however, loving a third neighbor, are merely two individuals, nothing more. This point will loom large in the final chapter of this book where a general analysis and critique will be given.

The most important thing that can be said in the world of technique and the city is the Gospel. Ellul has noted the irony of the fact that just as theologians are announcing that the essence of early Christianity was kerygma, the same (or other) theologians are recommending (and practicing) the incognito approach in evangelism!

> To evangelize means to go into groups and meetings of people who are not Christians. To evangelize is to declare a Gospel which enters the concrete interests, the anxieties and hopes of these people. It is not a good news which is abstract and spiritual.[90]

This evangelism, however, is not to be attempted through the technical means of propaganda.[91] Rather, it is to be personal evangelism, that is, an actual person communicating to other persons, about the person of Jesus Christ.

The previously discussed matter of awareness of reality implies communicating this awareness to people around us, both in words and by the character of our life and presence. This is, first, the negative task of assaulting idols and slave-masters, demythologizing, desacralizing, relativizing, and rejecting idealisms, commonplaces, orthodoxies, illusions, ideologies, and propaganda. Ellul concludes The New Demons with this comment:

> To smash these idols, to desacralize these mysteries, to assert the falseness of these religions is to undertake the one, finally indispensable liberation of the person of our times.[92]

This, however, must be accompanied by the second, more positive, task of evaluating trends and events at a deeper and broader level; providing "benchmarks," "reference points," "sighting points"; warning of consequences; and showing the true character, significance, and meaning of things.[93] It is particularly important to engage in criticism of the means employed in various activities.

The tendency of the world is always to "close up" to a limited set of options. This is especially true of technique which pushes inexorably toward the "one best way." In conflict situations, adversaries harden into narrow positions. The role of Christians is, thus, to introduce "the Wholly Other"--to introduce a "breach" and open up situations. Christians should be an inexhaustible source of creative alternatives--ones that permit human personality to have space for expression. Once again, this calling is simply the incarnation of the Wholly Other, a repetition of God's "normal" relationship to human history.

In conflict situations, the Christian's role is to reconcile adversaries, calm passions, and restore respect, dialogue, and communication. Christians should help explain competing sides to each other.[94] The tendency has been for Christians to jump on various bandwagons, political and otherwise, and intensify disputes by endorsing one side or another. This is not to say that Christians will never be found on one side or another, but that wherever they are, they will help their side to understand the opposition.[95] In Ellul's view, no "issue" is more important than a life which might be jeopardized if passions heat up and take over.

Christians are also called to ameliorate the conditions that oppress people. In his 1948 Presence of the Kingdom, Ellul puts it this way:

> What the Church ought to do is to try to place all men in an economic, intellectual, yes, and also in a psychological and physical situation, which is such that they can actually hear this Gospel--that they can be sufficiently responsible to say "yes"

> or "no," that they can be sufficiently alive for these words to have some meaning for them.[96]

Ellul has three qualifications to make on this work. First, Christian love and care for the poor must be indiscriminate and reach the "truly poor" and not just the poor who have caught the eye of the mass media. Second, Christian love is essentially "interindividual," and thus impersonal charity can be no substitute for establishing personal relationships as servants of the poor family down the block. Third, there is the "vast domain of the psychic."

> Social psychologists tell us, moreover, that modern man is living in a state of anguish, of anxiety and fear, that he suffers from psychological loneliness, that he is a prey to the rise of the irrational (which is a source of suffering), to nebulous beliefs.... I would think that here we are exactly at the point at which the Church and Christians can act.[97]

It is important to recognize that Ellul has never been anything but an advocate of Christian presence on the side of the poor and the outcast, whether international or local. The specific issue he raises in all this, however, is whether Christians are fulfilling their specific and unique calling, to which only they might be able to contribute.

We are also to do well the mundane work of administering cities, businesses, and even politics.

> The radical devaluation of everything in society is accompanied by the revaluation (the only one) that everything, by the grace of God, may be able to serve the kingdom.[98]

It is not, after all, technique or the city that are to be rejected. Rather, it is the ideology of technique and the power of the city. The relativization of everything is accompanied by an attribution of complete seriousness to the relative! If these affairs are demythologized and desacralized, and if certain limits are not transgressed (through violence, domination, exploitation, etc.), Christians will properly participate in them, although with a different meaning.

As a final consideration, Ellul's discussion of work and vocation must be entered in this picture. The fact that

Christians quite properly participate in work or city management, as described in the preceding paragraph, does not mean that it is thereby a Christian activity. That is, it is necessary, relative, and limited--but not specifically Christian. This is because of Ellul's strong emphasis on the uniqueness and specificity of what is Christian. Thus, in discussing work, he insists that work is at best a matter of necessity. It should not be confused with vocation, although they are related. One's vocation is a kind of counterpoint to one's work which manifests freedom.[99] Thus, in his own case as he describes it, Ellul works as a professor; but his vocation is his voluntary service at a local halfway house in Bordeaux. Work, he suggests, is a result of the fall, just as in the city.

This final example from Ellul's urban-technological ethics points up another major problem in his thought. Just as his doctrine of the "New Creation" in the form of the Church is rather weak, so too his doctrine of Creation is weaker than Scripture will permit. His attempt to make work in any form a result of the fall involves him in a twisted interpretation of the Genesis story ("till the earth and subdue it" etc.). As Harvey Cox has noted in his article "The Ungodly City," it is quite possible to view the city as elementally constituted by the quest for human fellowship, and not just as a rebellious selfish quest for security. That is, to extend Cox's argument, the city, like work and even techniques, may be seen in the pre-fall Garden of Eden as part of the created order. It might also be argued that, given Ellul's emphasis on the eschatological character of Christian ethics, where Jesus Christ is understood as the "eschatological man" who lived out fully the "presence of the end" in this world, both the city and work can validly be seen as "Christian." This discussion will be resumed in the final chapter, but it must be noted here that Ellul's basic approach need not lead to the conclusions he reaches on work (or technique, or the city), even if his point on ideology and the powers is well-taken.

* * *

Despite its shortcomings and omissions, Ellul's urban-technological ethic provides a perspective and even a program which is realistic, positive, and creative, and which serves that Church which looks to Jesus Christ and Scripture for the Word of God. The charge that Ellul fails by being too pessimistic or fails to give enough concrete suggestions is weak. A better charge is that he does not draw his program together in any one article or book and so permits these negative reactions. He is given to overstatements--some of which are inexplicably contradictory unless his total work is understood, and his dialectical prophetic style and calling are understood.

All one has to do to appreciate Ellul's work on this problem is to examine the work done on urban ethics by Max L. Stackhouse, Ethics and the Urban Ethos; Harvey Cox, The Secular City; Donald W. Shriver, Jr. and Karl A. Ostrum, Is There Hope for the City?; Craig Ellison (editor), The Urban Mission; Roger S. Greenway, Calling Our Cities to Christ; and others as well. Though each of these studies makes a contribution of one kind or another, the biblical input is in every case extremely limited. Ellul's Meaning of the City--in combination with Apocalypse, The Technological Society, and his other works--is a sustained and penetrating analysis of both the sociological and theological perspectives on the city and technique.

As we shall see even more clearly in the final chapter, Ellul may sound as though he has the final word in terms of the sheer force of his way of expression. But he has often said that his purpose is to stimulate Christians to think out for themselves the meaning of their faith. His own statements come not just out of his study and reading, but out of experiences in the city and university of Bordeaux and the Reformed Church of France. Thus his voice deserves to be heeded. But his purpose is accomplished only if his hearers grapple with the issues in their own time, place, and style.

## NOTES

1. The New Demons, pp. 70-87.
2. Meaning of the City, p. 153.
3. "Mirror of These Ten Years," Christian Century, 87 (Feb. 18, 1970): 201. This essay is essential for an understanding of Ellul's work. It appeared originally as a contribution to the "How My Mind Has Changed" series. It is also available in D. Peerman and A. Geyer, eds., Theological Crossings (Grand Rapids, Mich.: Eerdmans, 1971), pp. 41-50.
4. Hope in Time of Abandonment, p. 274.

5. Ibid., p. 279. On Ellul's sociology see Katherine Temple, "The Sociology of Jacques Ellul," Research in Philosophy and Technology, Vol. 3 (1980), pp. 233-261; John Boli-Bennett, "The Absolute Dialectics of Jacques Ellul," pp. 171-201 in the same volume; and David C. Menninger, "Jacques Ellul: A Tempered Profile," The Review of Politics, 37 (April 1975), pp. 235-246.
6. Hope in Time of Abandonment, pp. 280-281. In passing, the profound similarity of method in Ellul's sociology and theology (denied or, at least, ignored by Ellul) should be noted. The primacy of individual experience and subjectivity, the impatience with textual and historical details, the bracketing of deeper "dogmatic" issues, and the passion for broad, common currents (throughout Scripture or throughout the world), etc.
7. Presence of the Kingdom, p. 33.
8. "Between Chaos and Paralysis," Christian Century, 85 (June 5, 1968): 747.
9. The Technological Society, p. 3.
10. La Technique ou l'Enjeu du siècle.
11. Technological Society, p. xxv.
12. Ibid., p. 19.
13. Ibid., p. 43.
14. Ibid., p. 21.
15. The Technological System (New York: Continuum, 1980).
16. Menninger, op. cit., p. 239. Raymond Aron's "Introduction" in Volume I of his Main Currents in Sociological Thought (2 vols.; Garden City, N.Y.: Doubleday, 1968), pp. 1-11, gives an excellent introduction to sociology in the Marxist tradition (as compared to the more analytical, statistically-oriented American tradition). Ellul's "On demande un nouveau Karl Marx!" Foi et Vie, 46.3 (Mai 1947): 367, indicates Ellul's high assessment of Marx: "Marx est le seul homme de son temps qui ait saissi l'ensemble des problèmes sociaux, politiques et économiques dans leur réalité, qui ait correctement posé les questions de la civilisation du XIX siècle." Of course, this is no longer the nineteenth century, so the Marxist analysis needs revision and updating, a task Ellul believes he has carried out.
17. James Y. Holloway, ed., Introducing Jacques Ellul (Grand Rapids, Mich.: Eerdmans, 1970), p. 168.
18. The Betrayal of the West gives Ellul's discussion of

this Eros/Agape conflict in the history of the West; Technological Society, pp. 23-64, gives Ellul's history of the rise of technique.

19. The New Demons, pp. 1-17, lays to rest any possible misconceptions that Ellul longs nostalgically for medieval Christendom.
20. Cf. Autopsy of Revolution and De la Revolution aux Revoltes.
21. Technological Society, pp. 64-147.
22. The New Demons, pp. 70-80.
23. See Leo Marx, The Machine in the Garden: Technology and the Pastoral Ideal in America (New York: Oxford, 1964). The quotation from Carlyle is on page 170.
24. See Emile Durkheim, The Division of Labor in Society (New York: Macmillan, 1933); Max Weber, From Max Weber: Essays in Sociology, edited by Hans H. Gerth and C. Wright Mills (New York: Oxford University Press, 1946), pp. 196-244.
25. Herbert Marcuse, One-Dimensional Man (Boston: Beacon Press, 1964); John Kenneth Galbraith, The New Industrial State (Boston: Houghton Mifflin, 2nd rev. ed., 1971); Rene Dubos, So Human an Animal (New York: Scribner's, 1968); C. Wright Mills, The Power Elite (London: Oxford University Press, 1959); Lewis Mumford, Technics and Civilization (New York: Harcourt, Brace, and World, 1934); Technics and Human Development (New York: Harcourt, Brace, and Jovanovich, 1966, 1967); and The Pentagon of Power (New York: Harcourt, Brace, and Jovanovich, 1964, 1970); Theodore Roszak, The Making of a Counter-Culture (New York: Doubleday, Anchor Books, 1968, 1969); Alvin Toffler, Future Shock (New York: Bantam, 1971).
26. A. Rupert Hall, Scientific American, 212 (Feb. 1965); 125; see also Thomas G. Donnelly, "In Defense of Technology," Christian Century, 90 (Jan. 17, 1973): 65-69; and Ellul's response, Christian Century, 90 (June 27, 1973): 706-707.
27. Victor Ferkiss, Technological Man (New York: New American Library, Mentor Books, 1969), pp. 35-36.
28. Apocalypse, p. 13.
29. Meaning of the City, p. xviii.
30. Ibid., pp. 1-9.
31. Ibid., p. 3.
32. Ibid., pp. 9-10n.
33. Ibid., pp. 10ff.
34. Ibid., pp. 15ff.

35. Ibid., pp. 23ff.
36. Ibid., p. 26.
37. Ibid., pp. 30-32.
38. Ibid., p. 32.
39. Ibid., p. 39.
40. Ibid., pp. 44ff.
41. Ibid., p. 54.
42. Ibid., p. 59.
43. Ibid., p. 63.
44. Ibid., p. 73.
45. Ibid., p. 94.
46. Ibid., pp. 94ff.
47. Ibid., pp. 113ff.
48. Ibid., pp. 135ff.
49. Ibid., p. 136.
50. Ibid., pp. 156-157.
51. Ethics of Freedom, p. 312.
52. Meaning of the City, pp. 163ff.
53. Ibid., pp. 174-179.
54. Apocalypse, p. 24.
55. Ibid., p. 146.
56. See Oscar Cullmann, Christ and Time (Philadelphia: Westminster, rev. ed., 1964), pp. 191-210; The State in the New Testament (New York: Scribner's, 1956), pp. 93-114; Hendrik Berkhof, Christ and the Powers (Scottdale, Pa.: Herald, 1962, 1977).
57. For Ellul's view of the powers, see The Ethics of Freedom, pp. 144-160; Apocalypse, pp. 152-153 and passim; and "Notes Preliminaires sur 'Eglise et Pouvoir,'" Foi et Vie, 71.2-3 (Mars-Juin 1972): 2-24.
58. See Ellul, "La Technique et les premiers chapitres de la Genese," Foi et Vie, 59.2 (Mars-Avril 1960): 97-113; "De la Mort," Foi et Vie, 73.2 (Mars-Avril 1974): 1-14.
59. Ethics of Freedom, pp. 37-50.
60. Technological Society, p. xxix.
61. Ibid., p. 429.
62. Jeffrey K. Hadden, "Is God a Country Boy?" Journal for the Scientific Study of Religion, 12 (March 1973): 120-121.
63. Gibson Winter, JAAR, 40 (March 1972): 118-122.
64. Harvey Cox, Commonweal, 94 (July 9, 1971): 351-7.
65. Ibid., p. 355.
66. For what I believe is a more balanced discussion see David W. Gill, "Biblical Theology of the City," International Standard Bible Encyclopedia (Grand Rapids, Mich.: Eerdmans, rev. edition, 1979), Vol. I, pp.

713-715.

67. Introducing Jacques Ellul, p. 6.
68. "Mirror of These Ten Years," p. 201.
69. Presence of the Kingdom, pp. 7-8.
70. Ibid., p. 17.
71. Ibid., p. 42.
72. Ibid., p. 118.
73. Ibid., pp. 96ff.; Propaganda: The Formation of Men's Attitudes and A Critique of the New Commonplaces expand on this problem in great detail.
74. False Presence of the Kingdom, pp. 188-189.
75. Presence of the Kingdom, p. 121.
76. Violence, p. 148.
77. Presence of the Kingdom, pp. 8-11.
78. "Between Chaos and Paralysis," p. 749.
79. Ibid., p. 748.
80. See Prayer and Modern Man and Hope in Time of Abandonment, pp. 258-274.
81. See Betrayal of the West, pp. 169-180.
82. "Search for an Image," The Humanist (Nov-Dec. 1973): 22-25.
83. Autopsy of Revolution, p. 276.
84. Ibid., p. 257.
85. The Ethics of Freedom, p. 210.
86. Ibid., p. 210n.
87. Ibid., p. 478.
88. Cf. "Mirror of These Ten Years."
89. Ethics of Freedom, p. 298.
90. False Presence of the Kingdom, p. 103.
91. New Demons, pp. 215-216n.
92. New Demons, p. 228.
93. False Presence of the Kingdom, pp. 186ff.
94. Ibid., pp. 190ff.
95. Violence, pp. 138ff.
96. Presence of the Kingdom, p. 142.
97. False Presence of the Kingdom, p. 184.
98. Ethics of Freedom, p. 312.
99. Ibid., pp. 495-510.; see also "Work and Calling," Katallagete (Fall-Winter, 1972). An excellent critique of Ellul's view of work is given in Udo Middelmann's Pro-Existence (Downers Grove, Ill.: Inter-Varsity Press, 1974), pp. 20ff.

## CHAPTER FIVE

# POLITICS AND THE NATION-STATE

We have already noted that Ellul identifies two poles in the new "sacred" of our society. One of these is technique. The other is the state.

> Our society is more than technological. As the various techniques developed in one ever-broadening sector, at first along parallel, then along converging lines, the power of the state also developed.... Technology has become the basis of political policy; the state has been technologized extensively.[1]

As in the previous case study, we will examine first Ellul's sociological studies of politics and the nation-state. Second, we will follow his search in Jesus Christ and Scripture for the Word of God to this area of life. Finally, we will attempt to summarize and critique the political ethics that comes out of this perspective.

## SOCIOLOGY OF POLITICS AND THE NATION-STATE

Two of the most important modifications of the human institution called the state derive from the impact of nationalism and technique.

> From the nation as a simple fact in the eighteenth century, there emerged in the nineteenth century the nation as an ought-to-be. All peoples must constitute themselves as a nation. It was the era of nationalism, in which peoples enclosed within an empire were under compulsion to liberate themselves,

> as in the case of the Austro-Hungarian empire. Conversely, peoples separated into principalities should unite to form a nation, as in Italy and Germany.[2]

Nationalism has proven more important in the development of the modern state than communism, tribalism, or any other collective identity. Ellul cites the African example, where European-style nationalism is routinely imposed by Africans after the European colonizers are thrown out. Katanga, Biafra, the Southern Sudan, and many other examples reflect this orgy of nationalism.[3]

The important point here is that the rise of nationalism has been accompanied by the "fusion of the state with the nation to form the nation-state."[4] The state takes charge of the life of the nation, and is ordainer of its activities.

> In all western countries (including the U.S.S.R. and the United States) the state is taking the nation in hand. It assures the whole of its indispensable services. It combines all the national forces and concentrates them. It resolves all national problems. Conversely, the nation finds its expression only in a powerful state, which is the coordinator if not the centralizer and the orderer. The fusion is complete. Nothing national exists outside the state, and the latter has force and meaning only if it is national.[5]

Thus the nation appeals to the state for greater management, direction, leadership, justice, and equality. "In all of these ways the state assumed functions which were formerly the province of private groups."[6]

Although the fusion of nation and state is of major importance, the relationship with technique (as defined in the preceding chapter) is of even greater significance. "From the political, social, and human points of view, this conjunction of state and technique is by far the most important phenomenon of history."[7] The state has always used techniques of various types. But, like the state itself, these techniques were always limited--e.g., military, financial, judicial techniques. Though the state exercised a political function there was no developed political technique until the twentieth century. Three reasons in particular have brought technique and the state together. First, individuals and private businesses began penetrating areas (e.g., transportation, education, welfare) which affected large masses of the people through the application of technique. The state could no longer remain disinterested. Second, the extreme expense of many applications of technique required resources and guarantees that only the state could provide. And third, there was a transformation in the conception of the role of the state as natural and traditional groups disappeared or lost their power. The "nation" took over, in turn, as the major theme.[8]

Stimulated and challenged by private technique, the state reacted in part by taking over areas (and their techniques) which were formerly private. It also began developing its own state technique. The state has been progressively transformed into an enormous technical organism, with its bureaus, technicians, and methods. The traditional role of the politician comes thereby into conflict with that of the newer technicians and bureaucrats (a development to which we will return below). The technician views the nation as an affair to be managed (and exploited) and makes judgments on the basis of efficiency. There is a progressive suppression of ideological and moral barriers to technical progress. The "dictatorship of the bureaus" becomes much more determinative of the options of the state than the constitution or any political doctrine. The trend is toward the totalitarian state, Ellul argues. The state absorbs more and more of the citizen's life as it, quite logically, takes over more and more techniques and the responsibility for coordinating them. In this development, justice becomes more and more of an abstraction; "order" and "security" are put in the place formerly occupied by justice. Finally, while the state is served by technique, it also serves technique and supports its further development. It is important to observe the global similarities of various governments, i.e., the U.S.A., U.S.S.R., West and East Germany, China and Japan, the emerging African nations, and South Africa. At the level of current events and political doctrines they are quite different, but their technical and bureaucratic organization is fundamentally the same and is growing in obedience to the same sociological necessities.

Ellul follows this discussion of the nation-state and its modern development in relation to technique in _The Technological Society_ with a longer analysis of politics in relation to this situation in _The Political Illusion_ (1965). In Ellul's definition, "political matter" (_le politique_) is "the domain and sphere of public interests created and represented by the state."[9] Politics (la politique) is "action relative to this domain, the conduct of political groups, and any influence exercised on that conduct." Ellul also endorses Max Weber's definition: "Politics is the leadership by a political body called the state, or any influence exerted in that direction."[10] He also quotes approvingly a definition by Goguel and Grosser:

> Politics is the whole of behavioral patterns and institutions concerning public affairs, which help create power, control actions through such power, and ultimately try to replace those who exert it.[11]

In his The Politics of God and the Politics of Man, Ellul says that "real political action" means "the discharge of a directive function in a party or state organism."[12]

Our era has seen a powerful "politization" take place. That is, "everything is political" and this political matter arouses our passions. There is a tendency to treat all problems as political problems. The moving force behind this is the growth of the state. The problem is the "citizen in the clutches of political power."[13] On the other hand, it is not just that the growing state intervenes in our life more frequently; it is also the case that individual members of the masses are more actively participating in politics.

Traditionally, politics has had two characteristics: (1) an effective choice among several options, encompassing both ends and means, present and future, was possible and sought; and (2) a certain amount of time for reflection, choice, and implementation was required.[14] Today, Ellul argues, those two requirements are not met. Thus, all of today's politization really means that people are frenetically active in what are truly "ephemeral" and superficial matters.[15] The most important element in ephemeral politics is "current events," although most elections and "political activities" are not much deeper. Current events must be studied in the newspaper and mass media so that one will be "informed" and capable of participating.

From four points of view, Ellul argues, there is a basic contradiction between the concern for the "immediate" and authentic political thought. First, a certain distance and elapse of time are necessary for the latter. In the present situation, however, even the educated and trained person is becoming incapable of grasping a political reality. Second, in authentic political thought, one must reflect on the sum of known events within a particular framework or set of concepts. The volume and discontinuity of information works against this. Third, immersion in the news produces ignorance of various levels of political affairs; the mass media level out these phenomena. Fourth, the "political spectacle" grabs attention and raises false problems. Thus, modern man is becoming a man without memory, without foresight, without freedom. "As radical as it may appear, I am not afraid to reverse the proposition ... and to claim that a man who reads his paper every day is certainly not a politically free person."[16]

Thus, the traditional free play of political forms is an illusion. "Necessity is the root of our great fundamental policies."[17] Authentic political decisions are still possible, of course, but they are increasingly limited. Part of this trend is the reduction of values to facts. For example, "justice" means the fact of equal distribution. The integration of peoples and nations into power blocs also reduces the possibilities for decisions. The size and complexity of issues means that necessity plays a greater role than free choice. "Efficacy" has become the primary criterion of political action. "It is not the best man who wins, but the most powerful, the cleverest; and all these terms can be reduced to one: effectiveness."[18]

The idea that politicians lay down the "ends" and technicians develop "means" is illusory. The true choices depend on technicians who prepare solutions, and other technicians who implement these solutions. Fiscal techniques, police methods, energy programs, etc., are in the hands of specialists. Political decisions are subordinated to technical evaluation. Ideology remains, but an authentic revolutionary power and a passion for radical transformation are gone.

Politics is increasingly autonomous today. It is an illusion to cling to the idea that politics is subject to moral values or religion, or that the Church or the University are an important counterbalance. Machiavelli's efficiency is the law of politics and the state. Even though Max Weber's dictum that force is the specific law of the state is correct, Ellul goes further to say that force is now a total monopoly of the state.[19] The state prevents other groups from using any force. The law is not a significant check on this monopoly: if the facts and technical needs conflict with the law, the latter is changed. Today, state force is extended to psychological as well as physical areas. The basic principle is that the more the power of the state grows, the more values are suppressed or disintegrated. Only a limited state can accept opposition from the "good" or the "just" outside itself.

It is thus essential to recognize the autonomy of politics today. Even relationships among political figures are determined not so much by the interplay of values and ideals as by the singleminded quest for "success" via the shortest route possible, including force, blackmail, pressure, deals, and propaganda. To interpret political facts and events by some spiritual or moral theory is thus naive. To demand anything more is hypocritical:

> If a citizen without actual political responsibility claims that politics should be guided by a moral canon, and judges the acts of political men according to that canon, he is the very hypocrite that he accuses the politician of being.[20]

Political affairs today exclude moral values almost by definition. Politics is not the place for fine feelings, humanism, or human warmth. Thus, Ellul argues, we must analyze politics as it exists and not pretend it were otherwise. And we must maintain a certain distance between political facts and ourselves as individuals. Politics is not the only or the best place to express personality or fulfill oneself.

Ellul's analysis then turns to public opinion.[21] Public opinion is necessary to all regimes for the masses are encouraged to enter the political arena and express the "popular will" on which government today allegedly rests. Facts become "political facts," however, only to the extent that public opinion forms around them. These facts are not often experienced directly, but are perceived through the mass media in the form of words and images. Since neutral information does not move public opinion, information must be turned into propaganda. Propaganda is the "fact conditioned so as to make it fit into the prevailing climate of opinion and enter into a debate in which it had a role to play."[22] Information must be "staged" properly; "values" (values vocabulary) must be injected.

The average, informed citizen cannot personally confirm most of these "facts." Social and collective stereotypes have for this reason become more decisive than personal experience. Thus, propaganda creates "political problems," and the political person "will act in relation to political facts as public opinion knows them."[23] Political acts are more important for their propaganda or public opinion consequences than for "real" consequences. Any action must conform to a set of facts known by public opinion and must take account of those who control the instruments capable of reaching public opinion. The result of all this is that propaganda (or public opinion) and political action are paralyzed and reduce each other to mere appearances. The real control is held by the autonomous technician.

The standard reaction to all of this analysis is that the educated, enfranchised, and informed citizens must regain control of the state and the political process. But this "control of the state" is the first major aspect of the "political illusion."[24] This illusion rests on an outmoded view of the state which fails to take account of the nature of bureaucracy. The president, congress or parliament, and law courts do not, fundamentally, control the state's operations; the vast body of bureaus and centers have the control. The modern state is composed to two contradictory elements: political personnel and bureaucratic administrative personnel. The true political problems that concern the daily life of the citizens are in the hands of the various bureaus. Nobody grasps or controls the whole operation. And even if a decision is made by a political figure, it is then taken over by the bureaus for implementation--and it may be far different by the time it is enacted, if at all.

The bureaus obey inviolable laws of operation: specialization, rationalization, anonymity, secrecy, organization, and efficiency are the most basic.[25] Bureaucracy is omnipotent and authoritarian by its own nature. Democracy does not control bureaucracy but rather organizes the masses in relation to the bureaus. For politicians to gain and retain power, there must be methodical action, development of party bureaucracy, and skillful manipulation of public opinion in the "world of images." This means, in turn, that politicians are rendered incapable of true political action and decision.

The second major aspect of the political illusion is the belief that citizens can participate effectively in political life.[26] Certainly any radical disagreement cannot be tolerated within the state. "Organized democracy" drowns out radical opposition. The party system only helps to organize the masses. Participation is a psychological need, but it is strongly determined by propaganda and is effective only at the ephemeral level.

The third aspect of the political illusion is that there are "political solutions" to nearly every problem of life.[27] This belief is anchored deeply in the hearts of citizens of the West, Ellul says. Politics can solve administrative problems, and it can resolve some problems of urban and economic organization and development. But it emphatically cannot deal with personal life, questions of good and evil, etc. The true political problem arises only when contradictory elements permit an accommodation, and then the solution will be limited, not total. Politization of human problems also means that we personally identify with state programs, thus accepting vicarious and general responsibility--but deferring it to tomorrow, and escaping the immediate and personal demands of dealing with our neighbors and our problems.

Politics, then, cannot achieve values such as "justice." Justice requires a longer-range analysis of factors in a situation. It requires us to engage in actions that are not necessary but gratuitous. And justice demands generosity, especially to the weaker party. The autonomy of politics and its pervasive bureaucracy, which obeys only technical necessity, overrules all other values.

Finally, we must raise the question of revolution. The world is filled with revolutions today. Indeed, Ellul argues, revolution is the "profane" to the new sacred of the state.[28] But, like sex in relation to technique, revolution is a delirium and explosion today that replaces the ruling elite but ends up in a total reinforcement of the sacred state. Just as sex becomes a matter of technique, revolution leads to the all-powerful state. Just as the technical object is sexualized, so too we see today the self-proclaimed "revolutionary state." In short, what Ellul performs is the "autopsy of revolution" as we observe it today.

> Whether we like it or not, a type of constant revolution has existed since 1789. Each successful revolution has left the state enlarged, better organized, more potent, and with wider areas of influence; that has been the pattern even when revolution has assaulted and attempted to diminish the state.[29]

> The same applies to post-1944 revolutions. I stress the fact that in each case dictatorship or the exercise of power by one man is not the important element; it is the institutional transformation, the creation of a more rational, all-embracing, efficient, and systematic state, which with its far greater sphere of influence, has become the "state/nation" and the "state/organization," whatever its constitutional form or ideology.[30]

In short, "revolution is finally the crisis of the development of the state."[31]

Has Ellul read the sociological data correctly in regard to the nation-state and politics? In "Watergate and the Thought of Jacques Ellul," Duane Miller argues that the Watergate affair substantiates Ellul's description of technique, propaganda, and politics at a number of critical points.[32] Saul K. Padover's only negative remark about The Political Illusion is that he is "clearly more cogent in his description than in his prescription."[33] Joseph Walsh's review is also generally enthusiastic, although "one can object to the constant overstatement of his case, as when he treats the masses as totally gullible and manipulable by the mass media."[34] In these two comments, the two major objections to Ellul's sociology of politics are reflected: his over-generalization and his lack of prescribed alternatives to the situation.

## NATION-STATE, POLITICS, AND THE WORD OF GOD

Ellul's theological counterpoint to his sociology of the nation-state and politics is primarily the book The Politics of God and the Politics of Man. Before turning to that work, however, it must be recalled from the preceding chapter that Ellul views the biblical concept of the "powers" as deeply meaningful for our understanding of the reality of the state (as well as of the city, technique, money, etc.).[35] This understanding of the demonic character of the state is further developed in his recent interpretation of the Apocalypse.

In Apocalypse Ellul interprets one of the two "beasts" as being political power.

> I will not hesitate to say that the first designates authority, political power in the global, universal sense. The second, propaganda; that is, the establishment of a privileged, exemplary, and magnified relation between the power and man.[36]

The beast symbolizes the absolute power of the political in the abstract sense, with propaganda as its cohort. This power wields the sword and brings death, decides punishment and captivity. It is not only naked force but is seductive and has the capacity to make itself adored. Though the beast is wounded it comes back stronger than ever. In each of these details, of course, Ellul sees an exact description of the state and the political order.

This power of the state is given to it by none less than the great Dragon.

> The power of the state is not of the natural, naturalistic, sociological order; it comes from the power of chaos, from the destroyer; as admirably organized, regulated as it is, it always expresses chaos. The more state order reigns, the more the disorder of the Dragon prevails. Such is the message of the Apocalypse on the state. And precisely because it expresses a spiritual power, men, who feel it deeply, worship it.[37]

This interpretation of the demonic character of the state in the Apocalypse corresponds to Ellul's interpretation of the temptation of Jesus to receive the kingdoms of the world by bowing down to Satan.

> To attain power in any manifestation man has to bow down to Satan and worship him. There is no legitimate power as such. Acquisition of power in this world is linked to service of the prince of this world.[38]

The second beast is the "false prophet" in the Apocalypse. This false prophet is in the form of a lamb but speaks as the dragon. It acts by the power of the word. The organization of power is the state; the animation of this power is by propaganda.

> This beast ... persuades men to raise up the

> image of the other, the image of the state. It animates this image and gives it the word.... It puts its words in the mouth of the state; by it the state speaks, makes itself known, identified, obeyed. We are then before the extraordinary work of the animation of dead structure, or a sterile organization, of a mechanism of power, which becomes living and vital presence. That which actually fills all these roles is exactly Propaganda.[39]

The "sign on the forehead," Ellul argues, symbolizes the way propaganda engenders an intellectual belonging to the state and politics. Propaganda creates this ideology of the political and adoration of the state and everything political. It creates the affirmation that the political is All and has primacy over everything else.

> What the Apocalypse describes under the form of two beasts is not only a state but rather the state; not only a particular political (of right or left, etc.) but the primacy of the political.[40]

The description of the great judgment (the bowls, etc.) culminates in the destruction of the beast (the political power) and the woman (the prostitute) riding on the beast.[41] The woman, as we mentioned in the preceding chapter, represents the great city, the summation and symbol of all technique and human culture--and this rides on the state and political power! In the Final Judgment, of course, it is only Satan who is destroyed, not the work of man per se. While Ellul has presented a thoroughly negative, demonic interpretation of the state, it is the state-as-rebellious-power that Ellul is indicating as the villain. The state and politics as limited, human affairs, detached from this demonic, sacred, totalitarian power is another matter (indeed, the goal of Ellul's presentation). What we wrestle with, however, is such "principalities and powers" even while being certain that they have been conquered finally by Jesus Christ.[42]

The Politics of God and the Politics of Man explicates Ellul's dialectical position in regard to politics, "between the modern concrete political reality and the reading of an example ... of both the meaning and nonmeaning of politics."[43] It is a commentary (of sorts) on the Second Book of Kings, "the most political of all the books in the Bible."[44] The figures of Elijah and Elisha dominate the stories of II Kings. The mission of Elijah is to maintain the purity of the religion of the Eternal and the holiness of God.

> But the task or vocation of Elisha is very different. He is a prophet, not of purity, but of power. He affirms that God is King.... The kingdom of God has drawn near, completely changes political life like everything else.... God is the God of all peoples. He reigns over all kings. He directs world politics.... When we are told that the kingdom is at hand, this has a political sense too, and the political sense is the one which Elisha brings out.[45]

The revelation in II Kings is characterized by two concerns: politics and political problems on the one hand and the relationship between God's action and human freedom on the other.

First, II Kings is mostly concerned with politics in the narrow sense of "political problems," i.e., Israel's political relations with Syria, Edom, Egypt, and Assyria. The topic is not theoretical politics of ideal politics, but practical politics in a time of crisis. A significant factor in the politics of II Kings is the internal spiritual condition of the people of God. The whole book shows both the importance as well as the relativity of politics for the people of God.

> The Bible shows us that the church is not just a spiritual matter, that politics is not just simply a human action of no concern to us. It may be that politics is the kingdom of the devil, but this certainly concerns us as Christians.... This meditation is also not unimportant in face of those who want politics to be the main action of men, and of Christians who think involvement in politics is essential and for whom everything is finally politics. In fact these texts show the relativity of politics, which is the sphere of the greatest affirmation of man's autonomy, of his revolt, of his pretentious attempt to play the role of God.[46]

Though the institution of the state is related to the question of political activity, the two must also be differentiated, Ellul argues. To recognize the validity of a legitimate state power and authority and to be subordinate do not imply that one necessarily leaps into whatever passes as "political action." A real wrestling of conscience, a search for the Word of God must precede our political activity.

> The real problem is that of active participation in real political action, that is, the discharge of a directive function in a party or a state organism. In this alone one is engaged in politics; the rest is a matter of opinion, obedience, or debate, but it is in no sense politics. Now the problem that is posed in the Second Book of Kings is exclusively the problem of political action and not that of the state.[47]

As stated earlier, Scripture will not provide us with a systematic political program in answer to this problem. It will, however, show us examples of how God works.

This brings us to the second aspect of the revelation in II Kings. That is, the issue which Karl Barth called the "free determination of man in the free decision of God." How do God's action and human action interrelate? Related to this issue is the role of the prophet as the translator and explicator of God's Word to the people. We will return to the matter of the prophet in more detail in the final chapter. We have, in the preceding chapter, discussed briefly the relation between God's creation and the subsequent choice of the city by humanity. This, as we saw, did not result in God's rejection of humanity (in the End!) but rather in God's decision to adopt human work, though purified, stripped of its demonic power, and renewed. In _The Politics of God and the Politics of Man,_ Ellul discusses another example of this relationship: the choice of monarchy by Israel. Here again, the original decision is not God's prescription (the contrary); but God accepts it, transforms it, redeems it, and yet permits the consequences of the rebellious decision to develop to a certain extent.

When God speaks, it changes situations and it changes the hearers. Autonomy or irresponsibility is no longer possible. And yet it is not a Word which is imposed mechanically or without dialogue.

> We discern here an aspect of God's wisdom, of his art of governing the world, the divine action which is made up of respect for man, of finesse, of subtlety, of pedagogy, of choice, of successive adaptations. Yet all of this is also inserted into God's

> omniscience and omnipotence which has prepared everything in advance no matter what may be the solution that each man finally adopts, that God leaves each man free to adopt.
>
> Thus God's action in politics will continually have for us the appearance of vocation, appeal, and address, and then judgment, outburst, and wrath.
>
> It will continually have for us the appearance of grace, of timid approach, of liberation, then of rigor, of inflexibility in attaining its specific end, and sometimes, if rarely, of a miracle which intervenes to overthrow the course of events, of history, and of life.[48]

Ellul then turns to the stories in II Kings in search of illumination of politics by the Word of God. He turns first to the story of Naaman the leper, a man of war and enemy of Israel. Naaman the politician automatically turns to another politician, the king, to get help for his problem. Yet God chooses to work through the humble means of a servant girl and then the prophet Elisha.

> Again we have the self-contemplation of political power which thinks that everything should be arranged at the political level by political means, and that everything has political signification. The text teaches us that everything does not have to have a political signification and that everything is not necessarily a concern of political powers.[49]

Despite his political position, Naaman is not treated by God or God's servants any better or differently than anyone else.

What is also surprising are the apparent results of the episode: relations between Israel and Syria do not seem to be improved and, in fact, war breaks out between them not long after. But a man has been healed and converted. The "Church" has been planted in Syria. These results are not insignificant in themselves, but they do not count greatly on the political and international scale. In a world which often yields to the idolatry of politics and the state, Ellul sees this episode as an indication of God's simultaneous interest and disinterest in the political world.

God's freedom is expressed in his choice of means: humble, loving, serving, liberating.[50] God will save Samaria not through bombs, elections, the courage of soldiers, the skill of generals, or the politics of a king, but through rejects and outcasts, through the Word, through a miracle. Political actions are important, but we have no reason to be triumphant about them. In all of our political passions, military and revolutionary storms and dramas, there is more noise than weight. If we take our electoral politics and weapons so seriously, we should also take seriously the fact that God laughs at much of our overserious and pretentious strutting around. These are the lessons Ellul discerns in the stories of Naaman and Joram.

From the story of Hazael, Ellul draws the lesson that, in the political context, the man of God does not proclaim a special political Word or Command of God. The political power cannot in principle recognize God as the true God. The role of Elisha is not to tell the state what it should do; rather, he tells the politician what will happen. It is a "nonpartisan" identification of the meaning and significance of what is happening--a fulfilling of the commission to be the "watchman on the wall." The Christian does this on behalf of God, but, again, it is not a matter of proclaiming a divine command with accompanying glory and power.[51]

One of the themes in II Kings (and which is alluded to in other parts of the Scripture) is the "sin of Jeroboam." This sin, which plagued many of Israel's kings, was to use God in the interests of politics. This is the special problem of Ahaz.[52] Both the experience of Jehu and that of Ahaz involve the problem of ends and means. In both cases, God is exploited as a means to a political end. Prophecy and worship are exploited and degraded. We are indeed responsible for the choice of means that we make; and it is true that the Holy Spirit is efficacious. Nevertheless, the identification of objectives, ends, and means must not follow the pattern of Jeroboam.

In a society ruled by technique, in politics as well as most other areas, the question of efficacy is extremely important. Ellul suggests that the effects of the Holy Spirit are of two types. First, there are the

> mysterious spiritual effects which we cannot measure and which are found both on earth and in heaven. These are totally his (the birth of faith, the effectiveness of prayer) and will appear visibly only at the end of the age.[53]

But the Holy Spirit also produces effects which are "temporal, visible, and concrete." These include miracles in the material world, conversion in the moral life, effects on the body, on psychology, sociology, and history in the world. "These temporal effects are inexplicable apart from the Holy Spirit in spite of man's ever new pretension that he can explain everything on a purely human level."[54]

The action and efficacy of the Holy Spirit are "integrated into the nexus of the psychosociological causes and effects which are their basis, occasion, and expression."[55] God works, however, in league with man. Man is "summoned to participate in one or other of the actions of the Holy Spirit, in the totality of the Work of God. He is summoned to provide the basis for the divine efficacy."[56] In this situation, how does one determine a course of action or participation? Ellul indicates two conditions.

First, "it must be an action governed by its objectives, which are themselves subordinate to the end."[57]

> The objectives to be achieved today are the universal knowledge and enjoyment of the gospel. The end is the coming of the kingdom of God. Everything else must be subordinate, whether at the level of objectives--happiness, science, art, etc.--or at the level of the end--justice, liberty, and peace.... The means must be compatible with the objectives and the end. They must conform and be of the same nature.[58]

If means are selected in accordance with this criterion, the Holy Spirit can empower them and make them effective. "The implication is that we cannot separate our objectives from the person of Jesus Christ."[59] Our work for peace and justice is entailed by the Gospel, but it has true meaning and is divinely efficacious only when it is rooted in a relationship to Jesus Christ as "prince of peace" and "sun of righteousness."

The second qualification of Christian efficacy is, in fact, that it is always found in a personal relationship with God in Jesus Christ. Thus, the first step toward efficacy is at "the level of personal unity."[60] It is personal, individual self-awareness and unity, in a relationship to God. Our responsibility is not for the total process but for our particular task. "Results are promised if we keep to our own level and use appropriate means."[61]

Our efficacy will usually appear a failure or fiasco by the world's criteria of measurement. But our efficacy is measured by faithfulness, not by success per se.

> The efficacy we seek can only be that of a radical alteration of the world and society. It is the efficacy of event as opposed to institution, of tension against the accepted line, of nonconformity. In sum, it is an efficacy which stands opposed to that of the world. Yet it is no less real. It is the efficacy of heretics and sectarians.[62]

Nonconformity is one index of true efficacy, for we are to be "existing as the incarnate presence of the Wholly Other."[63] That incarnation is what is really at stake for us. Elisha and Hezekiah were "successful" at this; Joram, Jehu, and Ahaz were not.

In the story of Rabshakeh, Ellul sees a description of the fundamental politics of the world.[64] He analyzes in particular Rabshakeh's two speeches, one political, the other propagandistic. Rabshakeh's political speech, composed of five arguments, is a hardline appeal to his weakened Israelite foes to be realistic and give in to him. In order, he argues the following: (1) What is needed in political action is sagacity, calculation, force, and power; values, sentiments and opinions, and justice and truth are unimportant relative to power and success. (2) Any diplomatic or military miscalculation will backfire with serious political consequences. (3) If Israel will submit to Assyria, she will be given gifts and even military hardware (horses!). (4) Religion and theology cannot be relied upon in the present crisis. (5) God has commanded the destruction of Israel anyway!

When his "political realism" fails immediately to move the Israelite people, Rabshekeh gives a propaganda speech, composed of three elements: First, he attacks their leaders, thus trying to separate the people from the leaders. Second, he promises happiness, affluence, and no more injustice if they will abandon their leaders. Third, he scornfully tells them that their situation is hopeless and that God will not deliver them.

This episode leads directly into Ellul's last study, Hezekiah, one of the leaders attacked by Rabshakeh. Hezekiah responds to the political crisis by tearing his clothes, retreating, and repenting in the temple. He appears weak and cowardly to the world. But Rabshakeh has mocked the living God and this has pushed the situation beyond the merely political to a question of God's honor. There is a "suspension of the political."[65] Ellul suggests that we are in a similar situation today, although "I cannot prove this, but I know it in the same way as I know that I myself an alive."[66] In such an extreme situation, only retreat and prayer are appropriate. In Hezekiah's case, God acts by warning, by judgment, and by miraculous, shattering execution, attacking the pride of the elite. As long as politics is relative, Christians can act in that arena.[67] But if God has been totally excluded and mocked and it is a time when "God has turned away" and if the state and politics have become the beast, the sacred, then Ellul asks, Is any form of continued participation radical enough to make the needed impact? As Ellul listens to the message of II Kings, the Word of God seems to him to answer "No."

The major critical question raised by Ellul's reviewers of The Politics of God and the Politics of Man is, as we have noted in earlier chapters, whether his method of interpretation is adequate. Walter Brueggemann, whose review was cited earlier, thinks that "this is bold exegesis and at many points most suggestive."[68] But Ellul's approach as a whole does not require the specific conclusions he reaches. Although Brueggemann agrees with most of Ellul's ideas, he worries that the method opens the door to other, equally subjective but socially dissimilar and perhaps retrogressive approaches. David A. Hubbard, also cited earlier, dislikes the subjective, typological method, as well as the "ultimate pessimism" and the lack of specific applications and illustrations related to contemporary politics.[69]

Richard S. Hanson finds Ellul's orthodoxy "stern and narrow" in one paragraph of his review, and "open and humble" in the next; his writing is "lively and vivid" but also "wordy and boring."[70] In contrast to Brueggemann and Hubbard, Hanson (also an Old Testament scholar) says that "his commentary is strictly biblical all the way. He never strays from or goes outside the text." Clearly, Hanson is himself rather "dialectical" in expression (at least) and perhaps this is necessary for an appreciation of Ellul's exegesis.

Ellul's commentary is, in some cases, rather loosely tied to the text in its original sense. In others (e.g., Rabshakeh's speeches) his commentary is tighter and downright brilliant by any standard. As discussed in Chapter Three, Ellul's intention is for us to read the stories of II Kings in the context of (1) the whole canon, i.e., the threads that run from Genesis to Revelation which concern politics and the state and (2) the incarnation of Jesus Christ. It is these two controls that Brueggemann and Hubbard overlook in their concern for the possible subjectivism of Ellul's approach.

The Word of God in Scripture illuminates our understanding of politics and the nation-state by establishing a familiar twofold pattern. (1) At best, the state is a limited organ of administration of the commonweal. Political action has serious, but nevertheless relative, importance in modifying the actual direction or orientation of the state. Modest, humble, and limited, the state and politics can be entirely valid affairs. (2) At worst, the state, animated by the _exousia_ of conquest and domination, becomes the "beast." A totalitarian monster, then, the state extends its power in every direction, dominating wider geographic regions, penetrating all social groups, manipulating and adjusting the inner spirit of the individual as well as the external life. In this situation, the state obeys only its own internal imperatives. Political affairs, political discussion, and political action are then, despite appearances, increasingly restricted to a very ephemeral level of reality.

The Apocalypse very clearly depicts this demonic character of the sacred state and, at the same time, reveals the final judgment of God. At the End, the state beast is damned while now purified human works (including, therefore, human political work) are incorporated into the New Jerusalem. This eschatological separation of the "work" from the _exousia_ provides the standpoint from which to judge our current political existence. In the Second Book of the Kings, we have examples of this separation. The state and political affairs are given only their true, relative significance. God works sometimes through, sometimes outside of, the state and the political arena.

The Word of God in Jesus Christ in regard to the state and politics is not given an extensive elaboration by Ellul in any one place. Jesus' refusal to bow down to Satan in order to receive political authority over the kingdoms of the world indicates again the connection between Satanic power and political domination. The periodic opposition of the state and the political authorities to Jesus, culminating in his crucifixion, also points up the opposition of the beast of the state to the Lamb of God. In general, however, it is the relativity of politics that Jesus teaches and exemplifies:

> The texts of the New Testament show that neither Jesus nor later his disciples ever engaged in or showed any interest in politics. What we are told about the state is theological. What we are told about conduct in relation to it is not at all political. We are to obey, to show honor and respect, and to offer prayers.[71]

While a lively political life was possible for those interested, in the first century, it was also possible to avoid politics then much more than today. We may not be able to avoid politics today (indeed, we are called to be "in" the world of our era), the fundamental lesson of Jesus Christ remains appropriate: politics should be relativized, the nation-state should be desacralized.

Ellul's description of Jesus as disinterested in politics is of the same order as his description of the "impossibility" of a Christian ethics. That is, if we accept Ellul's narrow definition of what politics (or ethics) is, he is probably correct. As a literary device to emphasize the distinctiveness of Christianity, this is understandable strategy. However, just as Ellul's "ethics" are finally and truly another species of ethics, so also there is a sense in which Jesus was very "political" but in an unusual way. John Howard Yoder's *Politics of Jesus* is an example of a study proceeding from this perspective: Jesus' program was apolitical only if we restrict the meaning of "politics" to a narrow, traditional usage. Ellul, in fact is not always consistent himself in this matter. In the quotation above he lists "prayers" as a nonpolitical activity. In *False Presence of the Kingdom*, however, he says that prayer is precisely a political act.

> For example, it is precisely the demonic character of the power which makes prayer the most important political action that the Christian could possibly take, prayer which is a sharing in the struggle of Jesus Christ, prayer that the authorities might be brought under subjection, prayer that they might be exorcised, prayer that their power might be turned toward justice and good. Prayer is much more important than all the declarations, demonstrations, elections, etc.[72]

## POLITICAL ETHICS

Ellul's political ethics builds from the approach that was described in the preceding chapter.[73] The same process of cultivating awareness, then engaging in action, applies in relation to the nation-state and politics. "Incarnating the Wholly Other" remains the paradigm guiding all Christian participation in the world, political or otherwise. All of this will not be repeated here, but the present discussion presupposes the general approach described earlier.

In relation specifically to politics and the nation-state, the major problem to which Ellul gives attention is the idolatry of the state and the religious fervor of political action in relation to that idol. Thus, in his biblical studies he emphasizes the importance of personally denying the state and politics that sacred status. Not only in our own political life but in our effect on others the impact should be to demythologize and desacralize the state as *exousia*. Incarnating the End means, in this case, damning the "beast" that lurks in the political realm.

Despite the criticism that Ellul offers little or no advice on how to respond to the sociological situations he describes, he has, in the case of the nation-state and politics, described an agenda which goes some distance toward meeting this need. In *The Political Illusion*, for example, after saying that depolitization and apolitical attitudes are not in themselves an answer, Ellul says the "state will retreat only when it meets an insurmountable obstacle. This obstacle can only be man, i.e., citizens organized independently of the state."[74] The crucial change is in behavior and in freedom from illusions. Political affairs must be demythologized and restored to a limited status. Personal life must be developed; private life and individuality are required.

This approach will lead to the restoration of "tensions" in public life. The theme of adjustment must be fought and rejected. Freedom has meaning only in the face of constraint; growth only occurs in the face of conflict and tension. What is true at the personal level is also true for a healthy collective or political life. The state must be limited and forced to deal with true opposition at a fundamental level. Thus we must create positions from which to struggle with the state and stop asking the state for help.

In short, Ellul argues, we need a revival of "democratic man."[75] Democracy has no meaning unless it is based on individual liberty. The clumsy, mediocre, maladjusted individual must be allowed space to evolve spontaneously. Democracy is not efficient! There must be a radical questioning of "progress," materialism, consumerism, and security. What is required is rationality (not rationalism and not irrationality), a restored communication and language, a restored respect, a maintained differentiation (not adaptation and adjustment).

In Autopsy of Revolution, Ellul describes the "necessary revolution."[76] The revolution that is needed "must be executed on the individual level by the individual's recovery of control over the systems of integration."[77] It consists in "attacking all instruments of mediation which alienate human beings from one another and from society." "A measure of flexibility must be found.... The arbitrary nature of personal judgment and the experience of passion" must be cultivated. Obviously this risks "massive regression" and certainly inefficiency, but it is the only way.

Since the state is the most vital issue today, the necessary revolution must espouse an anti-statist and anti-nationalist viewpoint. Since the society is technological, the revolution must struggle against the transformation of society into a technological body. This will require a sacrifice, including decreased efficiency in all areas (productivity, total yield, etc.), a lowered standard of living, reduction of large-scale public programs, and the erosion of mass culture. All of this will also require the rediscovery of individuality, individual autonomy and uniqueness, the development of consciousness, and a revival of democratic citizenship (in the sense described in Political Illusion). Awareness must be associated with reason, contemplation (a breach in the frenetic activity of the technological society), and the creation of new values around which to regroup and from which to struggle.

Fifteen years after the publication of Ellul's Presence of the Kingdom he wrote False Presence of the Kingdom as an attempt to clarify the political implications of that earlier work. In Ellul's view the church is too adapted to the world and, moreover, both incompetent and irresponsible in much of its political involvement. The primary purpose of the church in the world, including its politics, is to bear witness to Jesus Christ, to "proclaim the Wholly Other."[78] Secondly, as ambassadors for Christ our function is "to introduce tensions."[79] This means "true tensions" in the sense of combatting the larger forces that threaten to become totalitarian, such as the state or technique. On the more ephemeral level, the opposite is true: there we should relativize, defuse issues, and calm passions.

In a section entitled "The Biblical Question Mark," Ellul argues that the Bible suggests an attitude of obedience, good works, and prayer in relation to the state.[80] The Bible indicates that political authority is willed by God, but "at the institutional level, this applies to persons only (the ruler, the king) ... never the regimes."[81] The biblical texts are still further from endorsing institutions or abstract doctrines of the state. Ellul argues briefly that the latter certainly existed during biblical times; politics was not merely personal at that time or this. Finally, it is in this passage that Ellul argues that prayer is particularly important as a political act because of the demonic character of the state.

Finally, Ellul indicates nine points for "The Orientation of Christians."[82] (1) The Christian life is one and inclusive of the political life; there is no separation of spiritual and temporal or political in the Bible. Politics is valuable primarily insofar as it arises as a prior condition for the Gospel and the faith. Thus, the Christian stance in politics should be specific and unique, and it should be so in virtue of its relationship to the End-in-the-Present which guides our life.

(2) The Church or Christian stands in a relationship of permanent tension in the political world, and for this reason can be and should be the factor that "opens up" the world through tension and challenge. (3) The starting point must be the Word of God as the basis for all Christian action. Thus, the Church should "bring about the event instead of trailing it, submitting to it, explaining it."[83] (4) The Church should intervene on her own level, within her own competence. That means concentrating on two categories of world problems in particular: first, the identification of the basic, key points around which the world is organized and developing, and second, the "vast domain of the psychic," including the problems of anxiety and loneliness.

(5) Growing out of the preceding point, the Church

should exercise a genuinely prophetic function of warning of coming developments which may still be modified or averted while situations are fluid. (6) The Church has the ministry of reconciliation--humanizing situations, introducing creative alternatives, moderation, and understanding. (7) Again, related to points (4) and (5), the Church may lend help to the world by providing benchmarks, sighting points, and identifying the stakes involved in situations. (8) There is the stern duty of desacralization. This means a rejection not of human works but of the religion built on them to glorify humanity. It means reducing the state and politics to their legitimate function of managing the material interests of the collectivity.[84] Christians, by their conduct, should profane the various idols and sacreds, including the state, money, and technique. The hope and love of Christ must, of course, be proclaimed along with the destruction of the myths and idols.

(9) Finally, Christians must open up the world--a task which was already implied in (2). This is accomplished first through preaching, then by participating without accepting the myths, and third by injecting humor and relativism into the activities of the world in which we participate.

Ellul's Ethics of Freedom repeats and, to some extent, extends this perspective and program in his chapter on "Concrete Implications." Rather than formulating abstract, theoretical systems in his volumes on the ethics of freedom, holiness, and love, Ellul intends to "begin at each point with the ethical situation, e.g., the Christian as a free man in politics, the Christian as a saint in politics, the Christian as an agent of love in politics."[85] Ellul follows this with his customary rejection of the twin temptations to plunge into politics or to abstain. Neither approach manifests freedom.

There are two signs of freedom in Christ in politics today. The first is simply "the exercise of choice and presence" in politics.[86] The particular party we choose or place we intervene is not unimportant; on the other hand, it is not necessarily for specifically Christian reasons that we choose one place over another. It is, of course, better to run a city well than poorly, to uphold the interests of the poor, etc. Nevertheless, the important thing is to be present as a witness for Christ and to demonstrate the unity across party lines which is possible in Christ. The second sign of freedom is the relativization of politics, a normal consequence of the first point. We are to contribute to freedom by indicating the relative and provisional nature of politics, thus restoring the health of democracy. This relativization must lead us to treat seriously these relative problems, but refuse to go further.

"Dialogue with the sovereign" is another concrete implication of freedom in politics.

> What is needed is that power should be confronted by someone else who uses other means, who says other things, and who even says them to the true sovereign beyond the state.[87]

It is essential for the health of the nation and the political arena that power not merely be in encounter with itself. We must "shatter the solitude of power." The conditions for such personal dialogue are (1) that the state have no religious pretensions and that it permit something or someone different from itself to exist alongside itself, and (2) that the Christian have something distinctive to say (as suggested in the preceding discussions on the "watchman on the wall" theme). In particular this dialogue should attack the political religion and should bring a certain ambiguity to the sphere of the state authority. This dialogue also includes the role of watchdog on the state's (or politician's) affirmations and promises, calling it into account so that its actions correspond to its words.

This dialogue may proceed from various positions, including the individual "prophet" outside, or a political office within the system. In an unexpected aside, Ellul says that "Christian political movements have their place."[88] In a fully expected argument, Ellul offers his own view of the most serious position to adopt today: anarchism. The global, totalitarian drift of the contemporary nation-state must be met with an equally radical response, and that, Ellul suggests, can only be anarchism. He is not advocating anarchism as a doctrine or as an organizational solution, but as a strategy for this time and situation in which democracy and the party system is a bureaucracy-ridden trap which further stabilizes the all-powerful nation-state. As for concrete organization, one may or may not associate with anarchist groups, situationists, or pacifists.

In relation to the "fight for freedom" around the world today, Ellul suggests that, in general, Christians should support all such movements.[89] The Christian belongs alongside the humiliated, the poor, the offended. The oppressed should find Christians at their side. However, we must be sure that the freedom we help to win is authentic, and thus our association with liberation movements is not unconditional. We cannot associate with movements that intend the destruction of Christianity (that is, the Gospel). We must also be critical about the means employed in any struggle and eschew all violence, torture, and manipulation of public opinion. The means affect the end. It is important to be both a "conscience" and a critical, long-range analyst for any freedom movement in which we participate. As a final qualification, Ellul argues that after a revolutionary victory, our place must switch to the side of the new "out-group" in jail!

Ellul's final comments on the concrete implications of freedom in politics are directed toward "religious freedom."[90] The Christian should be an advocate of religious freedom for all. This is because God is not coercive, and his followers should not be either. Although it is true that Christianity is a revelation that opposes religion, we should fight for the freedom of other religious groups. This is also because the state is only secular and should be restricted, and because respect should be granted to all human beings made in the image of God. This position does not mean that religions are any less false or illusory, of course, and evangelism should proceed alongside our support for other religious groups.

* * *

Ellul's political ethic can be reduced to a few major guidelines. However, these guidelines can be elaborated to some degree (and Ellul has performed this elaboration to an "extent greater than his critics charge"). In the end, his ethical perspective is quite "potent" and applicable. It needs some "translation" and "application" for the sake of the faithful in the churches, who cannot be expected to wade through the volumes of argument and analysis provided by Ellul.

Two major questions remain, however. The first, and most important, concerns his interpretation of Jesus Christ and Scripture in relation to politics and the nation-state.[91] On the one hand, has he said too much? Has Ellul read too much into Scripture by imposing a dialectical method which borders on dualism, by a typological interpretation that exceeds the bounds of even his own theoretical commitments? Has he credited the fall and the exousia with more power and impact than is warranted? Conversely, has he said too little? For example, is John Howard Yoder closer to the "politics of Jesus" than Ellul? Certainly, Yoder finds much more content in Jesus and Scripture and gives much more specific content to Jesus' program (e.g., the renewed Jubilee legislation) than does Ellul (who tends to focus almost exclusively on Jesus Christ as paradigm of the "inbreaking of the Wholly Other").

The second question is whether he has adequately read the ethical stiuation, in terms of the rising power of the technical nation-state and the illusory character of most political activity. Has he minimized the human importance of "current events" (such as urban crime and violence, racism, war, Third World pride and dignity, etc.) in his determined "plunge" to the intermediate level of the "currents"? Finally, has his sociological method and its conclusions tinted his interpretation of Scripture (or conversely) to an excessive degree?

In raising these questions, it should be clear that I believe he has engaged, to some degree, in most of these aberrations, overextensions, or impositions. Since most of these criticisms apply to the preceding work on urban-technological ethics, as well, they will be developed and analyzed in the next and final chapter.

## NOTES

1. Autopsy of Revolution, p. 268.
2. New Demons, p. 82.
3. Cf. Autopsy of Revolution, pp. 270-273.
4. New Demons, p. 83; cf. Technological Society, pp. 237-238.
5. New Demons, p. 83.
6. Technological Society, p. 238.
7. Ibid., p. 233.
8. Cf. Technological Society, pp. 228ff., for the argument summarized in these paragraphs.
9. Political Illusion, p. 3.
10. Ibid., p. 12.
11. Ibid., p. 16.
12. Politics of God and the Politics of Man, p. 14.
13. Political Illusion, pp. 8-11.
14. Ibid., pp. 25ff.

15. Ibid., pp. 49-67.
16. Ibid., p. 63.
17. Ibid., p. 66.
18. Ibid., p. 35.
19. Ibid., p. 72.
20. Ibid., p. 91.
21. Ibid., pp. 96-135.
22. Ibid., p. 105.
23. Ibid., p. 124.
24. Ibid., pp. 136-162.
25. Obviously, obeying the "law of efficiency" does not always or necessarily result in what we can personally experience as an efficiently operating bureau. Cf. John Wilkinson's comment, Technological Society, p. xi.
26. Political Illusion, pp. 163-184.
27. Ibid., pp. 185-198.
28. New Demons, pp. 84-87.
29. Autopsy of Revolution, p. 160.
30. Ibid., p. 161.
31. Ibid., p. 163.
32. Duane R. Miller, Christian Century, 90 (Sept. 26, 1973): 943-946.
33. Saul K. Padover, Saturday Review (April 29, 1967): 27-28.
34. Joseph L. Walsh, Commonweal, 87 (Oct. 13, 1967): 56-57.
35. It is with reference to the state and political authority that the discussion of the meaning of exousia by Cullmann, Berkhof, Barth, Yoder, Morrison, and others has been most actively pursued.
36. Apocalypse, p. 92.
37. Ibid., pp. 94-95.
38. Ethics of Freedom, p. 57.
39. Apocalypse, p. 96.
40. Ibid., pp. 96-97.
41. Ibid., pp. 185ff.
42. This distinction is clearly made in Ellul's Violence, pp. 162-166. See also "Rappels et Réflexions sur une théologie de l'Etat," in Jacques Ellul, et al., Les Chrétiens et l'Etat (Tours: Maison Mame, 1967), pp. 129-180.
43. Apocalypse, p. 13.
44. The Politics of God and the Politics of Man, p. 13.
45. Ibid., p. 11.
46. Ibid., pp. 13-14.
47. Ibid., p. 14.

48. Ibid., p. 22.
49. Ibid., p. 29.
50. Ibid., pp. 61-62.
51. Ibid., pp. 74ff.
52. Ibid., pp. 121ff.
53. Ibid., p. 135.
54. Ibid.
55. Ibid.
56. Ibid.
57. Ibid.
58. Ibid., p. 136.
59. Ibid., p. 138.
60. Ibid.
61. Ibid., p. 139.
62. Ibid., p. 141.
63. Ibid., pp. 141-142.
64. Ibid., pp. 143-161.
65. Ibid., p. 167.
66. Ibid., p. 169.
67. Ibid., pp. 170-171. In his _Hope in Time of Abandonment_, Ellul argues that this era is, in fact, an age of the silence of God.
68. Walter Brueggemann, _JBL_, 92 (Sept. 1973): 470-471.
69. David A. Hubbard, _Christian Scholar's Review_, 3.2 (1973): 172-173.
70. Richard S. Hanson, _Interpretation_, 27 (April 1973): 238-240.
71. _Ethics of Freedom_, p. 370.
72. _False Presence of the Kingdom_, p. 112.
73. The final section of Chapter Four on "Ellul's Urban-Technological Ethics."
74. _Political Illusion_, p. 202.
75. Ibid., pp. 224ff.
76. _Autopsy of Revolution_, pp. 233ff.
77. Ibid. The quotations in this paragraph are on pp. 259-269.
78. _False Presence of the Kingdom_, p. 40.
79. Ibid., p. 52.
80. Ibid., pp. 109-117.
81. Ibid., pp. 110-111.
82. Ibid., pp. 176-211.
83. Ibid., p. 102.
84. Ibid., p. 203.
85. _Ethics of Freedom_, p. 369.
86. Ibid., p. 378.
87. Ibid., p. 385.
88. Ibid., p. 394.

89. Ibid., pp. 398ff.
90. Ibid., pp. 435ff.
91. For purposes of comparison, see John Howard Yoder, *The Politics of Jesus* (Grand Rapids, Mich.: Eerdmans, 1972); *The Christian Witness to the State* (Newton, Kan.: Faith and Life, 1964); John C. Bennett, *Christians and the State* (New York: Charles Scribner's Sons, 1958); *The Radical Imperative* (Philadelphia: Westminster, 1975); Oscar Cullmann, *The State in the New Testament* (New York: Charles Scribner's Sons, 1956); and Karl Barth, *Community, Church, and State* (Gloucester, Mass.: Peter Smith, 1968).

## CHAPTER SIX

# THROUGH AND BEYOND ELLUL'S ETHICS

A dozen or so years ago, just after the American publication of To Will and to Do, a hopeful little essay by Stephen Rose was titled "Whither Ethics, Jacques Ellul?" Rose concluded: "We must wait for the constructive portion of Ellul's ethics to see where he will center down as a Christian thinker."[1] Since Rose's essay in 1970, Ellul has produced more than enough articles and books to be able, at this point, to describe where he "centers down." The Meaning of the City, The Politics of God and the Politics of Man, Hope in Time of Abandonment, Apocalypse, and, above all, The Ethics of Freedom have all appeared in American editions since 1970.

Of course, Ellul's ethics, as he has planned the work, remain incomplete, but more is on the way. La Foi au prix du doute (Paris: Hachette, 1980) is a provocative study of faith in the modern world that is scheduled for American publication in 1983. This volume is related to Ellul's "Ethics of Holiness" (nearly completed by Ellul as of February 1983), much as the book on hope was related to The Ethics of Freedom. The second half of his "Introduction" (To Will and to Do was the first half) has been written but held up by Ellul for further revision. The volumes on love and the ethics of relationship are still in the planning stages.

As Ellul's work has proceeded, so has the discussion and debate concerning the role of Scripture and Jesus Christ in contemporary Christian ethics. Has Jacques Ellul made a contribution which might be significant in this discussion? I believe he has, although not all of his proposals are equally persuasive. Certainly, his work in ethics is emerging more and more in the recent literature discussing options in Christian ethics. Among his most important contributions is the very challenge his work presents to other Christian ethicists. His swashbuckling attempt to contribute to theological ethics, biblical exegesis, and sociology can only be welcomed. The failure to build bridges between these disciplines, bemoaned by Brevard Childs, James Gustafson, and others, will not be due to a lack of effort on Ellul's part!

In this concluding chapter, attention will first be directed to six contributions which Ellul's work makes to contemporary Christian ethics. In each case, I wish to recognize and applaud Ellul's "promise" while also noting real or potential "problems" that attend his approach. Finally, Ellul's contribution will be located in a discussion of the "prophet" and the "ethicist."

## THE PROMISE AND THE PROBLEMS

The following six topics range from methodological issues to concrete areas of application in normative ethics. There is a certain amount of overlap among these discussions, and preceding sections should be kept in mind as new topics are approached. There are doubtless other ways of setting up this concluding analysis, but by following this approach the whole of Ellul's work is brought into view at one or more points, and, as he has said, his work must be viewed and interpreted as a whole.

### A. Dialectical Method

If there is one characteristic which permeates every thought and every analysis rendered by Jacques Ellul, it is that his work is thoroughly dialectical. "I am a dialectician above all; I believe nothing can be understood without dialectical analysis."[2] Contradiction, opposition, and paradox are ever-present in anything Ellul has in view. Axiomatic-deductive, linear logic is rejected. Rationalistic "scientism"--the worship of empirically demonstrable facts (and nothing else)--is damned. Understanding, whether of Christianity or of society, results from a true perception of the various antithetical factors and forces at work.

On the broadest level, there is the dialectical nature of Ellul's career and publications. On the one hand there is the sociological description of the world; on the other is the biblical-theological articulation of the Word. It is a "composition in counterpoint."[3] These are two perspectives that shed light on our experience, yet cannot be synthesized into a unified "Christian sociology" or "social Christianity." Corresponding to this dialectic of the world and the Word is the dialectic between (the world of) necessity and freedom (of the Word of God).

In general terms, Ellul agrees with Hegel's description of the "positivity of negativity." That is, the negative pole of any dialectic has a positive value. The end of dialectical contradiction and interaction is the end of life, whether on an individual or a social level. Life implies movement, change, and development through the interplay of opposing forces. Change in this manner is not necessarily progress. On this point Ellul disagrees with both Hegel and Marx. But, for Ellul, innovation and mutation, revolution and conversion, are in themselves a manifestation of life. Thus, not only between his sociology and his theology but also within each of these areas, Ellul describes (and to a certain extent promotes) dialectical contradictions.

In his sociological work, Ellul typically sets up dialectics of appearance versus reality, individual versus world, life versus abstract forces, surface events versus "maincurrents," and so on. His method is always that of identifying opposing factors and letting them interact in stark contrast and contradiction--never creating a systematic, noncontradictory, causally interrelated model.

In his theological, biblical, and ethical studies, Ellul says that his "method is the dialectic in accordance with which the biblical revelation is given to us."[4]

> I am profoundly convinced that from the beginning ... Jewish thought, then Christian thought, is, and <u>can only be</u>, dialectical. It is there, and not with the Greeks, that the dialectic is enrooted, and a biblical text cannot be understood except by inserting it in the network of contradictions, the crises and the historical resolution of the crises.[5]

Thus, there is the contradiction between the "impossibility" and the "necessity/possibility" of Christian ethics. There is the profound contradiction between God's "No" of condemnation to humanity and human works and his "Yes" to the same. On the one hand, the fall is total, and nothing remains--no natural law, no conscience, no justice or goodness. The works of fallen humanity--the city, etc.--are beyond redemption and reform. And yet, God graciously adopts these works, although purified and given new meaning. More emphatically by far than Karl Barth, Ellul proclaims the universal salvation of all human beings.[6] Still, there is no way of mediating this dialectic in any intellectual sense: evangelism remains essential.

This Biblical dialectic is also expressed in terms of the End, the Eschaton, the Kingdom of God versus the Present, the Immanent, the Kingdom of the World. The situation of the Christian is to be "in" the world and yet "not of" the world. The Christian cannot escape this tension.

> Thus we seem to be caught between two necessities, which nothing can alter: on the one hand it is impossible for us to make this world less sinful; on the other hand it is impossible for us to accept it as it is.... To be honest, we must not accept this tension of the Christian, or of the Christian life, as an abstract truth. It must be *lived*, it must be realized, in the most concrete and living way possible.[7]

> But our dialectic, that of the Bible, operates between the historical powers and the metahistorical power that is historicized. It is the only true dialectic possible. The final dialectic. Every other being penultimate and relative.[8]

Any synthesis or resolution of antithetical factors and forces takes place in terms of crisis and life--not in terms of an easy intellectual operation, or a peaceful transition to a new condition. The crisis of resolution happens in an "explosion," a moment of illumination, destruction, and re-creation. While the resolution changes the situation and modifies the forces which led to that point, a new dialectical tension emerges. Life is thus a continuous process of tension, conflict, and resolution, followed by further tension, conflict, and resolution.

> So far as the solution is concerned, it cannot be a rational one: it can only be a solution in terms of *life*, and the acceptance of forgiveness given in Jesus Christ. In other words, it is in receiving, and in living the Gospel that political, economic, and other questions can be solved.[9]

Both Ellul's theological and sociological works place decisive importance on individual life. As the individual experiences the tension of the dialectical contradiction in which he or she exists and then refuses to escape this tension by conformity or withdrawal, an existentially valid resolution is possible in terms of choice and action bringing the Wholly Other into the Here and Now.

Ellul's dialectical method often proves very illuminating. Human life is pervaded by contradiction and paradox. When biblical theology is taken seriously, this sense of paradox is radically intensified, above all because of the transcendence and holiness of God. The dialectical method refuses to collapse this tension, but rather recognizes it totally. The freedom of God and the complexity of the world are acknowledged. No pretense is made of dominating and encapsulating reality (including God) within a finite, rational, logical system. Man is not the measure if one follows a dialectical approach such as Ellul's.

The danger of oversimplification is, however, equally present in dialectical and nondialectical thinking. Ellul's dialectic is so intransigent that phenomena tend to be "pushed" toward contradictory loci. Mediating factors and phenomena are sometimes ignored, sometimes violated, and, even when acknowledged, relegated to nonempirical status. That is, for example, if God adopts human works (and Ellul says he does) we know that only from the standpoint of the Eschaton and can make no certain judgments about the status of various human works around us. To be sure, we have some "leads" and some guidance for life, but this is temporary, distinctly relative to this deeper dialectic, and at times both arbitrary and inconsistent in Ellul's hands.

Thus, Ellul's preferred description of God is the "Wholly Other." Ellul's dialectic makes him emphasize this characteristic of God more than any other. It is interesting to note that, in this choice, Ellul has chosen to identify with the earlier Karl Barth and with Søren Kierkegaard, rather than follow Barth's own development as described in his essay "The Humanity of God."

> What began forcibly to press itself upon us about forty years ago was not so much the humanity of God as His <u>deity</u>--a God absolutely unique in His relation to man and the world, overpoweringly lofty and distant, strange, yes even wholly other. 10

> What expressions we used--in part taken over and in part newly invented!--above all, the famous "wholly other" breaking in upon us "perpendicularly from above," the not less famous "infinite qualitative distinction" between God and man, the vacuum, the mathematical point, and the tangent in which alone they must meet.[11]

> Where did we really go astray?... At that time we worked almost exclusively with the concept of diastasis, only seldom and incidentally with the complementary concept of analogy.[12]

As we shall see in a later section below, the incarnation of God in Jesus Christ means one important thing for Ellul, dwarfing all others in significance; i.e., the Wholly Other is fully embodied in one unique individual, historical person.

Since the primary concern of this book is with North American Christianity, and since dialectical thought of this sort is more common in Europe (especially France) than here, Ellul's dialectical method can be an important and illuminating contribution for us. He has exploited it to its full potential in examining both the world and the Word. And yet, ultimately, in my judgment, his great strength can pose problems due to his unrelieved and absolute application of dialectical method. What begins to illuminate the paradox and complexity of life and Christian ethics, can end with an overly simple reduction. We shall see specific instances of this limitation or distortion later on.

A final peril must also be noted in passing. That is, Ellul's extremely dialectical way of thinking and speaking occasionally makes analysis and communication difficult. Ellul is often accused of internal contradiction. Usually these complaints are the result of a failure to understand his dialectic and his paradoxical way of expression; i.e., the contradictions are intentional and are supposed to describe realities that are themselves contradictory. However, it is also true that such a constant barrage of contradiction can cloud over false as well as true contradictions. Hasty and sloppy expression sometimes contains verbal contradictions uncalled for by the reality being described and yet difficult to detect because part of a torrent of dialectical contradictions. Part of this will be excused later on the basis of Ellul's "vocation" and its literary conventions. But that does not mitigate the problem for those reading his works.

## B. The Intermediate Focus

In addressing Ellul's use of Scripture and his sociological focus, I pointed out earlier that his target in both cases is an "intermediate" level of form and movement. In his sociology he wants to go below the surface phenomena, the "waves," by which he means "current events," elections, speeches, slogans, personalities, and so forth. And yet he does not want to descend all the way to the "depths," to the deepest constants of human and social life such as the need for power or food. Instead, he wants to examine the intermediate level of the powerful currents and forces which shape our lives. By this he refers to technique, the growth of the nation-state, urbanization, and so forth.

In the case of his theology and biblical interpretation, the same sort of focus obtains. Ellul is impatient with "surface" details of a historical and literary character. But he is also generally devoid of discussion of the "attributes of God," and other questions of classical dogmatics. What he seizes on are themes and concepts which can be pursued in their flow throughout the canon--*or* he insistently interprets particular books or passages in relation to what he sees as broader continuities in Scripture. Thus, the cosmology of the "*exousia*," the impact of the fall, the role of the Word and the prophet, the city, and the Word of God in Christ surface in nearly every passage he examines--sometimes to our surprise!

Here again, Ellul must be applauded for his accomplishment. His work can be understood in terms of the commonplace about the trees and the forest; Ellul is a "forest" viewer, not a "tree" analyst. An analogy which also illuminates his orientation is that of a ship whose passengers are quarreling, divided, and hungry, and yet which has sprung some very threatening leaks. Ellul's focus is on the common fate of the ship and its passengers, in light of which the quarrels and hunger seem relatively less important. Of course, in terms of his biblical interpretation he does not identify only the threats and the negative challenges; there are common themes on the grace or positive pole as well.

In an age of specialization and "micro" studies, Ellul's theology and sociology are welcome "macro" analyses. His study of the city in Scripture and in relation to Jesus Christ is nothing short of brilliant, although as a pioneering effort it has weaknesses in various specific places. Similarly his analyses of technique, the nation-state, revolution, and religion, are extraordinarily illuminating.

It cannot be said that Ellul is uncaring or ignorant of the "surface" phenomena which he relativizes. Most of his biblical studies show a broad familiarity with the critical literature of the field, and he periodically engages in what could be called "critical" exegesis himself. He commends the work of the "greater scholars" such as Conzelmann, Campenhausen, and von Rad, but complains that in the hands of second-rank scholars these same critical methods are "disastrous."[13] The question, however, is whether Ellul has overreacted. There needs to be a true dialectic between the "whole" and the "parts" where each corrects the other, or serves the other. We have observed in earlier chapters that Ellul's intermediate-level biblical theologizing is sometimes guilty of straying rather far from the texts with which he is working. Sometimes this is a result of too much dependence on a typological interpretation.

Thus, in his biblical interpretation Ellul is usually helpful, always provocative, but occasionally irresponsible in imposing a broad interpretation on passages or events which cannot sustain its weight. In the other direction, this "intermediate level" can be faulted for not being related more carefully or explicitly to the "deeper" theological waters. Ellul's passing references to Karl Barth's theology--that he is a conditional Barthian, etc.--are helpful in understanding these roots. Nevertheless, Ellul's debt to Kierkegaard's Christian philosophical theology appears to be even more profound than his acknowledged debt to Karl Barth. We can figure out much of this theological orientation by inference, but Ellul might help his readers (and his own writing) by being more attentive to his theological presuppositions.

What has been said about Ellul's biblical theology can be repeated for his sociology.[14] That is, he shows broad familiarity with microsociology, statistical studies, etc., and occasionally uses them in his own arguments, and not just as whipping boys. While he damns "current events" he shows rather thorough familiarity with the same! He can be accused of overgeneralizing and inadequate interaction with the detailed data of social experience, although this does not so much invalidate as qualify his major theses. It is also true that Ellul could be helpful by relating his work at the intermediate level to his deeper philosophical commitments. As in the case of biblical theology, we must infer his underlying philosophical conceptual framework indirectly.

Ellul is highly persuasive in what he affirms, much less so in what he denies (explicitly or implicitly). Thus, he has made a strong case for the importance of the city, the exousia, technique, and the nation-state. The question remains whether there are other currents--crosscurrents, perhaps!--which have equal, or nearly equal, importance, and yet which are dismissed finally as merely surface phenomena by Ellul. It is my judgment that he is guilty on this last score. José Miranda's Marx and the Bible, to which reference was made earlier, argues that

> reality consists above all in the outcry of the poor who have been crushed by history and in the very dialectics of the history which yearns to heed this outcry in a definitive way.[15]

Poverty and hunger and their alleviation are as integral to social history, and to biblical theology, as is the growth of the city and yet these concerns are somewhat arbitrarily relegated to the level of "surface" phenomena.

A second example, of a different kind, is the quest for dignity and individual or group worth. The biblical motifs are well-known ("being addressed, named, and redeemed by God," etc.). In the recent decolonization movements in the Third World, Ellul relativizes this sort of concern with a warning about the penetration of technique and the Western nation-state into the new framework. We do not have to deny the validity of Ellul's point to acknowledge an equally important crosscurrent at work in this part of the world, i.e., the achievement of racial or cultural dignity and pride. Thus, while the Third World is in one respect more dependent on the West and its framework, it is simultaneously more feisty and independent, and this development is already of major significance for the course of world history.

In short, Ellul's focus on intermediate-level currents in both Scripture and the world is generally very helpful. The questions that are raised by this choice of focus are of two kinds: first, has this focus been productive of the best identification of what are in fact the definitive forces in our history and society? On this score, Ellul appears to have been accurate, as far as he goes, in the phenomena he identifies at this level, while he is suspect on a few counts where he might have neglected or overlooked other forces and phenomena deserving equal emphasis. Second, the intermediate level has to be responsibly related to the other two levels of analysis. In this case, the verdict on Ellul's work is again mixed. He has given some attention to this relationship, especially of the intermediate to the surface level. It may be that his emphasis on the intermediate level is unbalanced and that more or less equal emphasis should be placed on the other two levels.

## C. The Individual

Another feature common to Ellul's sociology and theology is the great emphasis on the individual. In *The Political Illusion*, for example, Ellul says, "Whether we like it or not, all depends entirely on the individual."[16] By this Ellul means a recovery of true, individual democratic citizenship. In *Autopsy of Revolution*, the same point is made:

> Revolution no longer can remain a struggle between an exploiting and an exploited class: the struggle itself reinforces the totalizing tendency of society and advances it. Yet because revolution must always emanate from the diametrical opposite of the organism under attack, if that organism is truly totalitarian its sole antithesis is the individual.[17]

The revolution we need must "be executed on the individual level by the individual's recovery of control over the systems of integration."[18] In his recent work, *The Betrayal of the West*, he continues:

> Never has society been in a better position over against the individual. Never has society been so exalted, and never has it so utterly denied the individual.[19]

In his essay for *The Humanist*, Ellul suggests that both the West and the Third World are in need of a view of the future and a collective project--and this "collective project can only be stirred by a new thrust of the individual."[20] Quotations of this sort could be multiplied from Ellul's sociological writings.

The same emphasis is found in his theological-ethical writings. The sociological arguments come into play in these writings as well. But this individualism is also grounded in a theological understanding of freedom before God.

> The fact that freedom is a choice of acts in terms of love for others means that we are faced with a purely individualistic ethics. This freedom can be demonstrated only by individual acts in individual cases.[21]

While this is not "private" it is still individualistic, and any social transformation will come "from below by the accumulation of a vast number of individual decisions."[22] Thus "Kierkegaard, it seems to me, alone can show us how to start."[23] The "radical subjectivity" and "passion" of Kierkegaard/Ellul's beloved individual is fundamental.

What we have then is a basic dialectic between the individual on the one hand and the collective forces of our society and history on the other. This fundamental dialectic is argued on sociological and on biblical-theological grounds. We have, in the preceding section, acknowledged the contribution as well as the problems of Ellul's focus on these collective forces and powers. Given the collectivistic ideology of our era--where the mass media combine with public education and the vast, growing centralized state to flatten out differences among people and regions and integrate everyone into an undifferentiated mass society (bringing some benefits, to be sure)--a renewed emphasis on autonomous individual life and consciousness is quite appropriate. This is especially valid because Ellul is clearly not advocating pure selfishness; it is individualistic but not privatistic, in his terms.

A careful reading of Ellul on this issue is imperative. On a superficial level, Ellul's individualism might appear to encourage the phenomenon we have recently witnessed in America in such books as <u>Looking Out for Number One!</u> Ellul's relativization of social programs aimed at aiding the poor at home or abroad is quite acceptable so long as one understands his call for "absolute seriousness" with respect to the relative. His call for individualism is acceptable so long as it is not a pretext for selfish privatism. Unfortunately, a rather extensive and careful reading of Ellul is required to prevent such misunderstandings.

Even a call for careful reading is not enough, however. Ellul's extreme dialectic has led him to "push" all groups and collectivities toward the pole standing against the individual. For every hint that an intermediate group might be helpful in combatting technique and the nation-state, there are a hundred others which condemn such groups as instruments of adaptation to the technological society.

> In this perspective, revolution must act against the mounting ascendancy of groups over individuals. I am concerned here not with the over-all problem of society, but rather with the prevailing attitude that an individual must be part of a group or be nothing: community-mindedness, team spirit (in the individual's immediate circle of existence), group projects, and group leisures. People who claim that intellectual or scientific pursuits now require "teamwork," who set up religious and political action "committees," who hold that individuals can do nothing on their own, are manifesting not a socialist attitude, but the developmental conditions of a technological society such as ours. They are molding themselves in the image of their own necessities. Their reasoning is totally confused: the combining of individuals into groups is represented as a revolutionary concept (specifically by identifying it with socialism and hypostasizing the principle that man exists only through and in his relationships to others), but it is, in reality, merely a reaffirmation of the imperatives governing the operation of our structures.[24]

When Ellul discusses the Church, it is most frequently in condemnation of its adaptation and conformity, its bureaucratization and impotence. Certainly Ellul is correct in identifying this adaptive, integrative function as an important (negative) potentiality of intermediate groups. And his call for a reasserted individualism is appropriate--as far as it goes.

What is underemphasized is the positive potentiality of intermediate groups. Although The Political Illusion concludes on the individualistic note, there is one point at which Ellul pays tribute to this positive possibility of intermediate groups:

> We must try to create positions in which we reject

> and struggle with the state ... in order to permit the emergence of social, political, intellectual, or artistic bodies, associations, interest groups, or economic or Christian groups totally independent of the state, yet capable of opposing it, able to reject its pressures as well as its controls, and even its gifts. These organizations must be completely independent, not only materially but also intellectually and morally.... 25

In his early Presence of the Kingdom, Ellul suggests that "rebuilding parish life" is essential. 26 Several years later, Ellul argues the need for a vital church life in False Presence of the Kingdom:

> I know the objection that "the Church is only the Church in mission and evangelizing." Yes, of course, but we must not forget the counterpart: the Church as a holy people, as a sacrificing people, as ambassador (that is, belonging to another power), as a body (that is, organically distinct, different from other bodies and not lost in the indiscriminate mass)... !
>
> What I am saying is that we are sending into the world babes in arms, who are not yet ready for adult tasks, that there is a preparation, both spiritual and intellectual, ethical and sociological, meditative and active, which is in no way being given to the Church, nor to those in the Church whom we are urging to become involved in the world. 27

And finally, in the Ethics of Freedom, "It is on the basis of a church which is a strong body and community" that the layperson is capable of living out freedom. 28

The quotations above would appear to answer the objection made earlier. This is not quite true, however. This is, first of all, because these infrequent affirmations tend to get lost in the overwhelming dialectic of individual versus collectivity, the latter viewed negatively nearly all the time. Secondly, the individual retains primacy even in the discussions giving positive value to an intermediate group like the church. The value of the group is almost exclusively in its aid to a rebuilt individuality, which in turn is the revolutionary factor.

From a biblical standpoint, the individual has tremendous value and potentiality. Yet this is paralleled by an emphasis on the value and potentiality of the new community: it is neither superordinate nor subordinate. By way of example, St. Paul's call for nonconformity to "this age," for sacrificial giving of one's body, for transformation of one's mind, and for conformity to the will of God (in Romans 12, arguably Paul's most "systematic" presentation of his ethics) is followed immediately by the warning, "Do not think more highly of yourself than you ought to think." Rather, he goes on to say, remember that you are one, and only one, member of the body of Christ, that all members are necessary to the functioning of this body. In a review essay on The Ethics of Freedom, I put it this way:

> My point is that much more could be, and needs to be, said about the role of the "body of Christ." After all, the New Testament envisions believers never as isolated individuals per se but as "individual members of a body, whose head is Christ." And while the collective structures and forces of our society have "powers" active in them, the body of Christ has the "power of the Holy Spirit." The presence of God's Spirit is not merely an individual matter, nor the accumulation of "individual presences" when we gather together. Further, New Testament social ethics makes a distinction between "love of neighbor" and "love of the brethren": both are essential, but they are not strictly identical. I am saying not that Ellul denies this but that it is the least developed aspect of his ethics. This is the point at which an Anabaptist conscience has most to say to brother Kierkegaard and his Danish Lutheran experience and to brother Ellul and his French Reformed experience![29]

In short, Ellul's dialectic of individual versus technological society or nation-state is neither the only nor the best one, although it is valid and helpful in its own right. From the standpoint of Christian ethics the two-directional relationship of the individual member and the body of Christ (and the similar concept of the family, although I have not discussed it here) is a better way of describing the pole that stands over against technique and the state. Ellul's call for a "new thrust of the individual" is definitive of a new social paradigm, of course. It is not a call to selfish privatism.

It is a radical challenge to a monistic technological mass society. And yet, both theologically and sociologically we have every reason to expect that this self-conscious, autonomous individual will simply be crushed by the "powers." Only the New Creation, the New Community, can stand up to the old one.

## D. Ethical Method

Ellul's ethical method reflects his understanding of the dialectic of God and the world. In terms of the categories of philosophical ethics, Ellul places great emphasis--indeed, almost exclusive emphasis--on the "nonmoral value," on "the Good," which stands over and informs all normative ethics. This Good is, of course, the Wholly Other God who is also love incarnate. Ellul virtually ignores the questions of metaethics--how the ethic is grounded and justified. The justification of Ellul's approach is primarily subjective, based on the "leap of faith." To the extent that there is a justification offered or implied, it is what Chaim Perelmann would classify as a "structure of reality" argument.[30] That is, Ellul constructs a model of reality and experience and, in effect, asks if this model does not best "fit" our observation and experience.

It is on the category of "normative ethics" that our evaluation of Ellul's method must focus. He has said that "there are no normative ethics of the good, but there are ethics of grace, which are quite the opposite."[31] As suggested earlier, if this were really true, Ellul should simply point his finger toward God and be quiet! The fact is that his "ethics of grace" <u>are</u> a species of normative ethics--distinctive but not "opposite." One of Ellul's great accomplishments is precisely this articulation of a particular normative ethics which is persistently and deeply rooted in a concept of the nonmoral Good. Ellul has taken upon himself the "mission" of developing an ethics from a Barthian point of departure and in this he has gone a fair distance.

Ellul's rejection of ethics as being "of the order of necessity" is valid as a literary device which aims at establishing the uniqueness of Christian ethics. What Ellul is rejecting, finally, is not ethics, but a particular type of ethics: naturalistic, rationalistic, humanistic, technical, etc. What differentiates Christian ethics from others is the particular character of its nonmoral Good. The living God, whose will is the Good, implies a dynamic character to normative ethics which defies permanent, comprehensive codification. The constancy of God's love and justice implies a continuity to our normative ethics. The intervention of God into closed situations, breaking them open to new possibilities of freedom, provides a powerful paradigm by which to judge our own action and character.

Thus, while Ellul has done a great deal to spell out some normative ethical guidance in relation to the will of God, the Good, he pulls up short. He has stipulated (and stigmatized as fallen) an ethical definition which, after being exhaustively analyzed and rejected, makes his own normative ethical formulation more ambivalent and (perhaps) half-hearted than it needs to be. An ethicist need not be a legalist in order to be considerably more "systematic" than Ellul has been.

In philosophical terms, Ellul engages in normative ethics and erects a "system" which may be compared with other ethical systems and approaches, whether he wants to admit this "family resemblance" or not. In theological terms, the admission of this resemblance need not be seen as a capitulation to the fall! If the fall brings with it the knowledge of good and evil and various attempts to construct an ethics defining its own good and evil, that need not be the starting point for our understanding of ethics. Prescriptive ethics can be defined as the concern for the "ought" over against the "is"--indeed the etymology of the words ethics and morals (derived from <u>ethos</u> and <u>mores</u>, in Greek and Latin, respectively) suggests a more inclusive definition than Ellul gives. Prior to the fall, God spoke and commissioned man and woman with an "ought." In Ellul's ethics, that Word of God addressed to man and woman is the heart, the core of ethics, and not some slicing of human activities into good and evil, right and wrong. God adopts human language of all types in order to express this will. There is no theological requirement for Ellul to impugn ethical discourse as such. The reason is to be found in Ellul's particular application of the dialectic, and in his vocation, a subject to which we shall return in the final section of this chapter.

Ellul's choice of the Pauline "virtues" of faith, hope, and love, and his pairing of these with holiness, freedom, and relationship may turn out to be the most brilliant advance he has made in doing ethics in the Kierkegaardian-Barthian tradition. For, while St. Paul gives the most explicit attention to these virtues, they appear also in the rest of the Apostolic writings and, as such, provide an intriguing summary mediation of biblical life and faith centered on Jesus Christ. Ellul's promised volumes on the ethics of holiness/faith and relationship/love will provide us with a better basis on which to judge the potential of this method.[32]

## E. The Word of God in Jesus Christ and Scripture

This study began with the affirmation that for a Christian ethics to serve the Church, it is necessary that the central figure of Christianity, Jesus Christ, be given major and ongoing importance as the Word of God to our ethics. The stumbling blocks of cultural and historical differences and Jesus' cosmology and eschatology have been noted, along with the remarkable willingness of vast numbers in the contemporary Church to accept (or overlook) these factors in profound commitment to the leadership of Jesus Christ.

Ellul's strong affirmation of Jesus Christ as the Word of God to ethics has already been noted. Ethics flows out of the relationship with Jesus Christ . Our works should proceed "directly from the action of Jesus Christ in us."[33] Jesus Christ is the one in whom "the Word of God is fully expressed, explained, and revealed."[34] All of history is affected and modified by his incarnation, and its meaning is dependent on his Parousia. The crucifixion and resurrection of Jesus Christ are the hub on which both terrestrial and celestial events turn and have meaning.[35]

Ellul's greatest contribution is, in line with his ethical method, to direct attention to the person of Christ as Lord, and not, first of all, to any specific program or teaching. The unifying theme that Ellul finds in the meaning of Jesus Christ is that of the intervention of the Wholly Other in the Here and Now. This discrimen becomes the paradigm for Christian ethics: "Because Christianity is the revelation of the Wholly Other, that action must be different, specific, singular, incommensurable with political or corporate methods of action."[36] This is not to say that maladjustment is a value in its own right, although Ellul comes perilously close to implying this at times. Rather, this call for uniqueness is God's response to the fateful closure of the fallen world in on itself, obeying only its own imperatives, laws, and necessities. Ellul's identification of this basic paradigm is true enough to Jesus Christ and appropriate enough to a contemporary world desparately in need of creative alternatives and imagination, that he must be applauded here.

When this basic understanding of the Incarnation becomes the master theme for interpreting the rest of Jesus Christ's significance, the results are mixed. As a means of getting at the profound significance of Jesus' choice of nonpower, servanthood, and sacrificial death--in opposition to power, domination, and self-exaltation--the paradigm works out well. In relation to violence, the pursuit of wealth, or exploitation of the weak, Ellul's emphasis on being "Wholly Other" is liberating.

In relation to the "temptation of Christ" episode, questions begin to arise about the appropriateness of this interpretive principle. What Jesus rejects is not so much necessity as it is necessity-as-manipulated-by-Satan. For example, is the temptation of bread a commentary on how Christians are to relate to the problem of hunger (much less all natural necessity), as Ellul argues? These three temptations, he says, are representative of all the tests faced by Jesus later on. It is not at all clear that Ellul's interpretation is exhaustive enough, although he should be granted the validity of his one point, viz., that Jesus introduces the Wholly Other in freedom from necessity.

In contrast to Ellul's approach to Jesus for ethical content, John Howard Yoder attributes central importance to Jesus' "platform" in Luke 4. Good news for the poor, release to the captives, sight for the blind, freedom for the oppressed, etc.: these are the themes with which Jesus identifies his mission.[37] Yoder's success in articulating this "program" and relating it to the broader sweep of the Old and New Testaments indicates that Ellul's view (and use) of Jesus Christ while powerful is unnecessarily concentrated (restricted) to one point. Negatively, Ellul's use of Jesus Christ is very effective in freeing us from traditional options. Positively, however, his approach fails to develop Jesus Christ's teaching and example as fully as it might have been developed.

In each of the case studies--the city and the nation-state--Jesus Christ is brought into the ethic in a fairly central fashion. As suggested earlier, merely doing this is an advance and also a challenge to go further if possible. For making this beginning Ellul is to be credited. For not following through more completely, and for distorting some passages slightly, he must be faulted.

* * *

In regard to Scripture, Ellul has succeeded in moving beyond both "Conservative" and "Liberal" preoccupations. In doing so, he is following the strong lead of Karl Barth, of course. Without neglecting completely the critical historical investigation of Scripture or the uncritical respect for every "jot and tittle" of the "Conservative" Bible, he has moved beyond both. Three of his major contributions are his affirmation, borne out in practice as well, of the *relevance* of the whole canon of Scripture for today; his insistence on, and substantial demonstration of, the underlying *unity* of biblical revelation; and his attempt to *center* the canon on Jesus.

Ellul's *Apocalypse* and his *Politics of God and the Politics of Man* are excellent examples of the point about relevance. Both are species of biblical literature (Revelation and II Kings) which are easily relegated to less important status as we search the Scriptures for ethical guidance. Fundamentalists who are interested in these two documents are concerned primarily with authenticating the past historical record ("inerrancy") of II Kings and using the Revelation as the key to predicting future "prophetic" events (e.g., Hal Lindsey's *The Late Great Planet Earth*). Ellul, whether one agrees with the details of his interpretation or not, has certainly made these books come alive in a relevant way.

His *The Meaning of the City* and his discussion of the *exousia* and biblical cosmology demonstrate the second point, that Ellul has opened our eyes to a unity that might have escaped us. In doing so, he has shown remarkable similarity to Brevard Childs' work. What he has done is not, thus, particularly unique except in its relation to contemporary ethics. Whether this unity is ultimately rooted satisfactorily in Jesus Christ or not is the most difficult question. His attempt must be applauded, however, in light of the needs of the Church for such a relationship to be established. It is interesting to note also that John C. Bennett, hardly an "Ellulian" in other respects, makes a strong plea for centering our biblical interpretation on Jesus Christ.[38] The major question about Ellul's Christocentric hermeneutic is whether his occasional typological approach is acceptable or adequately argued. It could probably stand a good deal of improvement.

Ellul has avoided the "genre-reductionism" which was a concern for Birch and Rasmussen in their Bible and Ethics in the Christian Life.[39] Although he gives greatest emphasis to the theme of the intervention of the Wholly Other, he also uses Scripture to teach the importance of prayer, love, service, nonviolence, etc., and to illuminate the reality of politics, the city, and human works. In short, Ellul's use of the Bible in ethics is one of his greatest contributions in that he has shown how we can hear the Word of God in the context of a variety of contemporary problems, from a variety of biblical literature. And where he does not convince, he at least challenges us to do the job better ourselves.

In any use of Scripture on the broad scale attempted by Ellul, it is almost inevitable that some distortion and some omission will take place. We have already suggested that Ellul's discussion of the Incarnation of Jesus Christ is an example of making powerful but limited use of Jesus Christ; i.e., his teaching and example could be developed much more fully. Other examples of this underdevelopment would be Ellul's view of the Church (also mentioned earlier in the section on the individual), and the Holy Spirit (which Ellul mentions often but never really develops).

The biblical themes in relation to which Ellul's exegesis and theology must be called in question are Creation and Eschatology. The latter figures largely in Ellul's ethics; the former has virtually no place. The relationship of eschatology to ethics is fully admitted by Ellul, and he regards it as no stumbling block whatsoever. Christian behavior is shaped by the coming Kingdom of God. The End is the perspective from which we judge the present. All of this is frequently and persuasively developed by Ellul.

The problem with Ellul's eschatology is twofold: first, is he guilty of detemporalizing or "Platonizing" biblical eschatology? Second, does his concept of the exchatological judgment finally cut the nerve of ethics? As we have observed, Ellul uses the language of biblical eschatology boldly and frequently. He sounds as though he believes in the kind of temporal End (which would, of course, be the Beginning of something else), which Oscar Cullmann argues is required by the biblical terminology and concept of time.[40] More than occasionally, however, Ellul's eschatology appears to be detemporalized. The End is not, then, a historical End, but rather the realm of the Wholly Other, the Beyond. This End doesn't intersect with history, except in the form of individual "presence" and through a mysterious, "hidden" adoption of our works.

The second problem is just as thorny, i.e., is everyone and everything both condemned and saved? This is Ellul's argument, especially in Apocalypse. As in the case of the detemporalized End, a universal salvation has to wrestle with a vast number of biblical texts and make them say the opposite of what they appear to say. I do not intend to argue against Ellul's exegesis of specific texts, but merely to point it up as a major problem on the exegetical level. It is also a problem for the people of God, or at least a large number of them for whom Ellul's exegetical gymnastics will be unconvincing. And finally, if everyone and everything is finally brought into the kingdom of God (which, however, never quite comes!) what happens to the eschatological sanction on our behavior? What happens to Jesus' threats of eschatological judgment on those who have failed to care for the hungry and the poor?

Ellul's basic argument in favor of "universalism" is that anything less means that God has failed, that "there is an external limit to the love of God."[41] Thus, he says, it is not "theologically possible." This brings us, ironically, to the problem of Creation in Ellul's thought. For in his rejection of Creation themes in his ethics, is not Ellul overstating the triumph of evil in the fall? Though Eschatology is a much more significant theme in biblical ethics, the Creation theme is not as "non-existent" as Ellul suggests. Ellul's (and Barth's) suspect exegesis of Romans 1 and 2 is not the only problem. The fall has completely twisted, marred, and vitiated God's creation. All is darkness. Nothing remains. But wait a minute: is not marriage and cohumanity something of a survival, as Jesus and Paul teach it? Symptomatic of Ellul's "blinders" on the subject is the fact that in his Apocalypse, the only chapter of Revelation which he fails to mention (much less develop as part of his interpretation) is precisely Chapter Four, the hymn to creation!

Harvey Cox's essay on Ellul's view of the city suggests that instead of viewing the city as elementally an act of rebellion against God, we could follow Lewis Mumford's suggestion that the city is essentially the demonstration of the social nature and the desire for fellowship of and by humanity. The city has a two-faced history. Its rebellious side, beginning with Cain, has been well-described by Ellul.

But as the place of cohumanity the city has roots in the creation of Adam and Eve and their desire to live in the same place. Thus, early in Genesis, Melchizedek is king of Salem ("peace"), later to become Jebus, later still, Jerusalem. This approach permits us to make judgments on what in our cities is in conformity with the will of God and what is not. The distinctions are clearer and more identifiable than Ellul implies. The reason for this is that God's will for the city-as-cohumanity is not visible only at the End (although it is clearest there).

Ellul's view of work is even more difficult to sustain exegetically. Most commentators see work as being part of the commission before the fall. The sweat and toil aspects resulted from the fall. Not so with Ellul, for whom work in its entirety is nothing more than necessity and fallenness. What has been said with respect to the city and work can also be repeated for politics and the state. An eschatological, Christocentric ethics need not rule so decisively against a doctrine of creation. It is not theologically or ethically necessary, nor is such a rejection warranted by Scripture. Ultimately, a neat dialectical distinction such as Ellul's is a partial imposition on Scripture. A dialectical "system" can be as binding and restrictive as any other "system."

## F. Technique and Politics: Ethical Implications

We live in what Ellul calls "the order of necessity" and "the order of the fall." Both of these concepts prove very illuminating in Ellul's hands as he tries to penetrate the essential nature of the city and technique. The temptation is to want to view technique and the city as neutral objects and locate evil only in the "hearts" of greedy capitalists, scheming political power brokers, fascists, and street thugs. Ellul's approach helps to illuminate the structural character of evil or, conversely, the demonic potentialities of structures.

In his development of the eschatological perspective, the New Jerusalem, Ellul proclaims a vigorous hope for the future of the city and human works. The history of the city from the fall to the eschaton is illuminated by his biblical and sociological analyses. Focusing on the significance of the incarnation of Jesus Christ, which implies at least (1) desacralizing the city, (2) opening up the city by the intervention of the unique, the Wholly Other, and (3) caring for and loving the people in the city, we are given a number of (unsystematic) suggestions on how our life and behavior might reflect the presence of the End in urban-technological society.

Ellul's contribution can be appreciated especially when compared to other work done on urban ethics in recent years. On the broader level, as among Christians, there is a certain disagreement about the city. On the one hand are the scientific and technical optimists (and politicians), such as John Maddox (The Doomsday Syndrome) and Alvin Toffler (Future Shock), who agree that we face considerable problems but that they are surmountable through improved and expanded application of resources and techniques now within our reach.[42] On the other hand, as Morton and Lucia White's study, The Intellectual Versus the City, abundantly demonstrates, most of America's greatest intellectuals from Thomas Jefferson to Frank Lloyd Wright and Lewis Mumford have been anti-urban.[43]

As I have argued throughout this study, Christians caught up in this situation turn (or would like to turn) to the Word of God in Jesus Christ and Scripture for guidance in developing their perspective on this urban-technological society. There have been some notable attempts to meet this need. Harvey Cox (The Secular City), Max L. Stackhouse (Ethics and Urban Ethos), Craig Ellison (editor, The Urban Mission), and Donald W. Shriver, Jr. and Karl A. Ostrom (Is There Hope for the City?) all include some degree of dependence on Jesus Christ and Scripture.[44] In each case, however, this dependence is very restricted and, in some cases, open to serious question. In some respects, these four studies just mentioned are the kind of second step implied by Ellul's work, i.e., working out a more systematic urban ethics from a thoroughgoing biblical-theological basis.

Ellul's work on technique and the city is a great stride forward for Christians. Nevertheless, it can itself be improved. The greatest difficulty is Ellul's failure to see any survival of God's creation after the fall (and, to a lesser extent, his failure to retain a temporal eschatology). Ellul's argument that any survival means that the fall was only partial--i.e., that there are "unfallen" sectors of human personality, such as reason--is a "straw man." Everything can be marred and adversely affected by the fall without eradicating all traces of God's creation and freedom. In fact, if the fall was as total and the separation as complete as Ellul suggests, life itself would have ceased to exist. The point is that the dialectic between Jerusalem and Babylon is not only the Redeemed End versus the Fallen Present. It is also a dialectic with roots in both creation and fall, and with a resolution in the Last Judgment and the New Creation. Ellul has well-described the negative pole of Babylon. His biblical study would be vastly improved by a fuller development, slightly recast, of the positive pole.

* * *

What has been said about technique and the city holds true in relation to Ellul's work toward a Christian political ethic. His sociological studies are a provocative analysis of the situation in which our political life must be worked out. His biblical studies and theological reflections help us to develop an appreciation of the meaning and the non-meaning of politics. For that part of the Church which commonly resorts to Jesus Christ and Scripture for guidance, Ellul has at least opened the door and shown some intriguing possibilities.

Once again, Ellul is much better in describing the demonic possibilities of nation-state and politics than he is at suggesting the positive potentialities or a constructive alternative to the political illusion. This is again partly due to his extreme dialectic where the state and politics are fallen necessities, not created orders.

As an alternative approach, Karl Barth's essay "The Christian Community and the Civil Community" suggests a number of guidelines for the state and politics based on analogies with the Christian community.[45] Barth finds much more positive content than does Ellul. On the other hand, Barth's presentation is somewhat abstract and general. Ellul's political ethics is arrived at with the input of Jesus Christ and Scripture on the one hand and a sociological study of the nation-state and political illusion of today on the other.

## THE PROPHET AND THE ETHICIST

From the preceding section it should be clear that my conclusion is that Jacques Ellul has made a decisive contribution in both method and application in Christian ethics. In particular, six areas of contribution have been identified. In each case, however, the promise and contribution is accompanied by at least one problem, sometimes a very serious one at that. An overall problem with Ellul's work is that it is often difficult for the people in the Church to understand. If we are searching for a contemporary Christian ethics, it must be able to "hold its own" at the lay level as well as among the experts in the ethical guild. Ellul's work, as it stands, has some problems at both levels! I am convinced, however, that with a degree of refinement and "translation" these communication problems can be overcome.

It is important to note Ellul's opening words in To Will and to Do, the introduction to his whole series on ethics:

> It remains for me to say that I have no competence to write this book. I am neither a theologian nor a philosopher by profession. I possess none of the specialist's qualifications.... I am trying only to be a human being. I am trying to live fully in this age. I feel the anguish of those around me. I am acquainted with our general laxity in a society without structure and without rules. My trade is to reflect, and I have undertaken to do that as a man, nothing more. I shall run into many a problem which the specialists have studied hundreds of times. I approach these in innocence and with the fresh look of the incompetent.[46]

This expression of humility is seldom repeated by Ellul as he turns his attention to the task at hand!

Ellul has invaded the domain of the ethicist, and his work must be evaluated at that level. Along with a great deal that is good and positive, his work is also incomplete and less than satisfactory in other places--when evaluated as ethics. But there is one sense in which Ellul should be permitted to excuse himself as not being an ethical specialist. The fact is, ethicists, like any other specialists, should not listen only to each other. Fundamentally, in my opinion, in giving a hearing to Jacques Ellul ethicists will be listening to a prophet.

Ellul is not, of course, a prophet to the masses. Rather, he is a prophet to the intellectuals. He does not call himself a prophet and would be embarrassed to have others designate him as such. In The Politics of God and the Politics of Man, Ellul has described the role of the prophet.

> Man chooses his own action. But between this decision by man and God's decision we find the prophet. This man has received a revelation of God's intention either before or during the course of the enterprise. He announces and can bend or provoke, but there is no necessity or determination. One is in the presence of open possibilities here. This man also understands what the politician is wanting. He understands it in depth. He sees the reality behind the appearance of the action, and he discloses to the politician his true intention, his situation.
>
> Finally this man gives the meaning of it all, the true significance of what has happened. He brings to light the relation that exists between the free determination of man and the free decision of God.
>
> Thus the prophet plays a role which is radical and decisive and yet also independent, ex-centric, and disinterested.[47]

The prophet thus "provokes," "explains," and "risks." The prophet is traditionally in conflict with the king, the guardian of the institutional and the established. In this conflict the prophet is "absolutely the wholly other," "absolutely new and surprising," and he "disturbs our ritual, morality, and piety." The prophet is the "son of thunder who interferes and overthrows, affirming that God is not the God of the past or of the dead, but the God of the present and the living."[48] The prophet brings the Word of God to bear on "the actual, concrete situation of man," but "he does not bring any solution or engage in any action." He says: Listen to the Word of God and make your decision.[49] The prophet opens up situations by mediating the Word of God who is Wholly Other. Ellul's little study of Jonah emphasizes this correspondence between the role of the prophet and the role of Jesus Christ.[50]

If we turn from this biblical study of II Kings to some of Ellul's more autobiographical comments in other contexts, the correspondence with the role of prophet is remarkable. He has often said, for example, that no solutions or systems will be offered by him.

> I refuse to construct a system of thought, or to offer up some Christian or pre-fabricated socio-political solutions. I want only to provide Christians with the means of thinking out for themselves the meaning of their involvement in the modern world.[51]

In "Mirror of These Ten Years" Ellul repeats his conclusion that there is no comprehensive Christian system possible and there are no solutions for social, political, economic, or moral problems.[52] Instead, it is out of a profound knowledge of reality, i.e., the confrontation of opposing dialectical forces, that solutions will come. God puts the questions to us and we provide the answers.

> For it is only out of the decision he makes when he experiences this contradiction--never out of adherence to an integrated system--that the Christian will arrive at a practical position.[53]

The clearest declaration of intention given by Ellul is quoted in the David Menninger article, alluded to in earlier sections of this study.

> I would say two things to explain the tenor of my writings. I would say, along with Marx, that as long as men believe that things will resolve themselves, they will do nothing on their own. But when the situation appears to be absolutely deadlocked and tragic, then men will try and do something. That's how Marx described the capitalist revolution and the situation of the proletariat --as something absolutely tragic, without resolution. But he wrote this knowing as soon as the proletariat sees his situation as without resolution, he'll start to look for one. And he'll find it.
>
> Thus it is that I have written to describe things as they are and as they will continue to develop as long as man does nothing, as long as he does not intervene. In other words, if man rests passive in the face of technique, of the state, then these things will exist as I have described them. If man does decide to act, he doesn't have many possibilities of intervention, but some do continue to exist. And he can change the course of social evolution. Consequently, it's kind of a challenge that I pose to men. It's not a question of metaphysical fatalism.

And later on:

> The purpose of my book is to provoke a reaction of personal reflection, and to thus oblige the reader to choose for himself a course of action.[54]

Ellul is a genius and a man of vast learning and erudition. His work demonstrates these characteristics over and over. His work can stand on its own as sociological or theological criticism and construction. But it is best appreciated if it is read as "prophecy" and challenge.

One of the most difficult to accept aspects of Ellul's work is this habitual overstatement, where he sounds as though life is all over, no political life or revolution is possible, etc., or where he proclaims the great victory of God or the radical transformation of human history by the Incarnation. Part of the reason for this overstatement is his persistent and radical dialectical method. But another reason, we can now see, is that he is writing in the heat of passion and concern and engages in rhetorical exaggeration to try to provoke the degree of response that will ultimately redeem a situation.

Like most prophets, Ellul's offense is not only his message but his style as well! Richard L. Rubenstein, for example, is thoroughly offended by Ellul's lack of "ordinary civility," "sustained intemperance," and "ungenerous way of dealing with his opponents" in The New Demons.[55] Another reviewer reacts to The Betrayal of the West by bemoaning Ellul's "continued petty, personal sniping at his colleagues," "crotchety ill-temper," "hectoring, sarcastic tone," and "jeering."[56] Both reviewers are justified in making these comments. And if Ellul offends others, he is himself guilty of "thin skin" and a persecution complex at times, e.g., bemoaning the fact that no one will listen to him and that his best efforts are useless. Like most prophets, Ellul is somewhat isolated, somewhat of a "loner."

This "prophetic" role is relative to the intellectual and academic community, of course, not the population in general. While Ellul is concerned with the laity in general, the Christian intellectual is Ellul's primary "prophetic target."

> It is quite true that the Christian intellectual is a layman, like other people in the Church. But it is also true that inevitably, as an intellectual, he

> has a somewhat peculiar function to fulfill, both in the world, and in the Church.... It is not his task to study speculative theology, but because his work involves him in the life of the world, in the activities of the world, he has to evolve some kind of practical theology. He must think out, very clearly, his situation as a Christian at work in the world, and he must think out his faith in its relation with the world. Thus, he has a very clear function to fulfil, and no one can take his place.[57]

This affirmation is part of Ellul's 1948 Presence of the Kingdom, which, as is often enough noted, is the initial summary of Ellul's chosen program. All of his subsequent work can be seen as an elaboration on the themes of Presence of the Kingdom.

For an ethicist, there are points where Ellul's approach needs revision or supplementation. As a prophet to the intellectuals, and especially to Christian ethicists, however, he is an important and much-needed voice and force. Ellul's style is always provocative and challenging, sometimes harsh and offensive, as he happens to hit a few innocent targets in his mad iconoclasm. My own review essay published shortly after the publication of The Ethics of Freedom, summed up his impact in these terms:

> Another way of describing the total thrust of The Ethics of Freedom, and most of Ellul's previous work for that matter, is to say that Ellul "takes everything away" from us. He removes our commonplaces and securities, destroys our idols, crutches, and supports, ruthlessly strips away our justifications, and attacks our conformity to the world and lack of faith in Christ. Both through sociological criticism and through biblical exposition, he leaves us with no way out, with the exits sealed off, with no hope. But wait! In this work, more than any since The Presence of the Kingdom (1948), Ellul gives it all back with what can only be described as an inspiring vision of hope and freedom.
>
> The effect of this strategy is to give all activists pause, to pull us back from our relentless plunge into frenetic activity in the world. We are helped to assess the reality of the world more profoundly and hear the Word of God more attentively. Then

we are led back into the fray in obedience to our Lord. After everything has been closed off, *The Ethics of Freedom* throws open the doors, batters down the walls, and opens out on a whole new life of freedom in service of God and our neighbor. "The radical devaluation of everything in society is accompanied by the revaluation (the only one) that everything, by the grace of God, may be able to serve the kingdom" (p. 312). It can hardly be disputed that this approach exemplifies, on the level of contemporary Christian ethical discourse, the pattern of "leaving all," "hating all," and embarking on the path of radical discipleship to Jesus Christ that is repeatedly given in the Gospels.[58]

## NOTES

1. Stephen Rose, "Whither Ethics, Jacques Ellul?" in James Y. Holloway, ed., *Introducing Jacques Ellul* (Grand Rapids, Mich.: Eerdmans, 1970), pp. 123-133.
2. Ellul to David C. Menninger, quoted in David C. Menninger, "Jacques Ellul: A Tempered Profile," *Review of Politics*, 37 (April 1975): 240; see also John Boli-Bennett's marvelous essay "The Absolute Dialectics of Jacques Ellul."
3. "Mirror of These Ten Years," p. 201; see also "From Jacques Ellul," p. 6.
4. *To Will and to Do*, p. 1. Jose Miranda, *Marx and the Bible* (Maryknoll, N.Y.: Orbis, 1974), especially pp. 201-292, is remarkable for its similarities to as well as differences from Ellul's (Marxist) social dialectics and biblical dialectics of faith.
5. *Apocalypse*, pp. 53-54. In his essay "On Dialectic," Ellul gives five examples of "biblical dialectic": (1) the Wholly Other God enters human history accompanying those who have rejected Him, (2) promise and fulfillment (the "not yet" and the "already"), (3) the whole and the remnant (universal salvation and the faithful remnant), (4) God's saving grace and human responsibility, and (5) history and *parousia* (continuity and contradiction of human history and eschatological New Jerusalem). In Clifford G. Christians and Jay M. Van Hook, editors, *Jacques Ellul: Interpretive Essays* (Urbana: University of Illinois 1981), pp. 291-308.

6. "Karl Barth and Us," Sojourners (December 1978): 24. See also Apocalypse, pp. 212-213, and passim.
7. Presence of the Kingdom, p. 17.
8. Apocalypse, p. 156.
9. Presence of the Kingdom, p. 18.
10. Karl Barth, The Humanity of God (Richmond, Va.: John Knox, 1960), p. 37.
11. Ibid., p. 42.
12. Ibid., p. 44.
13. Ethics of Freedom, p. 179.
14. See Katherine Temple, "The Sociology of Jacques Ellul."
15. Miranda, Marx and the Bible, p. 270.
16. The Political Illusion, p. 224.
17. Autopsy of Revolution, pp. 256-257.
18. Ibid., p. 259.
19. Betrayal of the West, p. 178.
20. "Search for an Image," p. 25.
21. Ethics of Freedom, p. 210.
22. Ibid., p. 478.
23. "Between Chaos and Paralysis," p. 749.
24. Autopsy of Revolution, p. 276.
25. Political Illusion, p. 222.
26. Presence of the Kingdom, p. 150.
27. False Presence of the Kingdom, p. 85.
28. Ethics of Freedom, p. 298.
29. David W. Gill, "Activist and Ethicist: Meet Jacques Ellul," Christianity Today, 20 (September 10, 1976): 1222.
30. Chaim Perelman and L. Olbrechts-Ortega, The New Rhetoric: A Treatise on Argumentation (Notre Dame, Ind.: University of Notre Dame Press, 1969), pp. 261ff.
31. To Will and to Do, p. 43.
32. Three recent authors who have assessed Ellul's ethics are J. Philip Wogaman, A Christian Method of Moral Judgment (Philadelphia: Westminster, 1976); Gene Outka, "Discontinuity in the Ethics of Jacques Ellul," in Clifford G. Christians and Jay M. Van Hook, eds., Jacques Ellul: Interpretive Essays (Urbana: University of Illinois, 1981), pp. 177-228; and Edward LeRoy Long, Jr., A Survey of Recent Christian Ethics (New York: Oxford, 1982). Wogaman labels Ellul an "evangelical perfectionist" (with John Howard Yoder) and stresses what he sees as Ellul's refusal of all moral compromise in a conviction that "Jesus Christ provides direct, unambiguous moral guidance." Outka

wrestles with Ellul's emphasis on the "discontinuity" between the morality of the world and Christian ethics. Long locates Ellul's approach to moral discernment (or norms) among "relational" thinkers and his approach to ethical implementation among those who "reject accommodation" and propose "intentional alternatives." None of these three critics is fully persuaded by Ellul, nor are their analyses comprehensive. In each case, however, the discussions are valuable for their thoughtful engagement with one or another aspect of his approach.

33. Presence of the Kingdom, p. 22; see also Ethics of Freedom, p. 7.
34. To Will and to Do, p. 27.
35. Apocalypse, pp. 47-48.
36. Violence, p. 148.
37. Cf. John Howard Yoder, The Politics of Jesus, pp. 34ff. See also Richard Cassidy, Jesus, Politics and Society (Maryknoll, N. Y.: Orbis, 1978).
38. Cf. John C. Bennett, The Radical Imperative (Philadelphia: Westminster, 1975), pp. 29ff.
39. See above, Chapter One.
40. Cf. Oscar Cullmann, Christ and Time (Philadelphia: Westminster, 1964).
41. Apocalypse, p. 213.
42. John Maddox, The Doomsday Syndrome (New York: McGraw-Hill, 1972); Alvin Toffler, Future Shock (New York: Bantam Books, 1970, 1971).
43. Morton and Lucia White, The Intellectual Versus the City (Cambridge, Mass.: Harvard University Press, 1962).
44. Harvey Cox, The Secular City (New York: Macmillan, 2nd ed., 1966); Max L. Stackhouse, Ethics and the Urban Ethos (Boston: Beacon, 1972); Craig Ellison, ed., The Urban Mission (Grand Rapids, Mich.: Eerdmans, 1974); Donald W. Shriver, Jr. and Karl A. Ostrom, Is There Hope for the City? (Philadelphia: Westminster, 1977).
45. Karl Barth, Community, Church, and State (Gloucester, Mass.: Peter Smith, 1968), pp. 149-189.
46. To Will and to Do, p. 2.
47. Politics of God and the Politics of Man, pp. 20-21.
48. Ibid., p. 47.
49. Ibid., p. 50.
50. Judgment of Jonah, pp. 11-18.
51. "From Jacques Ellul," p. 6.
52. "Mirror of These Ten Years," p. 200.

53. Ibid., p. 201.
54. "Jacques Ellul: A Tempered Profile," p. 241.
55. Richard L. Rubenstein, Psychology Today (November 1975): 18.
56. Edgar Z. Friedenberg, "Faithful Servant Old and Cross," Canadian Forum (Oct.-Nov. 1978): 42-44.
57. Presence of the Kingdom, pp. 96-97.
58. David W. Gill, "Activist and Ethicist: Meet Jacques Ellul," Christianity Today, 20 (September 10, 1976): 1222; see also David W. Gill, "Jacques Ellul: The Prophet As Theologian," Themelios (London), 7.1 (Sept. 1981): 4-14.

# SELECTED BIBLIOGRAPHY □

## I. PRIMARY SOURCES

### A. Books

#### 1. Sociology and History

Ellul, Jacques. Autopsy of Revolution. New York: Alfred A. Knopf, 1971. Translated by Patricia Wolf. Autopsie de la Révolution. Paris: Calmann-Levy, 1969.

________. The Betrayal of the West. New York: Seabury, 1978. Translated by Matthew J. O'Connell. Trahison de l'Occident. Paris: Calmann-Levy, 1976.

________. Changer de révolution: L'inéluctable proletariat. Paris: Editions du Seuil, 1982.

________. A Critique of the New Commonplaces. New York: Alfred A. Knopf, 1968. Translated by Helen Weaver. Exégèse des Nouveaux Lieux Communs. Paris: Calmann-Levy, 1966.

________. De la Révolution aux Révoltes. Paris: Calmann-Levy, 1972.

________. L'Empire du Non-sens. Paris: Presses Universitaires de France, 1980.

________. Histoire des Institutions. Paris: Presses Universitaires de France. Tome 1/2: L'antiquité. 1951/52; rev. ed., 1972. Tome 3: Le Moyen Age. 1953-1956; rev. ed., 1975 and 1980; Tome 4: XVIe-XVIIIe siècles. 1956; rev. ed., 1976; Tome 5: Le XIXe siècle (1789-1914). 1956; rev. ed., 1979.

________. L'Idéologie marxiste chrétienne. Paris: Le Centurion, 1979.

________. Métamorphose du Bourgeois. Paris: Calmann-Levy, 1967.

________. The New Demons. New York: Seabury, 1975. Translated by C. Edward Hopkin. Les Nouveaux Possédés. A. Fayard, 1973.

________. The Political Illusion. New York: Alfred A. Knopf, 1967. Translated and Introduction by Konrad Kellen. L'illusion politique. Paris: Robert Laffont, 1965; new postscript, 1977 edition.

________. Propaganda: The Formation of Men's Attitudes. New York: Alfred A. Knopf, 1965. Translated by Konrad Kellen and Jean Lerner. Introduction by Konrad Kellen. Propagandes. Armand Colin. 1962.

________. The Technological Society. Revised American edition. New York: Alfred A. Knopf, 1964. Translated and Introduction by John Wilkinson. Foreword by Robert K. Merton. La Technique ou l'Enjeu du siècle. Armand Colin, 1954.

________. The Technological System. New York: Continuum, 1980. Translated by Joachim Neugroschel. Le Système technicien. Paris: Calmann-Levy, 1977.

## 2. Theology and Ethics

________. Apocalypse: The Book of Revelation. New York: Seabury, 1977. Translated by George W. Schreiner. L'Apocalypse: Architecture en Mouvement. Desclee, 1975.

________. The Ethics of Freedom. Grand Rapids, Mich.: William B. Eerdmans, 1976. Translated and edited by G. W. Bromiley. Ethique de la Liberté. Labor et Fides, vol. 1, 1973; vol. 2, 1975; vol. 3, forthcoming.

________. False Presence of the Kingdom. New York: Seabury, 1972. Translated by C. Edward Hopkin. Fausse Présence au Monde Moderne. Paris: Les Bergers et les Mages, 1964.

_______. La Foi au prix du doute. Hachette, 1980.

_______. L'homme et l'argent. Delachaux et Niestle, 1953.

_______. Hope in Time of Abandonment. New York: Seabury, 1973. Translated by C. Edward Hopkin. L'espérance oubliée. Gallimard, 1973.

_______. The Judgment of Jonah. Grand Rapids, Mich.: William B. Eerdmans, 1971. Translated and Preface by G. W. Bromiley. Le Livre de Jonas. Paris: Foi et Vie, 1952.

_______. The Meaning of the City. Grand Rapids, Mich.: William B. Eerdmans, 1970. Translated by Dennis Pardee. Introduction by John Wilkinson. Sans Feu ni Lieu. Gallimard, 1975.

_______. La Parole humiliée. Paris: Editions du Seuil, 1981.

_______. The Politics of God and the Politics of Man. Grand Rapids, Mich.: William B. Eerdmans, 1972. Translated, edited, and Preface by G. W. Bromiley. Politique de Dieu, Politique des hommes. Editions Universitaires, 1966.

_______. Prayer and Modern Man. New York: Seabury, 1970. Translated by C. Edward Hopkin. L'impossible prière. Le Centurion, 1971.

_______. The Presence of the Kingdom. Philadelphia: Westminster, 1951. New York: Seabury, 1967. Translated by Olive Wyon. Introduction by William Stringfellow. Présence au Monde Moderne. Labor et Fides (Roulet Editions), 1948.

_______. The Theological Foundation of Law. New York: Doubleday, 1960. New York: Seabury, 1969. Translated by Marguerite Wieser. Le Fondement Théologique du Droit. Delachaux et Niestle, 1946.

_______. To Will and to Do: An Ethical Research for Christians. Philadelphia: Pilgrim, 1969. Translated by C. Edward Hopkin. Foreword by Waldo Beach. Le Vouloir et le Faire. (Recherches ethiques pour les chrétiens. Introduction, Tome I). Labor et Fides, 1964.

________. Violence: Reflections from a Christian Perspective. New York: Seabury, 1969. Translated by Cecelia Gaul Kings. Contre les Violents. Le Centurion, 1972.

3. Autobiography

________. In Season, Out of Season. San Francisco: Harper & Row, 1982. Translated by Lani K. Niles. Introduction by David W. Gill. A Temps et à contre-temps. Le Centurion, 1981.

________. Perspectives on Our Age. New York: Seabury, 1981. Edited by William H. Vanderburg. Translated by Joachim Neugroschel.

B. Articles

Ellul, Jacques. "Actualité de la Réforme," Foi et Vie 58.2 (Mars-Avril 1959): 39-64.

________. "A Little Debate About Technology: Replying to Thomas G. Donnelly," The Christian Century 90 (June 27, 1973): 706-707.

________. "Between Chaos and Paralysis," The Christian Century 85 (June 5, 1968): 747-750.

________. "Cain, the Theologian of 1969," Katallagete: Be Reconciled 2.1 (Winter 1968/69): 4-7.

________. "De la mort," Foi et Vie 73.2 (Mars-Avril 1974): 1-14.

________. "Ellul Replies on Violence," Christianity and Crisis 30 (Oct. 19, 1970): 221.

________. "From Jacques Ellul," in James Y. Holloway, ed., Introducing Jacques Ellul. Grand Rapids, Mich.: William B. Eerdmans, 1970. pp. 5-6.

________. "Jesus Christ," La Table Ronde (1968): 19-20.

________. "La Jeunesse force révolutionnaire?" La Table Ronde (1969): 150-168.

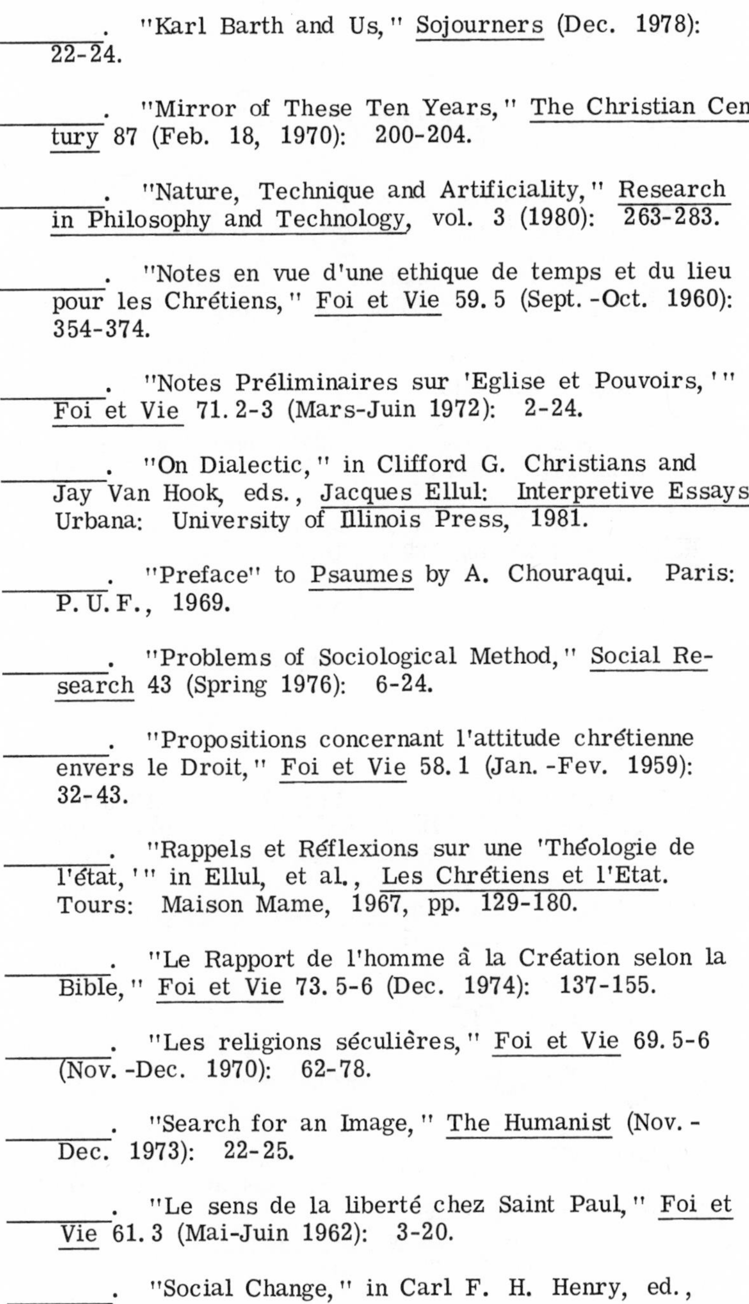

________. "Karl Barth and Us," Sojourners (Dec. 1978): 22-24.

________. "Mirror of These Ten Years," The Christian Century 87 (Feb. 18, 1970): 200-204.

________. "Nature, Technique and Artificiality," Research in Philosophy and Technology, vol. 3 (1980): 263-283.

________. "Notes en vue d'une ethique de temps et du lieu pour les Chrétiens," Foi et Vie 59. 5 (Sept. -Oct. 1960): 354-374.

________. "Notes Préliminaires sur 'Eglise et Pouvoirs,'" Foi et Vie 71. 2-3 (Mars-Juin 1972): 2-24.

________. "On Dialectic," in Clifford G. Christians and Jay Van Hook, eds., Jacques Ellul: Interpretive Essays. Urbana: University of Illinois Press, 1981.

________. "Preface" to Psaumes by A. Chouraqui. Paris: P. U. F., 1969.

________. "Problems of Sociological Method," Social Research 43 (Spring 1976): 6-24.

________. "Propositions concernant l'attitude chrétienne envers le Droit," Foi et Vie 58. 1 (Jan. -Fev. 1959): 32-43.

________. "Rappels et Réflexions sur une 'Théologie de l'état,'" in Ellul, et al., Les Chrétiens et l'Etat. Tours: Maison Mame, 1967, pp. 129-180.

________. "Le Rapport de l'homme à la Création selon la Bible," Foi et Vie 73. 5-6 (Dec. 1974): 137-155.

________. "Les religions séculières," Foi et Vie 69. 5-6 (Nov. -Dec. 1970): 62-78.

________. "Search for an Image," The Humanist (Nov. - Dec. 1973): 22-25.

________. "Le sens de la liberté chez Saint Paul," Foi et Vie 61. 3 (Mai-Juin 1962): 3-20.

________. "Social Change," in Carl F. H. Henry, ed.,

Baker's Dictionary of Christian Ethics. Grand Rapids, Mich.: Baker Book House, 1973, pp. 629-632.

________. "Sur le pessimisme chrétien," Foi et Vie 52.2 (Mars-Avril 1954): 164-180.

________. "La technique et les premiers chapitres de la Genèse," Foi et Vie 59.2 (Mars-Avril 1960): 97-113.

________. "Théologie dogmatique et spécificité du christianisme," Foi et Vie 70.2-4 (Avril-Sept. 1971): 139-154.

________. "Unbridled Spirit of Power," Sojourners 11.7 (July-Aug. 1982): 13-15.

________. "Work and Calling," Katallagete: Be Reconciled 6 (Spring 1973): 8-16.

________. "'The World' in the Gospels," Katallagete: Be Reconciled 7 (Spring 1974): 16-23.

## II. SECONDARY SOURCES

### A. Books

Aron, Raymond. Main Currents in Sociological Thought. 2 vols. New York: Doubleday, Anchor Books, 1968, 1970. Translated by Richard Howard and Helen Weaver.

Bahnsen, Greg L. Theonomy in Christian Ethics. Nutley, N.J.: Craig Press, 1977.

Barr, James. The Bible in the Modern World. New York: Harper and Row, 1973.

________. Fundamentalism. Philadelphia: Westminster Press, 1977, 1978.

Barth, Karl. Church Dogmatics. 13 vols. Translated by G. W. Bromiley, T. F. Torrance, et al. Edinburgh: T. and T. Clark, 1936-62.

________. Community, Church, and State: Three Essays. Gloucester, Mass.: Peter Smith, 1968.

_______. The Humanity of God. Richmond, Va.: John Knox Press, 1960.

_______. The Word of God and the Word of Man. Translated by Douglas Horton. New York: Harper and Row, 1957.

Bennett, John Coleman. Christians and the State. New York: Scribner's, 1958.

_______. The Radical Imperative: From Theology to Social Ethics. Philadelphia: Westminster Press, 1975.

Berkhof, Hendrik. Christ and the Powers. Translated by John Howard Yoder. Scottdale, Pa.: Herald Press, 1962, 1977.

Birch, Bruce C., and Larry L. Rasmussen. Bible and Ethics in the Christian Life. Minneapolis: Augsburg, 1976.

Bonhoeffer, Dietrich. The Cost of Discipleship. New York: Macmillan, revised and unabridged edition, 1959.

_______. Creation and Fall/Temptation: Two Biblical Studies. New York: Macmillan, 1959.

_______. Ethics. Edited by Eberhard Bethge. New York: Macmillan, 1955.

Braaten, Carl E. Eschatology and Ethics: Essays on the Theology and Ethics of the Kingdom of God. Minneapolis: Augsburg, 1974.

Cadbury, Henry J. The Peril of Modernizing Jesus. New York, 1937.

Cantin, Eileen. Mounier: A Personalist View of History. New York: Paulist Press, 1973.

Cassidy, Richard J. Jesus, Politics, and Society: A Study in Luke's Gospel. Maryknoll, N.Y.: Orbis Books, 1978.

Childs, Brevard S. Biblical Theology in Crisis. Philadelphia: Westminster Press, 1970.

_______. Old Testament Books for Pastor and Teacher. Philadelphia: Westminster Press, 1977.

Christians, Clifford G., and Van Hook, Jay M., eds. Jacques Ellul: Interpretive Essays. Urbana: University of Illinois, 1981. Includes essays by Martin Marty, David C. Menninger, Geoffrey W. Bromiley, Vernard Eller, John L. Stanley, C. George Bonello, Michael R. Real, Jay M. Van Hook, Clifford G. Christians, Gene Outka, Arthur F. Holmes, Kenneth Konyndyk, David L. Clark, and Jacques Ellul, with a bibliography by David W. Gill.

Cox, Harvey. The Secular City: Secularization and Urbanization in Theological Perspective. New York: Macmillan, revised edition, 1966.

________. The Seduction of the Spirit. New York: Simon and Schuster, Touchstone Books, 1973.

Cullmann, Oscar. Christ and Time. Translated by Floyd V. Filson. Philadelphia: Westminster Press, revised edition, 1964.

________. The State in the New Testament. New York: Scribner's, 1956.

Davis, Stephen T. The Debate About the Bible. Philadelphia: Westminster, 1977.

Durkheim, Emile. The Division of Labor in Society. Translated by George Simpson. New York: Free Press, 1933.

________. On Morality and Society. Edited with an introduction by Robert N. Bellah. Chicago: University of Chicago Press, 1973.

Ellison, Craig W., ed. The Urban Mission. Grand Rapids, Mich.: William B. Eerdmans, 1974.

Everding, H. Edward, Jr. and Dana W. Wilbanks. Decision Making and the Bible. Valley Forge, Pa.: Judson Press, 1975.

Ferkiss, Victor C. Technological Man: The Myth and the Reality. New York: New American Library, Mentor Books, 1969.

Florman, Samuel C. The Existential Pleasures of Engineering. New York: St. Martin's Press, 1976.

Frankena, William K. Ethics. Englewood Cliffs, N.J.: Prentice-Hall, second edition, 1973.

Galbraith, John Kenneth. The New Industrial State. Boston: Houghton Mifflin, second edition, Revised, 1971.

Greenway, Roger S. Calling Our Cities to Christ. Nutley, N.J.: Presbyterian and Reformed, 1974.

Guiness, Os. The Dust of Death. Downers Grove, Ill.: InterVarsity Press, 1973.

Gustafson, James M. Can Ethics Be Christian? Chicago: University of Chicago Press, 1975.

________. Christ and the Moral Life. New York: Harper and Row, 1968.

________. Christian Ethics and the Community. Philadelphia: Pilgrim Press, 1971.

________. Theology and Christian Ethics. Philadelphia: Pilgrim Press, 1974.

Harnack, Adolf. What Is Christianity? Translated by Thomas B. Saunders. New York: Harper and Row, Torchbooks, 1957.

Hengel, Martin. Christ and Power. Translated by Everett R. Kalin. Philadelphia: Fortress Press, 1977.

________. Victory over Violence: Jesus and the Revolutionists. Translated by David E. Green. Philadelphia: Fortress Press, 1973.

Henry, Carl F. H. Aspects of Christian Social Ethics. Grand Rapids, Mich.: William B. Eerdmans, 1964.

________. Christian Personal Ethics. Grand Rapids, Mich.: William B. Eerdmans, 1957.

________, ed. Baker's Dictionary of Christian Ethics. Grand Rapids, Mich.: Baker Book House, 1973.

Hiers, Richard H. Jesus and Ethics: Four Interpretations. Philadelphia: Westminster Press, 1968.

Holloway, James Y., ed. Introducing Jacques Ellul. Grand Rapids, Mich.: William B. Eerdmans, 1970. Essays by James Y. Holloway, Will D. Campbell, Gabriel Vahanian, Christopher Lasch, Julius Lester, Stephen Rose, Willaim Stringfellow, James W. Douglass, James Branscome, and John Wilkinson, with a brief note "From Jacques Ellul."

Houlden, J. L. Ethics and the New Testament. Baltimore: Penguin Books, 1973.

Kelsey, David H. The Uses of Scripture in Recent Theology. Philadelphia: Fortress Press, 1975.

Kierkegaard, Søren. Concluding Unscientific Postscript. Translated by David F. Swenson and Walter Lowrie. Princeton, N.J.: Princeton University Press, 1941.

________. Fear and Trembling and The Sickness unto Death. Translated by Walter Lowrie. Princeton, N.J.: Princeton University Press, 1941, 1954.

________. Philosophical Fragments. Translated by David Swenson and Howard V. Hong. Princeton, N.J.: Princeton University Press, 1936, 1962.

________. The Point of View for My Work as an Author: A Report to History. Translated by Walter Lowrie. New York: Harper and Row, 1962.

________. Works of Love. Translated by Howard and Edna Hong. New York: Harper and Row, 1962.

Lindsell, Harold. The Battle for the Bible. Grand Rapids, Mich.: Zondervan, 1976.

Lindsey, Hal. The Late Great Planet Earth. Grand Rapids, Mich.: Zondervan, 1970.

Long, Edward LeRoy, Jr. A Survey of Christian Ethics. New York: Oxford University Press, 1967.

________. A Survey of Recent Christian Ethics. New York: Oxford University Press, 1982.

Maddox, John. The Doomsday Syndrome. New York: McGraw-Hill, 1972.

Malantschuk, Gregor. Kierkegaard's Thought. Edited and Translated by Howard V. Hong and Edna H. Hong. Princeton, N.J.: Princeton University Press, 1971.

Marcuse, Herbert. One-Dimensional Man. Boston: Beacon Press, 1964.

Middelmann, Udo. Pro-Existence. Downers Grove, Ill.: InterVarsity Press, 1974.

Miller, William D. A Harsh and Dreadful Love: Dorothy Day and the Catholic Worker Movement. New York: Doubleday, Image, 1973, 1974.

Mills, C. Wright. The Power Elite. New York: Oxford University Press, 1956.

Miranda, José. Marx and the Bible: A Critique of the Philosophy of Oppression. Translated by John Eagleson. Maryknoll, N.Y.: Orbis Books, 1974.

Moltmann, Jürgen. Theology of Hope. Translated by James W. Leitsch. New York: Harper and Row, 1967.

Morrison, Clinton D. The Powers That Be. London: SCM, Studies in Biblical Theology, 1960.

Mounier, Emmanuel. Be Not Afraid. Studies in Personalist Sociology. Translated by Cynthia Rowland. London: Rockliff Publishing, 1951.

Muilenburg, James. The Way of Israel: Biblical Faith and Ethics. New York: Harper and Row, 1961.

Mumford, Lewis. The City in History. New York: Harcourt, Brace, and World, 1961.

________. The Pentagon of Power. Volume II of The Myth of the Machine. New York: Harcourt, Brace, and Jovanovich, 1964, 1970.

________. Technics and Civilization. New York: Harcourt, Brace, and World, 1934.

________. Technics and Human Development. Volume I of The Myth of the Machine. New York: Harcourt, Brace, and Jovanovich, 1966, 1967.

Perelman, Chaim, and L. Olbrechts-Tyteca. The New Rhetoric: A Treatise on Argumentation. Translated by John Wilkinson and Purcell Weaver. Notre Dame, Ind.: University of Notre Dame Press, 1969.

Rogers, Jack, editor. Biblical Authority. Waco, Texas: Word Books, 1977.

Roszak, Theodore. The Making of a Counter Culture: Reflections on the Technocratic Society and Its Youthful Opposition. Garden City, N.Y.: Doubleday, Anchor Books, 1969.

Rushdoony, Rousas J. The Institutes of Biblical Law. Nutley, N.J.: Presbyterian and Reformed, 1973.

Sanders, Jack T. Ethics in the New Testament. Philadelphis: Fortress Press, 1975.

Schnackenburg, Rudolf. The Moral Teaching of the New Testament. New York: Seabury Press, 1973.

Schuurman, Egbert. Reflections on the Technological Society. Toronto: Wedge Publishing Foundation, 1977.

Schweitzer, Albert. The Quest for the Historical Jesus. London: Black, 1954.

Shriver, Donald W., Jr. and Karl A. Ostruum. Is There Hope for the City? Philadelphia: Westminster, 1977.

Smart, James D. The Strange Silence of the Bible in the Church. Philadelphia: Westminster, 1970.

Stackhouse, Max L. Ethics and the Urban Ethos. Boston: Beacon Press, 1972.

Stringfellow, William. An Ethic for Christians and Other Aliens in a Strange Land. Waco, Texas: Word Books, 1973.

________. Free in Obedience: The Radical Christian Life. New York: Seabury Press, 1964.

Toffler, Alvin. Future Shock. New York: Random House, Bantam Books, 1970.

Toulmin, Stephen. Reason in Ethics. London: Cambridge University Press, 1970.

________. The Uses of Argument. London: Cambridge University Press, 1969.

Warnock, Mary. Existentialist Ethics. New York: St. Martin's Press, 1967.

Weber, Max. From Max Weber: Essays in Sociology. Edited by H. H. Gerth and C. Wright Mills. New York: Oxford University Press, 1946.

________. The Protestant Ethic and the Spirit of Capitalism. Translated by Talcott Parsons. New York: Scribner's, 1958.

________. The Sociology of Religion. Translated by Ephraim Fischoff. Boston: Beacon Press, 1963.

White, Morton and Lucia. The Intellectual Versus the City. Cambridge, Mass.: Harvard University Press, 1962.

Wilder, Amos N. Eschatology and Ethics in the Teaching of Jesus. New York: Harper and Brothers, revised edition, 1950.

________. Kerygma, Eschatology, and Social Ethics. Philadelphia: Fortress Press, Facet Books, 1966.

Winter, Gibson. The New Creation as Metropolis. New York: Macmillan, 1963.

Wogaman, J. Philip. A Christian Method of Moral Judgment. Philadelphia: Westminster Press, 1976.

Yoder, John Howard. The Christian Witness to the State. Newton, Kans.: Faith and Life Press, 1964.

________. Karl Barth and the Problem of War. Nashville, Tenn.: Abingdon, 1970.

________. The Original Revolution. Scottdale, Pa.: Herald Press, 1971.

________. The Politics of Jesus. Grand Rapids, Mich.: William B. Eerdmans, 1972.

B. Articles and Reviews

Boli-Bennett, John. "The Absolute Dialectics of Jacques Ellul," Research in Philosophy and Technology, Vol. 3 (1980): 171-201.

Brueggemann, Walter. Review of The Politics of God and the Politics of Man by Jacques Ellul, Journal of Biblical Literature 92 (Sept. 1973): 470-471.

Cerezuelle, Daniel. "From the Technical Phenomenon to the Technical System," Research in Philosophy and Technology, Vol. 3 (1980): 161-170.

Christians, Clifford G., and Michael R. Real. "Jacques Ellul's Contributions to Critical Media Theory," Journal of Communications 29.1 (Winter 1979): 83-93.

Cox, Harvey. "The Ungodly City: A Theological Response to Jacques Ellul," Commonweal 94 (July 9, 1971): 351-357.

Curran, Charles. "Dialogue with the Scriptures: The Role and Function of the Scriptures in Moral Theology," Catholic Moral Theology in Dialogue. Notre Dame, Ind.: Fides Publishers, 1972, 24-64.

Donnelly, Thomas G. "In Defense of Technology," The Christian Century 90 (Jan. 17, 1973): 65-69.

Eller, Vernard. "How Jacques Ellul Reads the Bible," The Christian Century 89 (Nov. 29, 1972): 1212-1215.

Fager, Charles. "Jacques Ellul: An Introductory Review," New Age (Dec. 1976): 50-55.

Friedenberg, Edgar Z. "Faithful Servant Old and Cross," Review of The Betrayal of the West by Jacques Ellul, Canadian Forum (Oct.-Nov. 1978): 42-44.

Gill, David W. "Activist and Ethicist: Meet Jacques Ellul," Christianity Today 20 (Sept. 10, 1976): 1220-1222.

________. "Biblical Theology of the City," International Standard Bible Encyclopedia (Grand Rapids, Mich.: Eerdmans, 1979 revised edition), Vol. 1, pp. 713-715.

________. "Bibliography: The Works of Jacques Ellul," in Clifford G. Christians and Jay M. Van Hook, eds., Jacques Ellul: Interpretive Essays (Urbana: University of Illinois, 1981), pp. 309-328.

________. "Eros and Narcissus on Trial," The Reformed Journal 30.9 (Sept. 1980): 26-29.

________. "Introduction to the American Edition," In Season, Out of Season by Jacques Ellul. San Francisco: Harper & Row, 1982, pp. v.-xiii.

________. "Jacques Ellul and Francis Schaeffer: Two Views of Western Civilization," Fides et Historia 13.2 (Spring-Summer 1981): 23-37.

________. "Jacques Ellul: The Prophet As Theologian," Themelios (London) 7.1 (Sept. 1981): 4-14.

________. "Ours Is Not a Secular Age," Review of The New Demons by Jacques Ellul, Christianity Today 20 (May 7, 1976): 840-841.

________. "Prophet in the Technological Wilderness," Catholic Agitator (Oct. 1976): 3-4.

________. "A Study in Contrasts: Bennett and Ellul," Radix 8 (July-Aug. 1976): 6.

Gorman, William. "Jacques Ellul: A Prophetic Voice," The Center Magazine 1 (Oct.-Nov. 1967): 34-37.

Gustafson, James M. "The Place of Scripture in Christian Ethics: A Methodological Study," Interpretation 24 (Oct. 1970): 430-455.

Hadden, Jeffrey K. "Is God a Country Boy?" Review of The Meaning of the City by Jacques Ellul, Journal for the Scientific Study of Religion 12 (March 1973): 120-121.

Hall, A. Rupert. "An Unconvincing Indictment of the Evils of Technology," Scientific American 212 (Feb. 1965): 125-128.

Hansen, Richard S. Review of The Politics of God and the Politics of Man by Jacques Ellul, Interpretation 27 (April 1973): 238-240.

Heddendorf, Russell. "The Christian World of Jacques Ellul," Christian Scholars Review 2.4 (1973): 291-307.

Hubbard, David A. Review of The Politics of God and the Politics of Man by Jacques Ellul, The Christian Scholars Review 3.2 (1973): 172-173.

Landes, George. Review of The Judgment of Jonah, Interpretation 26 (Jan. 1972): 98-99.

Long, Edward LeRoy, Jr. "The Use of the Bible in Christian Ethics: A Look at Basic Options," Interpretation 19 (April 1965): 149-162.

Lovekin, David. "Technology as the Sacred Order," Research in Philosophy and Technology, Vol. 3 (1980): 203-222.

McFerran, Douglas D. "The Cult of Jacques Ellul," America (Feb. 6, 1971): 122-124.

McLuhan, Marshall. "Big Transistor Is Watching You," Review of Propaganda by Jacques Ellul, Book Week (Nov. 28, 1965): 5, 25-26.

Marty, Martin E. "The Protestant for This Summer," National Catholic Reporter (July 3, 1970): 17-18.

________. "Shattered Necessities," Review of Violence by Jacques Ellul, The Christian Century 86 (Sept. 24, 1969): 1223-1224.

Menninger, David C. "Jacques Ellul: A Tempered Profile," Review of Politics 37 (April 1975): 235-246.

Miller, Duane R. "Watergate and the Thought of Jacques Ellul," The Christian Century 90 (Sept. 26, 1973): 943-946.

Minnema, Theodore. "Evil in the Thought of Jacques Ellul," Reformed Journal 23 (May-June 1973): pp. 17-20.

Mitcham, Carl, and Robert Mackey. "Jacques Ellul and the Technological Society," Philosophy Today 15 (Summer 1970): 102-121.

Muelder, Walter G. Review of The Meaning of the City by Jacques Ellul, The Christian Century 88 (March 3, 1971): 299.

Nisbet, Robert A. "The Grand Illusion: An Appreciation of Jacques Ellul," Commentary 50 (Aug. 1970): 40-44.

Outka, Gene. "Discontinuity in the Ethics of Jacques Ellul," in Clifford G. Christians and Jay M. Van Hook, eds., Jacques Ellul: Interpretive Essays (Urbana: University of Illinois, 1981), pp. 177-228.

Padover, Saul K. Review of The Political Illusion, Saturday Review (April 29, 1967): 27-28.

Ray, Ronald R. "Jacques Ellul's Innocent Notes on Hermeneutics," Interpretation 33 (July 1979): 268-282.

Rubenstein, Richard L. Review of The New Demons by Jacques Ellul, Psychology Today (Nov. 1975): 18-19.

Shorter, Edward. "Industrial Society in Trouble: Some Recent Views," American Scholar 40 (Spring 1971): 334-336.

Sklair, Leslie. "The Sociology of the Opposition to Science and Technology, with Special Reference to the Work of Jacques Ellul," Comparative Studies in Society and History 13 (April 1971): 217-235.

Sleeper, C. Freeman. "Ethics as a Context for Biblical Interpretation," Interpretation 22 (Oct. 1968): 443-460.

Stringfellow, William. "Jacques Ellul: The Layman as Moral Theologian," Messenger (Dec. 3, 1970): 25-28.

Temple, Katherine. "The Sociology of Jacques Ellul," Research in Philosophy and Technology, Vol. 3 (1980): 223-261.

Theobald, Robert. "The House That Homo Sapiens Built," The Nation (Oct. 19, 1964): 249-252.

Van Hook, Jay. "The Burden of Jacques Ellul," Reformed Journal 26 (Dec. 1976): 13-17.

________. Review of The Ethics of Freedom by Jacques Ellul, Reformed Journal 27 (Feb. 1977): 26-27.

Walsh, Joseph L. Review of The Political Illusion, Commonweal 87 (Oct. 13, 1967): 56-57.

Wilder, Amos N. "The Basis of Christian Ethics in the New Testament," Journal of Religious Thought 15. 2 (Spring-Summer 1958): 137-146.

Wilkinson, John. "The Divine Persuasion: An Interview with John Wilkinson about Jacques Ellul," The Center Magazine 3. 3 (May 1970): 11-18.

________. "Second Edition: The Quantitative Society," The Center Magazine 2. 4 (July 1969): 64-71.

Winter, Gibson. Review of The Meaning of the City by Jacques Ellul, Journal of the American Academy of Religion 40 (March 1972): 118-122.

# NAME INDEX ☐

# SUBJECT INDEX